Constituents of Modern System-safety Thinking

Related titles:

Towards System Safety
Proceedings of the Seventh Safety-critical Systems Symposium, Huntingdon, UK 1999
Redmill and Anderson (Eds)
1-85233-064-3

Lessons in System Safety
Proceedings of the Eighth Safety-critical Systems Symposium, Southampton, UK 2000
Redmill and Anderson (Eds)
1-85233-249-2

Aspects of Safety Management
Proceedings of the Ninth Safety-critical Systems Symposium, Bristol, UK 2001
Redmill and Anderson (Eds)
1-85233-411-8

Components of System Safety
Proceedings of the Tenth Safety-critical Systems Symposium, Southampton, UK 2002
Redmill and Anderson (Eds)
1-85233-561-0

Current Issues in Safety-critical Systems
Proceedings of the Eleventh Safety-critical Systems Symposium, Bristol, UK 2003
Redmill and Anderson (Eds)
1-85233-696-X

Practical Elements of Safety
Proceedings of the Twelfth Safety-critical Systems Symposium, Birmingham, UK 2004
Redmill and Anderson (Eds)
1-85233-800-8

Felix Redmill and Tom Anderson (Eds)

Constituents of Modern System-safety Thinking

Proceedings of the Thirteenth Safety-critical Systems Symposium, Southampton, UK, 8-10 February 2005

Safety-Critical
Systems Club

 Springer

Felix Redmill
Redmill Consultancy, 22 Onslow Gardens, London, N10 3JU

Tom Anderson
Centre for Software Reliability, University of Newcastle,
Newcastle upon Tyne, NE1 7RU

British Library Cataloguing in Publication Data
A catalogue record for this book is available from the British Library

ISBN 1-85233-952-7
Springer Science+Business Media
springeronline.com

Typesetting: Camera ready by contributors
Printed and bound by the Athenæum Press Ltd., Gateshead, Tyne & Wear
34/3830-543210 Printed on acid-free paper SPIN 11316947

PREFACE

The papers in this book address topics that are of crucial importance in current safety thinking. The core of modern safety thinking and practice is a risk-based approach, and, not only is this a 'given' in all of the papers, but also one session of two papers is devoted to an exploration of the subject of risk. Another fundamental of safety engineering and management is the need not merely to achieve safety but to demonstrate its achievement in advance of deploying a system. This requires the construction of an argument (a safety case) that the system is adequately safe for its intended application, and the independent safety assessment of the argument. Both of these topics – the safety case and safety assessment – are addressed in papers in this volume. Indeed, they are recurring themes at the annual Safety-critical Systems Symposium, for both are in the process of development and change.

Another topic reprised in this book is accident investigation, for, whenever an investigation takes place, lessons are learned not only about the accident itself but also about the investigation process. Two papers in this book make strong contributions in this field. Then, there is the issue of commonality between the processes and techniques employed in safety and security engineering. Typically, the one discipline looks outwards and the other inwards, but they both take a risk-based approach and both employ techniques to identify and analyse the risks and processes to manage them. Yet there is little attempt by the two communities to come together, compare notes, and learn from each other. This Symposium has in the past invited papers that prompt such communication, and, again, this year's event points to similarities between the two disciplines and an inherent interdependence between them.

But the major themes are not mutually exclusive. Through them run common threads, including 'blueprints' for specification and definition, the use and development of technology, and the human factor. Safety is multi-dimensional, in both concept and practice.

On behalf of the Safety-Critical Systems Club, the promoter of the Symposium, we gratefully thank the authors for their contributions to the event and this book. And for the thirteenth successive year, we thank Joan Atkinson who so ably manages the Club's secretariat and organises the event's logistics.

FR & TA
November 2004

THE SAFETY-CRITICAL SYSTEMS CLUB

organiser

of the

Safety-critical Systems Symposium

What is the Club?

The Safety-Critical Systems Club exists to raise awareness of safety issues and to facilitate technology transfer in the field of safety-critical systems. It is an independent, non-profit organisation that co-operates with all bodies involved with safety-critical systems.

History

The Club was inaugurated in 1991 under the sponsorship of the UK's Department of Trade and Industry (DTI) and the Engineering and Physical Sciences Research Council (EPSRC). Its secretariat is at the Centre for Software Reliability (CSR) in the University of Newcastle upon Tyne, and its Co-ordinator is Felix Redmill of Redmill Consultancy.

Since 1994 the Club has had to be self-sufficient, but it retains the active support of the DTI and EPSRC, as well as that of the Health and Safety Executive, the Institution of Electrical Engineers, and the British Computer Society. All of these bodies are represented on the Club's Steering Group.

What does the Club do?

The Club achieves its goals of technology transfer and awareness-raising by focusing on current and emerging practices in safety engineering, software engineering, and standards that relate to safety in processes and products. Its activities include:

- Running the annual Safety-critical Systems Symposium each February (the first was in 1993), with Proceedings published by Springer-Verlag;
- Organising a number of 1- and 2-day seminars each year;
- Providing tutorials on relevant subjects;
- Publishing a newsletter, *Safety Systems*, three times each year (since 1991), in January, May and September.

How does the Club help?

The Club brings together technical and managerial personnel within all sectors of the safety-critical community. It provides education and training in principles and techniques, and facilitates the dispersion of lessons within and between industry sectors. It promotes an inter-disciplinary approach to safety engineering and management and provides a forum for experienced practitioners to meet each other and for the exposure of newcomers to the safety-critical systems industry.

The Club facilitates communication among researchers, the transfer of technology from researchers to users, feedback from users, and the communication of experience between users. It provides a meeting point for industry and academia, a forum for the presentation of the results of relevant projects, and a means of learning and keeping up-to-date in the field.

The Club thus helps to achieve more effective research, a more rapid and effective transfer and use of technology, the identification of best practice, the definition of requirements for education and training, and the dissemination of information. Importantly, it does this within a 'club' atmosphere rather than a commercial environment.

Membership

Members pay a reduced fee (well below a commercial level) for events and receive the newsletter and other mailed information. Without sponsorship, the Club depends on members' subscriptions, which can be paid at the first meeting attended.

To join, please contact Mrs Joan Atkinson at: Centre for Software Reliability, University of Newcastle upon Tyne, NE1 7RU; Telephone: 0191 221 2222; Fax: 0191 222 7995; Email: csr@newcastle.ac.uk

CONTENTS LIST

INDEPENDENT SAFETY ASSESSMENT

The IEE/BCS Independent Safety Assurance Working Group
David H Smith 3

Putting Trust into Safety Arguments
Jane Fenn and Brian Jepson 21

Independent Safety Assessment of Safety Arguments
Peter Froome 37

SAFETY AND SECURITY

Structuring a Safety Case for an Air Traffic Control Operations Room
Ron Pierce and Herman Baret 51

SafSec: Commonalities Between Safety and Security Assurance
Samantha Lautieri, David Cooper and David Jackson 65

ACCIDENT INVESTIGATION

Learning from a Train Derailment
Kevin Payne 79

Accident Investigations – Meeting the Challenge of New Technology
Knut Rygh 93

RISK AND ITS TOLERABILITY

Identification of Time At Risk Periods of Significance to ALARP
Justifications
Mark George 111

Developing and Using Risk Matrices
Michael Prince 129

ACHIEVING AND ARGUING THE SAFETY OF MODULAR SYSTEMS

Health Monitoring for Reconfigurable Integrated Control Systems
Mark Nicholson 149

Exploring the Possibilities Towards a Preliminary Safety Case for
IMA Blueprints
Graham Jolliffe and Mark Nicholson 163

Modular Certification of Integrated Modular Systems
James Blow, Andrew Cox and Paul Liddell 183

TECHNOLOGIES FOR DEPENDABILITY

The Effects of Timing and Collaboration on Dependability in the
Neonatal Intensive Care Unit
*Gordon D Baxter, Juliana Küster Filipe, Angela Miguel
and Kenneth Tan* 195

Applying Java Technologies to Mission-Critical and Safety-Critical
Development
Kelvin Nilsen and Adrian Larkham 211

INDEPENDENT SAFETY ASSESSMENT

The IEE/BCS Independent Safety Assurance Working Group

David H Smith
Frazer-Nash Consultancy Ltd.
Stonebridge House, Dorking Business Park,
Dorking, Surrey, RH4 1HJ.
d.smith@fnc.co.uk

Abstract

The purpose of this paper is to provide an introduction to the work of the IEE/BCS Independent Safety Assurance Working Group, including what has been achieved to date and looking at what needs to be addressed in the future.

1 Introduction

This paper describes the role of the Working Group, and provides an overview of the issues that can affect the ISA role and how the Working Group is trying to address them.

2 The Role of the ISA Working Group[1]

The Independent Safety Assurance Working Group was set up by the Institution of Electrical Engineers (IEE) and the British Computer Society (BCS) in September 2000 to promote and assist the role of the independent safety assessor (ISA). The Working Group is made up of representatives from a variety of industries representing the supply chain, namely: the regulator, the purchaser, the supplier and the independent safety organisations.

The Mission Statement of the Working Group is:

"To enhance awareness and knowledge of the concept of Independent Safety Assurance in the interests of the engineering profession"

where Independent Safety Assurance is provided by safety professionals fulfilling the role of an Independent Safety Advisor, Auditor or Assessor.

---

[1] Some of this text is based upon information held at the ISA WG website.

2.1 Aims

The aims of the Working Group are to:

- Provide a contact point for ISA professionals.
- Promote the ISA role of a safety professional as a means of providing independent safety assurance to the supplier, purchaser and user.
- Promote the ISA role of a safety professional in standards.
- Support the development of safety professionals.
- Provide support for professional ISA's by developing guidance and providing information that effects their role.
- Explore the concept of expanding the ISA role to include independent environmental assurance.

Although the Working Group is independent, it is subject to the direction of the IEE Inter-Institutional Group on Health and Safety and is affiliated to the IEE and the BCS.

2.2 Membership

Membership of the Working Group is open to safety professionals with extensive experience of working on safety critical projects / programmes. Since September 2000 there have been 14 meetings of the Working Group. Current members are from many different industry sectors, including:

- Standards makers – such as the UK Health and Safety Executive (HSE) and the MoD.
- Defence Equipment Manufacturers.
- Nuclear Power.
- Rail.
- Independent Safety Consultants.
- Professional Institutions.

The Working Group is endeavoring to widen involvement with other institutions and related safety groups as it is recognized that the ISA role applies to many systems not just those based on complex electronics.

From the very beginning the Working Group has recognised the importance of working together with those bodies involved in the development of safety standards, as well as those interest groups that have been set up by safety practitioners. This has led to the Working Group either inviting representatives from those parties to join the Working Group or to encourage Working Group members to participate and liaise with those other safety organisations.

3 Issues Addressed by the ISA WG

3.1 What is the role of the ISA?

A question that arises far too often, both from those looking to purchase ISA services, and even from ISAs themselves, is "what does an ISA actually do?" The question arises even though there are a plethora of existing safety standards, guidance documents, scholarly reports, etc. that all purport to provide the answer to that question, but none of them can be considered to give a definitive answer. The reasons for this are:

- Standards are usually produced to define what needs to be done, not how to do it.
- Where good guidance is incorporated into a standard, such as the many tables within Defence Standard 00-56 Issue 2, they are commonly used as if they were a normative part of the standard[2].
- The state-of-the-art changes so quickly that such guidance can easily become out of date.
- The role of the ISA cannot be fixed, it is not one such that a tick-in-the-box approach can, or should be undertaken.
- There are many different approaches, each of which can be perfectly valid depending on the requirements of the customer and the product involved.
- No-one is sure as to whether the role is that of a pure auditor, the provision of advice on safety issues, the assessment of processes and products, or a combination of all of these.

The Working Group investigated how guidance had been produced, and by whom and came to the conclusion that there was not one organisation that could be contacted to give definitive advice on how functional safety could be assured. It was recognised that the HSE took the lead regarding what could be considered as traditional safety issues, but it was felt that there was still a gap with regard to the detailed independent assessment of safety related processes and products.

As it has a very diverse membership, which is involved in the ISA role across many sectors of industry, the Working Group took the view that it was in a good position to be able to:

- Produce guidance that could be applied across the whole of industry, so that a common approach could be defined. This would be of benefit not only to ISAs, but also to those looking to use ISA services.
- Make such guidance readily accessible through its web site.
- Ensure that such guidance was kept up-to-date.

---

[2] Defence Standard 00-56 Issue 3 (MoD, 2004c) no longer includes such examples.

3.1.1 What's in a Letter?

One of the first tasks of the Working Group was to determine what the "A" in "ISA" stood for. This was not as simple as it at first appears, even though there were only three definitions that were in common use:

- Auditor.
- Assessor.
- Advisor.

Defining these terms was initially thought to be important, as the definitions would indicate the scope of an ISA's task. It has been the subject of previous debates, an example of the difficulty and angst it is able to generate was recorded in an ISA workshop held by the Defence Aerospace and Research Partnership in 2000 (DERA, 2000).

It was quickly decided that the Advisor role, whilst important, was not within the ISA role as defined in current international and UK standards. It was agreed that both the Auditor and Assessor could, as part of their role, provide some form of advice to customers; but that advice should not undermine their independence.

Following some quite enjoyable discussions, it was finally decided that a pure Auditor role would provide very little "added value" to a customer, especially if the auditing would take the form of "ticking the box". Checking that the requirements of standards have been met means very little without assessing the quality of such compliance. After all, it can be very easy to develop a Safety Case Report that has all the required headings but does not actually put forward a reasoned argument for safety. An audit would be able to check the headings, but only an assessment would enable a determination as to whether the arguments being put forward were valid.

It was therefore decided that the Independent Safety Assessor was the most important safety role, and that it would be expected that the Assessor would undertake safety auditing in order to obtain information on which to base judgements and assessments.

It was agreed that, in the real world, both the Auditor and Assessor roles would be asked to give some sort of advice on how to ensure safety issues were being addressed. It is extremely important that such advice is not so specific that the Auditor / Assessor in effect becomes part of the project team and could find it difficult to continue to function in an independent role.

3.1.2 Defining the Safety Assessor Role

The Working Group has developed the following definition for the Assessor role:

"Independent safety assessment is the formation of a judgement, separate and independent from any system design, development or operational personnel, that the safety requirements for the system are appropriate and adequate for the planned application and that the system satisfies those safety requirements."

The above definition was based on the Independent Safety Assessor competency description in the IEE/BCS/HSE competency guidelines (IEE, 1999).

3.1.3 Guidance on the Safety Assessor Role

The Working Group considers that for those involved in discharging the responsibility of an ISA, the key tasks are:

- Acquiring an appreciation of the scope and context of the assessment.
- Selecting and planning a cost-effective assessment strategy.
- Gathering relevant evidence.
- Forming a judgement including managing any outcomes.

The gathering of evidence is likely to be undertaken through a combination of auditing for conformance to planned arrangements, reviewing of project documentation and performing additional analyses.

The Working Group has identified that specific guidance on the following topics would be useful:

- How to actually undertake safety assessments and audits.
- The difficulties associated with the assessment of Commercial-Off-The-Shelf (COTS) components and how to address them successfully.
- The use of ISA Teams, rather than an individual ISA.
- How to read-across the requirements of different safety standards, especially where such standards appear to be in disagreement or conflict over what needs to be addressed in order to assure safety. This is especially important where projects are being undertaken in an international arena.

An increasing issue is that of the scope of the ISA role. Most large projects have a large number of subcontractors developing safety-related systems and subsystems. In many cases these subcontractors are supplying systems based on products that have been previously developed. These COTS systems may have been developed without taking into account the requirements of current safety standards, or have been produced in accordance with another country's safety standards or legislation. The Working Group has considered how to provide guidance to ISAs working on these types of projects.

Another aspect that requires discussion is that of an Independent System Safety Assessor (ISSA), who would take on responsibility for the ISA role across an entire project, for the customer, the main supplier as well as all the subcontractors. This would have the benefit of enabling a clear and consistent approach to addressing safety issues. The biggest problem that has been identified to date is who would pay for such an ISSA? The customer? The supplier? The regulator?

3.1.4 What's in a Word?

One aspect that the ISA Working Group has not been able to address fully so far is a detailed definition for is the meaning of the word "Independent." During extensive discussions no simple definition could be identified, as it could be said that "independence is in the eye of the beholder."

A Safety Consultant from a small consultancy contracted to provide the Safety Assessment role to a large multinational conglomerate would generally appear to provide an acceptable definition of "Independent". However, the perceived independence could be undermined if the financial well being of the consultancy was considered by others to be overly dependent on the continuation of such a contract.

Another problem that arose during the discussions was that when a large company, with many divisions based on separate sites, wanted to use their own safety specialists to undertake such roles. Whilst they could easily be independent of a particular project or product, or could even be part of a separate division or group, they could be considered to be working for the same company, and therefore could become vulnerable to managerial and commercial pressures; this is known to have happened in the past.

Therefore it was decided that the Working Group guidance on the meaning of the word "Independent" would be limited to advising on the use of the definitions contained within IEC-61508 (IEC, 1998) and other similar standards such as Defence Standard 00-56 (MoD, 1996), note that this is only guidance, not a definition. The role of the ISA is determined by the regulatory authority and the applicable standard. Thus, the contextual viewpoint of independent can change.

Some may find it extremely surprising that there has been such difficulty in coming up with a definition of "independent." However, many of the safety standards have the concept of different levels of safety requirements, differing levels of safety integrity; these all impact on the level of independence that is required of the ISA.

If those were the only issues that needed to be taken into consideration, then it would in all likelihood have been possible for the Working Group to produce a definition that would satisfy everyone, or at least the majority. However there are other issues that bring their own complications and difficulties to the discussion table:

- An ISA is commonly thought of as being "their ISA", "the customer's ISA", "our ISA." Can an ISA be truly independent if he is being contracted, and paid, by only one of the parties? Indeed there have been many cases where a programme has ended up with many ISAs, each being contracted by a different organisation, and commonly each with different and sometimes conflicting terms of reference. This can only increase costs and reduce confidence that safety is being addressed in a consistent and efficient manner.
- An ISA will usually work on many programmes, for many different customers, and can build up very valuable commercial knowledge that could, inadvertently or otherwise, be made available to a supplier's competitors or customers.

- Some ISAs work for companies that are themselves equipment suppliers. It can be very difficult for a competing company to consider these ISAs as being truly independent.

As stated previously, one important aspect of the ISA role is that of giving advice. There have probably been many cases where an ISA has heard a supplier say, tell me what you want me to do, then I'll go and do it and we will all be happy!"

To date most guidance on this issue states that the ISA should not give detailed advice on how to address specific safety issues. This has been mainly intended to ensure that the ISA does not become technically responsible for any detailed design or implementation aspects of a product; in some cases it has been taken to even preclude giving detailed advice on how to satisfy the requirements of safety standards.

There have been situations where an Independent Safety Advisor role has been undertaken during the early phases of a project, with the role changing to that of an Independent Safety Assessor as the project develops. This has enabled detailed advice to be given during the conceptual phases, but does not cause the ISA to become involved in generating product-specific safety evidence.

This approach can be extremely beneficial to both the developer and customer of the product. However, it requires an experienced and professional ISA who is able to identify when possible conflicts-of-interest and/or loss of independence may occur, and then act accordingly to ensure that assurance of safety is not compromised in any way.

These are all issues that need to be considered when attempting to come up with definitive guidance on the term "independent."

3.1.5 Who needs an ISA?

As well as providing guidance to those undertaking the ISA role, the Working Group has produced guidance aimed at those who might need to purchase ISA services. It was agreed that it would be improper to assume that such potential ISA customers would be safety experts themselves. Therefore the guidance produced has been aimed at the safety novice. Typical reasons as to why an ISA may be needed are:

- To comply with a Standard that requires an ISA.
- To provide assurance that a product is acceptably safe, both to the purchaser and the supplier.
- To aid in the demonstration to a regulator that your system is acceptably safe.

Because the safety assessment that is provided by the ISA is independent of any existing safety analysis and assessment that might have been undertaken internally, it provides confidence that safety claims are justified and that any weaknesses are identified and dealt with.

In some situations the use of an ISA is mandatory. For instance, when carrying out work in accordance with Defence Standard 00-56 Issue 2[3] or when developing safety critical systems for use in the UK railway industry.

In other cases, use of an ISA can be considered to be good practice. For instance, the generic functional safety standard IEC 61508 represents "current best practice" for safety-related electrical / electronic / programmable electronic systems (E/E/PES). The standard requires the use of independent safety assessment (called functional safety assessment in the Standard) where the degree of independence depends on the Safety Integrity Level of the system.

Independent safety assessment is intended to be retained in the industry-specific instantiations of the generic Standard. Within the motor industry, the MISRA (Motor Industry Software Reliability Association) Development Guidelines for Vehicle Based Software (MISRA, 1994) recommend the use of an independent assessor and/or auditor in order to act as an advocate for the level of confidence in the safety of the product delivered to the end customer.

As well as providing assurance of safety, using an ISA can help to focus safety planning and analyses. This can come about naturally by answering ISA questions and providing safety information to the ISA. In addition, an ISA is often able to offer generic guidance that does not compromise independence, as discussed above this can be particularly useful in the early stages of a project.

3.1.6 Making the Guidance Available to All

The Working Group has established a Web Site, which will be used to enable easy access to the outputs developed by the Working Group. The site is currently hosted on the IEE site and can be accessed at the following URL:

http://www.iee.org/Policy/Areas/isa/index.cfm

Since the Working Group Web Site came online, it has become increasingly popular as a source of safety information. The graph below shows the number of hits that have occurred since January 2004.

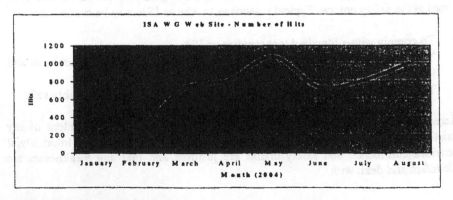

---

[3] Defence Standard 00-56 Issue 3 no longer mandates the use of an ISA.

At present the site contains the following freely available information:

- The aims of the ISA Working Group.
- A list of members of the ISA Working Group.
- The Working Group's definition of the term "ISA."
- Guidance on who needs an ISA.
- A downloadable copy of the UK MoD developed "Guidelines for ISAs." (QinetiQ, 2003)[4].
- A set of Frequently-Asked-Questions (FAQ) on the ISA role.
- A copy of the minutes of the most recent Working Group meeting.
- A contact email address for getting in touch with the Working Group:

    mailto:\\isa@iee.org.uk

If anyone or any organisation has documents that could be made available via the Working Group Web Site then please send an email to the contact address.

3.2 The ISA WG Seminar - Life Saving Second Opinions

During 2004 the Working Group members discussed ways to improve the general profile of the Working Group, as well as increase awareness among the engineering community of the guidance for ISAs that had been developed.

It was decided that the best way to undertake this was to hold a safety seminar, which was eventually held during June 2004 under the title "Life Saving Second Opinions." It was a deliberate decision not to have any reference to ISAs in the seminar title as it was felt that such a reference would have given the impression that the seminar was only for ISAs; rather than the much wider audience of engineers and managers that the seminar was aimed at.

Some of the topics addressed at the seminar are described below.

- It is recognised that the ISA Working Group is not the only body that is producing guidance on the role of the ISA. There is a major commitment within the UK MoD to ensure that its systems are safe. A highly visible result of this commitment is the existence of standards such as Defence Standard 00-56, which has been one of the main drivers of the use of ISAs in the UK.

    To date most of the advice that had been produced was aimed at the ISAs, and there was little information readily available to those intending to use ISA services. The UK MoD addressed this by producing a documented set of guidelines (MoD, 2004a) for use within the UK MoD's Integrated Project Teams (IPTs) which contains information on:

---

[4] This has been superseded by more recent guidelines which have been developed for the UK MoD, (MoD, 2004a), however, at the time of writing, this was not available for download from the Working Group web site.

- basis for the ISA role;
- relationships between the ISA and other organisations;
- selection of ISAs;
- expected expertise and competence;
- defining the scope of work.

The UK MoD contracted a member of the ISA Working Group to manage the production of this document, which contains much in common with that which has been discussed and agreed by the Working Group.

- There has been extensive work undertaken by members of the Working Group in order to identify how measurement of the safety process can be undertaken in order to determine whether the process is enabling safety to make a positive contribution to a development programme.

  This is a very difficult aspect to address, as the many different roles and organizations involved in a safety programme can have completely different concepts of what construes a positive contribution

- In order to explain how the ISA role is undertaken examples of ISAs working in the real world were described. One case study described the use of the UK Rail Industry Yellow Book (Railtrack, 2000), showing how the ISA role is undertaken within the Rail Industry: how Assessors are selected; the methods and tools used and how the results of such assessments are disseminated.

  Another study described the undertaking of the Independent Safety Assessor role within the UK motor industry, including how existing standards such as IEC-61508 sometimes have to be carefully tailored before they can be used effectively during a programme.

  Other topics included the wide range of customer expectations and contractual situations that could be encountered by an ISA, as these can easily impact on the ISAs responsibilities and independence and are a major influence on the success of the ISAs role.

  Information was also given on those important and difficult lessons that have had to be learnt by those acting as ISAs, including the need to:

- develop the scope of the ISA role with the customer as the project develops;
- use as many information sources as possible when assessing levels of risk;
- identify all those responsible for safety across all equipment and process interfaces;
- use a team of ISAs, so that specific areas of expertise can be applied, for example having an Independent Software Safety Assessor;
- document ISA findings in a form that a customer can respond to efficiently and effectively within agreed timescales;
- beware of situations where the ISA is required to prove that something is unsafe;
- address what is meant by "risk" in a clear and consistent manner;

- remember that the ISA is there to give confidence that safety is being addressed, the ISA is not responsible for safety on a project;
- add value to the project.

This seminar was considered to have been very successful in achieving its aims. In fact the seminar had the largest audience of any functional-safety-related event held in the UK during 2004.

4 Future Topics of Interest

4.1 Competency Assessment of Independent Safety Assessors

The main topic currently under discussion within the Working Group is that of the competence of those involved in the safety assurance role. It is widely recognised that there is no formal definition of what qualifications or experience should be expected of an Independent Safety Assessor. Indeed anyone could call himself or herself an ISA and define the role as one of:

- Independent Safety Analyst.
- Independent Systems Assessor.
- Independent System Advisor.
- Independent Safety Accreditor.

The Working Group considers it extremely important that there is a mechanism for those looking to use independent safety consultants to be able to check that the consultant is a Suitably Qualified and Experienced Person (SQEP) undertaking a recognised ISA role.

Other groups have also identified these areas of concern, such as the HSE and the UK Department of Trade and Industry (dti). The Working Group has undertaken extensive reviews of these schemes, which are summarised below.

- The IEE/BCS/HSE Competency Guidelines for Safety-Related System Practitioners (IEE, 1999)

   First issued in 1999 following extensive consultation with industry the guidelines were produced in order to help in the assessment of the competencies of staff working on various aspects of safety related systems. According to the guidelines the overall objectives of the study were to:

   - create sets of core competencies for mainstream practitioners in the field of Safety Related Electrical / Electronic and/or Programmable Electronic Systems;
   - increase the understanding of the basis for the definition of core competencies;
   - Allow organizations to undertake a self-assessment of competency requirements for identified safety roles.

Identified strengths of this approach include:

- can be applied on an informal self-assessment basis;
- is based on extensive industry involvement;
- describes different levels of expertise, (Supervised Practitioner, Practitioner and Expert);
- enjoys extensive industry take-up.

Weaknesses include:

- has no requirement for a formal independent assessment to be undertaken;
- is issued as guidance and is not intended as a description of "current-best-practice".

The Conformity Assessment of Safety Systems (CASS) Scheme

This was started in 1998 with the support of the dti, and is currently run by The CASS Scheme Ltd., which has developed an assessment scheme for safety-related systems based upon IEC-61508. According to the CASS Assessor Guide (CASS, 2000) the benefits of the scheme include:

- enhanced confidence in the safety of complex E/E/PES systems through the availability of an accredited assessment standard;
- reduced procurement costs by facilitating the reuse of assessed products;
- provision of a yardstick to national and regulatory authorities assessing "fitness for purpose" and best practice of installed systems;
- generation of a pool of assessors recognised as competent to undertake assessments in this field.

Identified strengths of this approach include:

- CASS is a formal assessment scheme;
- it includes a documented framework for undertaken competence assessment;
- whilst aligned with the requirements of IEC-61508, CASS have agreed to take on board the competency requirements described in the IEE/BCS/HSE guidelines;
- part of the assessment is in the form of an interview.

Weaknesses include:

- the CASS scheme is obliged to charge for the Assessor Registration at a level which will financially compensate a peer-review panel, and as a consequence the scheme is perceived as being expensive by members of the Working Group. This is in comparison with other schemes that might be undertaken as "in-house" projects using the IEE/BCS/HSE Competency Guidelines. The Working Group has discussed the issue of cost with the CASS organisation;

- whilst there has been some take-up of the Registered Assessor service covering Process Industries, Railways, and Nuclear Inspection, with Assessor scopes addressing both hardware and software aspects, there are still very few Registered Assessors;
- the IEC-61508 standard is not embodied in UK Law, therefore neither it, nor the CASS scheme can be mandated by any regulatory body;
- to date, take up of formal 3rd party accredited assessment of safety systems to IEC-61508 has been limited, with consequent limited demand to expand the Assessor Register. This has lead some who have considered becoming a Registered Assessor to take the view that there may be limited opportunity to recoup the registration costs.

- **The UK MoD Assessment Scheme**

The UK MoD, rather than an actual assessment scheme has various training courses that anyone intending to undertake an ISA role for the MoD must successfully complete:

- the Ship Safety Management Office, part of the Defence Procurement Agency, Sea Technology Group requires completion of their Ship Safety Management Training Course;
- the Defence Ordnance Safety Group has organised an Ordnance, Munitions and Explosives Safety Course that it considers as highly desirable for potential ISAs to complete.

UK MoD Integrated Project Teams are advised by the UK MoD Safety Offices to check that any personnel who are taking on safety tasks on their behalf satisfy the guidance provided regarding basic competence set out in the latest UK MoD guidance document (MoD, 2004a) and that they have at least attended a course such as those listed above

Identified strengths of this approach include:

- it is targeted at specific safety issues and provides guidance from recognised experts in the field;
- it should be relatively easy to manage.

Weaknesses include:

- it is UK MoD oriented and therefore of little benefit to those whose work is mainly non-MOD;
- it is basically an approved training course and record scheme, not an assessment scheme as such;
- it can actually be more expensive than CASS accreditation (however CASS accreditation is not regarded as equivalent to attendance at a designated course.)

Therefore the Working Group had discussed various ways in which the best elements of the above schemes could be used to develop a specific competence assessment scheme for ISAs.

One suggestion has been for the Working Group itself to set up a registration scheme for ISAs. This would have the following attributes:

- It would be based on the IEE/BCS/HSE Competency Guidelines.
- It would take the form of a peer assessment, undertaken by Working Group members.
- The assessment would be refereed by a nominated member of the IEE or BCS.
- It would be open to all, and would not be limited to those who were members of a professional institution such as the IEE or BCS.
- There would be no assessment interviews; the assessment would be of objective evidence put forward by the prospective registree.
- There would be no cost, other than an individuals time during the assessment.

This is generally considered to be a workable scheme, however there are some potential problems:

- Due to potential liability issues, registration could in no way be construed as any form of endorsement by any of the professional institutions, the Working Group or its members.
- As it could not be a mandatory scheme, it would probably suffer from a similar lack of take-up as the CASS scheme has.
- The scheme is not driven by Purchasers across many industry sectors so has limited appeal to those seeking 'registration'.
- It is unclear as to what "added value" such a scheme would give to purchasers of ISA services, especially as they currently tend to give such work to companies or individuals who they know well and who have a proven track record.
- The 'voluntary' nature of the scheme means that it will only exist for as long as those running it are prepared to donate their 'spare' time.

The Working Group still considers that the issue of recognising ISA competence and setting standards needs to be addressed and would welcome suggestions[5] from safety practitioners on this topic.

4.2 The Importance of Environmental Safety

Over the past few years there has been an increasing requirement for functional safety assessments to include environmental aspects, in order to determine whether a

---

[5] At the time of writing this paper the Safety Critical Systems Club had published an article in its newsletter (SCSCN, 2004) on the licensing or registration of software practitioners.

system is not only safe for the user but that any risks to the environment are effectively managed.

There has been significant work undertaken on this, including that by the UK MoD, which, during 2004 issued their Acquisition Safety and Environmental Management System (MoD, 2004b).

The Working Group is to consider how the ISA role could be expanded to address such issues.

4.3 The International Safety Role

An increasingly important role for UK based ISAs is the assessment of systems, components, etc. that have been developed to non-UK/EU standards. The most commonly encountered standards are generally U.S. standards such as:

- MIL-STD-882C & D[6].
- MIL-STD-498.
- RTCA/DO-178A.

It is quite common for ISAs to be asked about the equivalence of such standards, whether a component developed to say, MIL-STD-882C, is suitable for use on a project that is required to work to Defence Standard 00-56. This is especially important when the differing definitions of safety integrity have to be considered.

Not only is there a need for clear advice on such issues, but it is considered important that the UK safety community:

- Is aware of the existence, revision and creation of such standards.
- Can provide feedback to the developers of such standards.
- Are able to participate in the development and/or updates of such standards.

The Working Group will therefore be looking at ways in which an UK "safety voice" can be heard. This could include:

- Active participation on international/national standards committees.
- Production and/or collation of comments on such standards to be sent to the relevant standards bodies outside the UK.

4.4 Improving the ISA Working Group Web Site

It is hoped that the current Working Group web site will be improved over the coming years, with the intention of making it one of the main "safety portals" in the UK. It is recognised that there already exist some important safety web sites, such as those produced by the UK HSE, various university research groups, etc. The intention would not be to replace these sites, but to provide safety professionals with

---

[6] At the time of writing 882E was being considered by the US DoD.

a portal that would provide access to Working Group information and information on what was held at other locations.

The Working Group considers that the web site could be developed to include the following:

- Descriptions of typical ISA tasks and the issues that could arise.
- Case Studies based upon real occurrences written by real ISAs.
- Guidance on how to measure the effectiveness of ISAs and Safety Management Processes.
- A repository for reports addressing topics relevant to ISAs.
- Information and recommendations on publications (books, videos, etc) that might be useful to the safety professional.
- Links to other web sites with safety-related information.

5 Conclusions

The IEE/BCS Independent Safety Assurance Working Group aims to provide relevant and useful information and guidance on a wide range of topics of relevance to safety professionals, and to those who might need the services of such professionals.

The success or failure of the Working Group is dependent on the contributions made from the group members, as well as support from the wider safety community. It is hoped that through initiatives such as seminars and the Working Group web site, there will be increasingly successful engagement between the Working Group and the safety community.

This paper has described how the Working Group is supporting ISA practitioners and their customers through the provision of independent guidance on aspects such as competence and the scope of work, as well as disseminating information across the professional safety community.

6 Acknowledgements

The author wishes to thank the IEE/BCS ISA WG for assisting in the production of this paper and providing valuable comments. The author also acknowledges that some of the text in sections 2 and 3.1 is based on that at the ISA WG website, which is hosted by the IEE.

7 References

CASS (2000), The CASS Guide: Guide to Functional Safety Capability Assessment, Accredited certification to IEC 61508. 26 April 2000, Issue 2a.

DERA (2000), DERA/KIS/SEB/TR000944, Overview Report of the DARP HIRTS Independent Safety Auditors Workshop, November 2000.

IEC (1998), IEC 61508, Functional Safety of Electrical / Electronic / Programmable Electronic Safety-Related Systems, International Electrotechnical Commission, Geneva.

IEE (1999), Safety Competency and Commitment, Competency Guidelines for Safety Related Systems Practitioners, The Institute of Electrical Engineers, ISBN 0 85296 787 X.

MISRA (1994), Development Guidelines for Vehicle Based Software, ISBN 0 9524156 0 7, November 1994. Motor Industry Software Reliability Association.

MoD (1996), Defence Standard 00-56, Safety Management Requirements for Defence Systems, Issue 2, UK Ministry of Defence.

MoD (2004), STG/181/1/9/1, Guidance for Integrated Project Teams for Use in Contracting for Independent Safety Auditor (ISA) Services, Safety Management Offices Group, UK Ministry of Defence.

MoD (2004), Acquisition Safety and Environmental Management System (ASEMS), Version 2.0e, UK Ministry of Defence.

MoD (2004), Defence Standard 00-56, Safety Management Requirements for Defence Systems, Issue 3, UK Ministry of Defence.

QinetiQ (2003), ISA Guidelines for MoD Projects, Simon N Brown, QinetiQ, Malvern.

Railtrack (2000), Engineering Safety Management, Issue 3, Yellow Book 3, Volumes 1 and 2, Fundamentals and Guidance, Railtrack plc.

SCSCN (2004), Should software engineers be licensed, The Safety Critical Systems Club News Letter, Volume 14, Number 1, September 2004, Prof. John Knight, University of Virginia.

Putting Trust into Safety Arguments

Jane Fenn and Brian Jepson

BAE Systems, Warton Aerodrome,

Preston, Lancashire, PR4 1AX

Abstract

This paper describes one development of a concept that emerged from the Defence and Aerospace Research Partnership to enhance safety arguments by identifying and managing the argument's dependence on safety evidence.

1 Introduction

The application of Safety Engineering methodologies is relatively immature as an engineering discipline. Techniques are inconsistently applied within and across domains. Reaching consensus on 'best practice' is difficult, if not impossible, consequently, a plethora of standards have emerged which reflect various 'flavours' of safety engineering. Typically, these present a 'cook book' approach to safety techniques; leaving the rationale for selection and appropriate combinations of techniques largely implicit. Similarly, there is an implicit, and, as yet, unproven assumption in these standards that a good process necessarily yields a safe product. Many critics of these standards have observed that, whilst a good process is necessary, it is not sufficient to ensure a safe product.

A characterisation of these standards can be used to draw out some of the contentious areas and plot a timeline of the development of safety standards as we, in the UK defence industry, brace ourselves for migrating to issue 3 of Defence Standard 00-56[1].

Perhaps it's best to start with a standard that has been quite widely used within the safety community: DEF STAN 00-56 issue 2[2]. This standard proposes managing safety by means of risk matrices based on failure rates and hazard consequences and provides guidance on determining tolerability criteria. Systematic errors are handled by way of Safety Integrity Levels; SIL 4 representing the highest safety risk systems and SIL 1 the lowest. These SILs are mapped across to development processes, of which the software aspects are addressed in more detail in DEF STAN 00-55[3]. The explicit record of the safety of the system, as declared by the developer, is contained in the safety case.

The Australian equivalent standard is DEF AUST 5679[4]. A similar schema is used where 'Levels of Trust' are mapped to SILs for software; SIL 6 presenting the highest risk and SIL 1 lowest. Examples are then given for design, implementation and verification techniques, based on allocated SIL. Whilst this standard doesn't have an explicit safety case, the 'Safety Analysis Plan' requires some of the same types of information.

The more generic European standard IEC 61508[5] has SILs too, though these are somewhat different, with SIL4 systems intended to have the lowest hazardous failure rate. Detailed techniques are then presented, with recommendation categories dependent on SIL, which are intended to address both random and systematic failures.

Our American colleagues use MIL-STD-882. Issue C [6] of the standard identified 'Software Control Categories' which are similar to SILs, but then gives no advice on how these should be handled, other than referring out to DO-178B[7]. Issue D [8] of the standard simply requires the developer to identify, evaluate and reduce 'mishap' risk. The standard contains a 'Safety Compliance Assessment' which fulfils some of the role of a safety case.

Whilst it is not a safety standard in itself, it is increasingly common for companies to offer compliance with DO-178B in response to safety requirements. This standard uses 'Development Assurance Levels' (DAL) to reflect the rigour of process required, with Level A being the highest and Level E lowest. Tables of techniques are provided in the annexes of the standard, indicating which should be used for each DAL, and noting independence requirements for these techniques at higher levels. The 'Software Accomplishment Summary' contains some of the same elements as a safety case.

None of the above standards offers a rationale for these choices of techniques. Various authors have criticised the approach, including Penny and Eaton[9], who said *"...there is a need to shift from documenting how hard people have tried to develop a system to providing evidence and argument about the behaviour of that system"*.

Support for this argument certainly seems to be growing, as demonstrated by the change in emphasis of some of the later standards such as the CAA's SW01[10]. This standard has a concept of 'Assurance Evidence Levels' (AEL) which "identify the depth and strength of evidence that must be made available from the software lifecycle for the equipment approval process". Dependent on AEL, an indication on the type of 'direct' testing and analysis necessary is provided, as well as the requirement for 'indirect' evidence of the process coverage. Whilst this standard clearly makes product evidence its mainstay, it still does not deal with the rationale behind the choices or composition of evidence to support a safety argument.

DEF STAN 00-56 issue 3 pushes a step further in emphasising the need for both the product evidence AND the argument which shows how this evidence is composed. Kelly [11] says that *"Argument without supporting evidence is unfounded, and therefore unconvincing. Evidence without argument is unexplained – it can be unclear that (or how) safety objectives have been satisfied"*.

Goal Structured Notation (GSN) has been used for some years and is an ideal vehicle for communicating precisely this concept of how evidence is composed. Whilst it is entirely feasible to generate a safety case without using this notation, the clarity, oversight and structure that such a notation provides is difficult to provide textually, in particular. The observer can gain insight into the author's logical and ordered thought processes in arguing that a system is safe. However, GSN does have some limitations. The importance of each goal, relative to its peer goals, typically cannot be communicated. For example, a formal proof, as a solution to a goal, is represented in exactly the same way as historical evidence of safe operation of a similar system.

The overall confidence in the safety of a system is often referred to as 'assurance' or 'trustworthiness'. The level of assurance it determined from both the confidence in the decomposition from one goal to its child goal(s) and the confidence in the assurance of those child goals. What is needed is a method through which to indicate that confidence.

During discussions at the Defence and Aerospace Research Partnership (DARP) workshop in 2000, a concept was explored which has subsequently been researched by BAE SYSTEMS and the University of York. Two techniques have evolved, but share a common heritage and many similarities. Both techniques are still relatively immature and require large scale validation. This paper describes one of these, the SEAL approach, that is being developed within BAE Systems.

2   The SEAL approach

In April 2000 the High Integrity Real Time Systems Defence and Aerospace Research Partnership[12] debated the proposed revision of the Defence Standards 00-55 and 00-56. The purpose of the revision was to remove prescriptive requirements and re-focus on evidence-based demonstration of safety through the use of a Safety Case.

It was immediately obvious that removing inappropriate requirements would be beneficial: reducing unnecessary cost, encouraging wider use of civil standards and improving competition.

An evidence-based approach is desirable since it allows the available effort and attention to be focused on achieving safety and producing direct evidence of safety.

Other industry sectors are moving towards evidential approaches, one of the best examples being the CAA which has adopted an evidence-based approach for its Air Traffic System software standard [10].

One drawback with the evidence-based approach is the relative immaturity of safety case and safety argument methods, and the lack of experience in using evidence and argumentation as the main thrust of safety assurance. It was proposed that safety argument methods would need to be enhanced to provide a way of indicating the degree, or level, of dependence, or trust, being placed on each part of an argument. The term Safety Evidence Assurance Level (SEAL) was coined to describe this and the concept has been developing slowly ever since.

The SEAL approach stresses the importance of considering the collection of evidence that can be obtained to support the safety argument throughout the development and decomposition of the argument. At each stage of argument construction, the feasibility of obtaining supporting evidence of the necessary strength and quality needs to be considered. It would be ill-advised to continue with a system design and safety argument if you were not confident that evidence could be obtained to support the case being made.

SEALs and safety argument notations

In this paper we describe and give an example of SEALs being used in conjunction with safety argument fragments expressed in Goal Structured Notation (GSN). GSN is our preferred notation for arguments but SEALs could be used with safety arguments and safety cases expressed using other notations. However the benefit of using SEALs is dependent on the robustness of the argument and the degree to which that argument is decomposed into clear, succinct, atomic goals.

Space constraints do not permit an explanation of GSN in detail; readers who require further information are recommended to read Kelly1998[11].

3   What is a SEAL?

A SEAL (Safety Evidence Assurance Level) is defined as:

SEAL   *A SEAL is a qualitative statement of requirement for a degree of confidence in the evidence that a specific safety goal has been achieved.*

The SEAL for a goal is based on the contribution of that goal to the overall argument and the risk associated with failing to satisfy the goal. Allocating SEALs to goals allows the confidence in the safety argument to be validated through a more systematic evaluation of the evidence that is available or is expected to be produced in support of the goal.

In a GSN safety argument each goal in the argument would be tagged with a SEAL to indicate the degree of confidence that is required in the solution of that goal. A goal is solved by either a body of evidence that shows the goal has been achieved or a set of sub-goals that develop and refine the argument. The sub-goals would then be tagged with SEALs to reflect the degree of trust being invested in each part of the argument.

By definition a SEAL is a qualitative tag, but the levels are ordered from least confidence required through to most confidence required. The convention adopted is to use numbers as tags, with 1 being the lowest level and 4 being the highest. This looks very similar to SILs, and it has to be acknowledged that there are parallels, but the choice of 4 levels has a reason.

The range of SEAL levels is defined by the extreme values as shown in Table 1. The lowest represents a requirement for evidence with a very small amount of confidence. This is more than having no confidence but may not be sufficient on its own to support any goal. The highest level represents almost complete confidence in the evidence. We say almost complete because there will always be some residual doubt but it should be an insignificant amount. The choice of the number of intermediate levels is open. Too few would limit the ability to express the levels required for each goal in the argument and too many would make it difficult to interpret what each meant in terms of evidence.

SEAL	Description	Trustworthiness
4	highest level of assurance	Incontrovertible
3		Compelling
2		Persuasive
1	lowest level of assurance	Supportive

Table 1 Safety Evidence Assurance Levels

4 The SEALs process

The SEALs process is a part of the safety argument development process and as such should be performed in parallel with the system development. If the safety argument is developed in three major phases, Preliminary, Interim and Operational, as is often recommended, the evidence emphasis at each phase would be:

Safety Argument Phase	SEALs evidence consideration.
Preliminary. Sets out the basis for the safety case. No detailed arguments.	Taking into account the proposed design of the system and the main goals of the safety argument, consider whether it is feasible that the argument could be developed to the point where evidence of the appropriate integrity and quality will be available. Where the feasibility of the argument is in doubt, for example insufficient independence of goals, the system architecture may need to be revised.
Interim. Arguments developed such that the whole safety case is visible. Little or no evidence provided.	Taking into account the system design and its development process, can evidence be obtained or generated so that all the goals of the argument are satisfied? Does the argument structure adequately reflect the characteristics of the evidence that will be available?
Operational. Argument is complete with evidence provided.	Does the evidence satisfy the goals and does it have the qualities necessary to be confident that the goal is satisfied?

4.1 SEAL for a Top-level goal

The starting point of any safety argument is the top-level goal. It is the objective of the argument to show that this goal is achieved. A SEAL is assigned to the top-level goal to indicate the degree of confidence that is required in the combined evidence for the complete argument.

The SEAL of the top-level goal must therefore be related to the hazard that might arise if this goal were not achieved. A simple approach to allocating this SEAL is to use a risk matrix (see Table 2), similar to that used for SIL allocation in Def. Stan. 00-56 Issue 2 [2].

Failure Probability of Mitigating Factors	HAZARD SEVERITY			
	Catastrophic	Critical	Marginal	Negligible
No Mitigation				
Frequent	SEAL 4			
Probable		SEAL 3		
Occasional			SEAL 2	
Remote				
Improbable				SEAL 1

Table 2 Initial derivation of SEAL base on hazard severity and external mitigation

At this point it should be considered whether it is likely that evidence that meets the SEAL requirement can be obtained or generated for the top-level goal. If there is a high risk of not having the evidence, or of the evidence being too weak, you should re-consider the safety strategy and possibly modify the system, to provide additional mitigation, so that the evidence requirements are lower.

The initial SEAL is identified from severity of hazard but may also take into account time at risk, environmental or other external factors. The probability of these other mitigating factors is expressed in qualitative terms and used as per Table 2 to provide the initial SEAL for the safety argument top-level goal.

The top-level goal would be tagged with its allocated SEAL and this would then be used to define the requirement for each level of goal decomposition.

At each level of goal decomposition a SEAL is allocated to each sub-goal. The SEAL indicates the level of assurance required for that goal and its subsequent solution(s).

4.2   SEAL for a sub-goal

In the simplest goal decomposition, and to ensure safety, the SEAL for a sub-goal should be the same as that for the parent goal. Whilst ensuring safety, this is generally not a useful approach since it does not correspond to the notion of layered protection or defence in depth. The safety argument methods should support, and possibly encourage, the satisfaction of higher-level safety goals through multiple diverse arguments involving combinations of sub-goals. What is important is that the evidence available for each sub-goal can be combined to fully satisfy the parent goal.

We have identified three attributes of evidence that need to be considered when determining how well a combination of two or more sub-goals satisfy a parent goal. These attributes are Relevance, Coverage and Strength and are described below.

At the current state of the technology it is not possible to determine quantitative measures for attributes of evidence. Neither is it possible for us to define a calculus for combining the attributes. But in practice we are considering these issues every time we read or review a safety argument. We each make a judgement about whether the sub-goals actually satisfy the parent goal and whether any ambiguity or weakness in the argument is significant.

Using SEALs we hope to move forward by using a set of qualitative attributes to guide our judgement and hopefully make it more explicit. As mentioned previously SEALs place the emphasis on considering the evidence that is available, or may be generated to support a goal as it is refined down the goal structure. The attributes are therefore defined in terms of the evidence which solves the goals.

- **Relevance**
  This attribute represents the degree to which a body of evidence for a sub-goal applies to the parent goal. For example a sub-goal "Unit testing completed" is only partially relevant to a parent goal "No run-time errors possible" since testing is only a partial solution to showing the absence of run-time errors.

- **Coverage**
  This attribute represents the degree to which a body of evidence for a sub-goal addresses all possible subdivisions, instances or cases of a parent goal. For example parent goal "X causes safe shutdown" is only partly covered by a sub-goal "Xm causes shutdown when system in mode 'm'". In this example a number of sub-goals would be required to achieve coverage of all modes.

- **Strength**
  The strength of a body of evidence is the degree to which that evidence can be trusted. Formal Methods generate strong evidence, manual reviews are generally weak and evidence from testing is only as strong as the test process.

These three attributes are not completely distinct properties of evidence. In certain contexts aspects of relevance may be similar to coverage and sometimes strength is equivalent to relevance. What is important to the SEALs approach is that the three attributes are considered when allocating SEALs to sub-goals.

4.3   Allocating SEALs to sub-goals

When decomposing a parent goal to a set of sub-goals, a range of strategies may be employed. It is possible to classify these strategies according to the relationship between the goals involved and this has been one of the areas addressed by parallel research at the University of York on Safety Assurance Levels (SAL) [13] . This work requires all goal refinements to be reduced to a very simple set of decomposition strategies such that per-defined SAL allocation rules might be applied.

The experience of the authors suggests that real-world safety arguments typically involve, at some stages of goal decomposition, hybrid strategies which cannot be simplified. It is important to validate all the strategies used against the evidence attributes.

Having considered the relationship between parent goal and sub-goals using the three attributes, Relevance, Coverage and Strength, SEALs are allocated to each sub-goal to reflect the degree to which the parent goal depends on its sub-goals.

Possible outcomes are:

- Evidence is inadequate.

  If it is found that the evidence attributes for the sub-goals are inadequate to support the parent goal, then the safety argument cannot be supported and is destined to fail. Either the argument strategy needs to be revised to include additional sub-goals and evidence, or additional evidence-generating activities are required. In the worst case the system may need to be modified so that it is possible to construct a justifiable safety argument.

- Evidence is adequate.

    If the evidence is considered adequate to meet to the requirement of the parent goal, each sub-goal is given the same SEAL as the parent goal.

- Evidence is more than adequate.

    Where the decomposition strategy shows that the requirement for evidence is satisfied with respect to all the attributes, any redundancy or excess in the evidence may be used to optimise the evidence gathering activities. For example effort may be reduced where the evidence is more plentiful than necessary and increased in other areas where the evidence is less convincing.

The SEALs provide the basis for making judgements about the trustworthiness of parts of a safety argument. Providing the SEAL requirement is satisfied at each decomposition there is no need for pre-defined decomposition strategies and a range of options may be considered, including:

- Seal apportionment.

    Where two sub-goals can independently fully satisfy a SEAL n parent goal, these sub-goals may be each allocated SEAL n-1.

- Highlighting the need for independence.

    Where a goal decomposition uses the independence of sub-goal evidence as a factor in its justification, it is important to consider whether a derived requirement on independence of the sub-goal evidence is being implicitly introduced. Any derived requirements should be made explicit in the argument so that evidence supporting the independence can be obtained.

- Identifying backing.

    Where a sub-goal only provides backing evidence i.e. is not the main thrust of the argument, it may be allocated a lower SEAL.

4.4 SEALs and Evidence

As the safety argument is developed, SEALs are allocated to each sub-goal as described above, based on the collection of evidence attributes that are expected to be satisfied for each sub-goal. For a final or operational safety argument, actual evidence is provided as a solution to the terminal sub-goals.

It is a relatively easy step to ensure that the actual evidence obtained satisfies the SEAL of the last sub-goal. If the actual evidence is insufficient to satisfy the goal then the argument has failed, in the same way as if a sub-goal could not be justified against its parent. In this case the argument would have to be modified to incorporate additional sub-goals and evidence.

One important benefit of using SEALs is that the contribution of individual items of evidence to the overall argument is better understood. This makes it easier to assess the impact of changes in the evidence and allows balancing of stronger and weaker items. By contrast, in a safety argument without SEALs, it can be difficult to assess the impact on the top goal of the loss of any single item of evidence, particularly for maintainers rather than developers of the safety argument.

5 A simple example

Figure 1 shows a simple abstract example of a safety argument fragment expressed in GSN using SEALS. The following description elaborates on each element in the argument but it should be noted that this is an artificial example to aid understanding.

In this example safety argument fragment the top level goal (G0) is "Run-time errors will not occur". The context for this (Cntx0) states that failure of the system, due to run-time error or any other cause, is Catastrophic. Hence G0 is allocated SEAL 4 since we need the highest level of confidence that a run-time error will not happen. The justification (J0) records the rationale for this SEAL allocation.

G0 is decomposed using strategy (Strat0) into three sub-goals. This strategy is the combination of evidence from three independent sources, each of which supports G0. Before SEALs are considered for the sub-goals it is not obvious how much the argument depends on each source, only that it does have a dependence. The justification for the use of this strategy is recorded in J2.

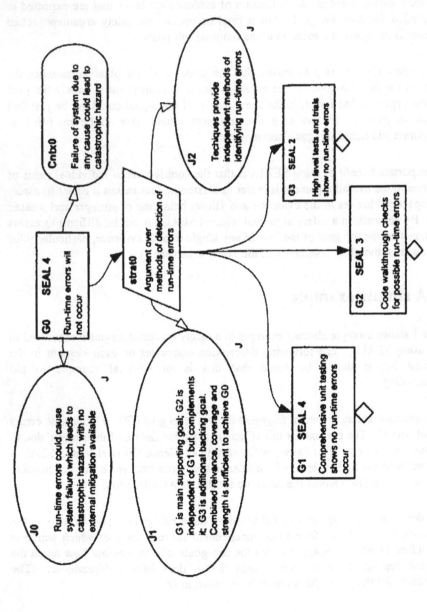

Figure 1 Example of using SEALs

Sub-goal G1 is "Comprehensive unit testing shows no run-time errors occur". Consideration of the evidence attributes of sub-goal G1 shows that it has high coverage, all possible run-time errors are addressed, and high relevance testing can find run-time errors. But unit testing only has medium strength since it is dependent on manual preparation and execution of test scripts.

Sub-goal G2 is "Code walkthrough checks for possible run-time errors". This has high coverage because all possible errors are covered, but its relevance is low since inspection is likely to be unable to detect arithmetic errors. Strength is also medium because of the manual nature of the process.

Sub-goal G3 is "Higher level tests and trials show no run-time-errors". Evidence for this goal has medium to low coverage because it cannot be inferred that all possible run-time error have been exercised by the tests and trials. Relevance is high because the test and trials are representative of operational use. Strength is medium because although significant errors would be detected and logged minor errors may have been missed.

The evidence attributes for each sub-goal are summarised in Table 3.

	Coverage	Relevance	Strength
G0 (Requirement)	**High**	**High**	**High**
G1	High	High	Medium
G2	High	Low	Medium
G3	Low	High	Medium

Table 3. Summary of evidence assessment at G0 decomposition

From this assessment we determine that G1 is the main leg of the argument but is not sufficient on its own to satisfy G0. G1 is therefore allocated SEAL 4 to show the argument has high dependence on it. G2 provides the additional support needed to satisfy G0. Because G2 is a lesser part of the argument and because the evidence attributes are lower allocate G2 SEAL 3. G3 adds little to the argument but does provide a level of backing to cover against the weaknesses of the other two sub-goals. As backing evidence we allocate G3 SEAL 2.

5.1   Variations on the example

This section describes other SEAL allocations and justifications that could be made based on the above example but where different evidence attributes were used.

1.   If G2 had High relevance.

In this case G1 and G2 would have equal contribution to the argument but neither would be sufficient on its own. If the evidence for G1 and G2 could be claimed to be independent then it could be argued that G1 and G2 should both be allocated SEAL 3. A derived goal to show the independence of the evidence for G1 and G2 would be introduced which would be allocated SEAL 4, because failure of independence would invalidate the whole argument. Achieving SEAL 4 for such an independence argument might be achieved by providing evidence that the unit testing and code walkthroughs were performed by different teams.

2.   If the coverage of G1 was medium.

In this case the combination of G1 and G2 would not be sufficient. Additional sources of evidence and associated sub-goals would be required to make a justifiable argument.

3.   If G3 was found to be false.

The argument structure uses G3 as backing for the other two sub-goals. If G3 becomes false because a run-time error is found during higher level testing or trials the whole argument would need to be revalidated.

6   Conclusion

Based on an concept identified during discussions about moving safety standards towards a more evidence based philosophy, a method has been developed to make the level of trust in safety arguments more visible. This method has been documented and initial trials have shown some benefit in helping both developers and readers of safety arguments understand the arguments being made.

In the future we expect to revise the method based on the results of trials.

7   Acknowledgements

The authors recognise the work done on safety cases and safety assurance by Tim Kelly and Rob Weaver of the University of York. The differences in approach and consequent debates have done much to help our understanding.

8 References

[1] Defence Standard 00-56, issue 3 – DRAFT – Safety Management Requirements for Defence Systems. 2003. UK Ministry of Defence.

[2] Defence Standard 00-56, issue 2 – Safety Management Requirements for Defence Systems. 1996. UK Ministry of Defence

[3] Defence Standard 00-55 - Requirements of Safety Related Software in Defence Equipment. 1997. UK Ministry of Defence.

[4] DEF(AUST)5679 – The Procurement of Computer-Based Safety Critical Systems. Australian Department of Defence.

[5] IEC–61508 - Functional Safety of Electrical / Electronic / Programmable Electronic Safety Related Systems. 1997. International Electrotechnical Commission.

[6] MIL-STD-882C – System Safety Program Requirements. 1993. US Department of Defense.

[7] RTCA DO-178B/EUROCAE ED-12B - Software Considerations In Airborne Systems and Equipment Certification. Radio Technical Commission for Aeronautics and EUROCAE.

[8] MIL-STD-882D – Standard Practice for System Safety. 2000. US Department of Defense

[9] Penny, J., A. Eaton, and P.G. Bishop. The Practicalities of Goal-Based Safety Regulation. in Aspects of Safety Management: Proceedings of the Ninth Safety-Critical Systems Symposium. 2001. Bristol, UK: Springer.

[10] CAA, SW01 - Regulatory Objective for Software Safety Assurance in Air Traffic Service Equipment. 1999. Civil Aviation Authority.

[11] Kelly, T.P., Arguing Safety - A Systematic Approach to Managing Safety Cases, in Computer Science. 1998, University of York

[12] Notes from a working group on 'Safety Standards' at the HIRTS DARPWorkshop. 18–19 April 2000, Harrogate. Available from: http://www.cs.york.ac.uk/hise/darp/index.php?link=events/past1.php

[13] R. A. Weaver, J. Fenn and T. P. Kelly. A Pragmatic Approach to Reasoning about the Assurance of Safety Arguments. Proceedings of 8th Australian Workshop on Safety Critical Systems and Software (SCS'03), Canberra, Australia 2003. Published in Conferences in Research and Practice in Information Technology Series, P. Lindsay and T. Cant (Eds.), vol.33, Australian Computer Society, 2003.

Independent Safety Assessment of Safety Arguments

Peter Froome

Adelard LLP,

London, United Kingdom

Abstract

The paper describes the role of Independent Safety Auditor (ISA) as carried out at the present in the defence and other sectors in the UK. It outlines the way the ISA role has developed over the past 15–20 years with the changing regulatory environment. The extent to which the role comprises audit, assessment or advice is a source of confusion, and the paper clarifies this by means of some definitions, and by elaborating the tasks involved in scrutinising the safety argument for the system. The customers and interfaces for the safety audit are described, and pragmatic means for assessing the competence of ISAs are presented.

1 Introduction

This paper is based on recent work carried out by Adelard for the UK Ministry of Defence (MoD), to produce guidance for project teams on contracting for Independent Safety Auditor (ISA) services.

It begins by explaining the origins of the Independent Safety Auditor (ISA) in the defence sector, and how the role has developed and expanded into other sectors, most notably the railways, over the last 15–20 years. It then describes the ISA role, by giving definitions of *independent, safety audit* and *safety advice*, and illustrates the scope of the role in terms of the way the ISA scrutinises a system's safety argument. The ISA's interfaces with the key customers are outlined, and the paper concludes with a discussion of competency assessment of ISAs.

As well as giving a factual account of the ISA role as captured in the new guidance, the paper provides some illustrations of potential difficulties and practical issues that arise.

2 Origins of Independent Safety Audit

The requirement for an Independent Safety Auditor for MoD projects first appeared in Interim Defence Standard 00-56 (Safety Management Requirements for Defence Systems), published in 1991 (MoD 1991). The aim was to provide an objective, independent opinion of safety that was lacking in defence projects at that time, except in certain special areas such as those covered by the Ordnance Board and the Chief Naval Architect.

Interim Def Stan 00-56 was written by Adelard under contract to the Directorate General Submarines (DGSM), the principal authors being Peter Froome and Robin Bloomfield. The ISA role was based on their experience during the Sizewell B Inquiry in the then CEGB's Health and Safety Department (HSD), which provided scrutiny of safety, independent from operations up to Board level, and was also the interface to the regulator (the Nuclear Installations Inspectorate or NII). Since there was no statutory regulator in the defence sector, the ISA role was intended to cover both independent scrutiny and quasi-regulatory responsibilities.

The role was originally entitled "independent safety assessor", but was changed to "independent safety auditor" at a late stage in the drafting by the Steering Committee that oversaw the development of Interim Def Stans 00-55 and 00-56. This change has led to confusion over the scope of the role ever since.

At the time, MoD was protected by Crown Immunity and safety was seen as largely the Contractor's responsibility, and therefore it was envisaged that the ISA would be appointed by the Contractor. Since the Interim Def Stan was published, the role has developed as a result of the changing legal framework and developing safety policy within MoD. Crown Immunity has been lifted: MoD is now a self-regulating organisation with regard to safety where it has been granted specific exemptions, disapplications or derogations from legislation, international treaties or protocols. The safety offices and safety boards provide this self-regulation within MoD, as defined in their respective safety management publications (e.g. MoD 2002a, MoD 2002b, MoD 2002c, MoD 2003). The ISA role is now founded on MoD safety policy that introduces independence into safety regulation by requiring or recommending that the "Duty Holder" (normally the Integrated Project Team or IPT Leader) seeks an ISA's opinion on the quality of the safety case for new or modified equipment. However, the ISA differs from a statutory regulator in having no executive authority or power of veto. The IPT accepts full responsibility for safety, and may overrule an ISA's recommendations.

The ISA is also important in other sectors. The ISA role (known as "functional safety assessment") is part of IEC 61508 (IEC 1998). The ISA also has an important role in the railway sector, where best practice as detailed in the Yellow Book (Railtrack 2000, RSSB 2003) recommends that Independent Safety Assessment is conducted with a level of rigour and independence that is related to the degree of safety criticality of the change. ISAs are also used in the automotive sector, where the role is mainly assessment with possibly some further analysis. Use of an ISA is not mandatory but automotive manufacturers see it as protection. Experience of the role in these different sectors is being shared through the IEE/BCS ISA Working Group, which is the subject of another presentation at this symposium.

The ISA role is becoming ever more challenging. Functional safety (i.e. the safety of data and commands, as opposed to "physical safety") is an increasing concern, especially with the widespread use of computers running commercial software packages. The MoD's new secure digital voice and data communications system, Bowman, is a "systems of systems" involving over a hundred individual safety cases with complex interdependencies, produced to extremely tight timescales where safety problems can lead to significant financial losses as well as loss of capability.

Provision of advice is also becoming increasingly important with the emergence of "goal-based" safety standards such as the CAA's SW01 (CAA 1999) and the Issue 3 of Def Stan 00-56 (MoD 2004). These standards require considerably more interpretation than older, prescriptive, standards. The ISA plays a key role in supplying this interpretation, while taking care to preserve their independence.

3 The Independent Safety Audit Role

As mentioned in the introduction, there has been uncertainty over the exact role of the ISA ever since it was invented. The role as currently defined in the MoD's safety management publications, Def Stan 00-56/2 (MoD 1996) and the Yellow Book (Railtrack 2000) is a mixture of assessment and audit. This has been investigated by the IEE/BCS ISA Working Group, which concluded that the role was likely to be a combination of auditing for conformance to planned arrangements, reviewing of project documentation, and performing additional analyses.

Underlying the ISA role is the fact that safety is fundamentally a property of the equipment, not the process used to develop it. Although processes are important for managing projects and ensuring the production of deliverables and other outputs that provide safety evidence, the judgement of whether an adequate level of safety has been achieved has to be made on the basis of the equipment properties and performance. Thus the ISA role has to include assessment and analysis.

This section explores the ISA role as it is carried out at the present time, firstly in terms of key definitions (*independent*, *safety audit* and *safety advice*), and then by considering how the ISA reinforces the safety case by examining the elements of a system's safety argument.

3.1 Definitions

3.1.1 Independent

The various safety standards and guidelines devote a considerable amount of space to whether the ISA should be from a separate department, separate organisation, etc., in order to be sufficiently independent. Formal requirements for independence based on Safety Integrity Level (SIL) are provided in IEC 61508 (IEC 1998) and the Yellow Book (Railtrack 2000), and JSP 430 (MoD 2002a) requires that the ISA is from an independent company, or is at least managerially independent up to board level.

However, the key consideration is that the ISA needs to be able to provide an expert, professional opinion without vulnerability to commercial, project or other pressure. Informally, this means that the ISA needs to be sufficiently independent that they are sheltered as far as practicable from pressure to modify their opinion, and that their career prospects are enhanced rather than damaged by carrying out a searching assessment.

The organisation that contracts the ISA must respect this independence. They should give the ISA substantial freedom to conduct the safety audit as the ISA judges to be appropriate. The relationship is similar to contracting an auditor in other areas, such as quality management or accountancy. An authorised ISA has the right and duty to raise significant concerns directly with the procurer or contractor, even when outside their agreed scope of work or terms of reference, and should raise unresolved concerns with the appropriate safety authorities and regulators.

The need for an independent auditor does not mean that the company that is the target of the audit has to accept someone from a competitor. Even if a non-disclosure agreement is signed, it is impossible to remove the information held in the ISA's head and it might be divulged unwittingly or under pressure from peers. The contracting organisation should negotiate a mutually acceptable ISA from an organisation that does not compete with the contractor, even though it may then be more difficult to find an ISA with appropriate domain experience.

3.1.2 Safety audit

Safety audit consists of the activities that enable an expert, professional, independent opinion to be reached on the safety of the system. Worded this way, it is clear that "traditional" auditing against planned arrangements is not sufficient, and expert document review and diverse analysis will generally form the majority of the ISA's work. Note that, in the defence sector, safety audit is targeted at both the contractor and the IPT.

Thus, for example, a contractor should not refuse to co-operate with the ISA over the provision of data to support failure rate claims, on the grounds that analysis of such data is not an audit function. This is not acceptable if the ISA judges the data to be an essential component of the safety argument.

The best way of identifying the safety audit activities on a particular project is to consider how the ISA will scrutinise the safety argument; this is examined in Section 3.2 below.

3.1.3 Safety advice

In order to maintain their independence, the ISA cannot give specific advice or contribute directly to the safety argument. However, an ISA may provide general advice on the acceptability of a proposed safety argument, which facilitates the procurer's or contractor's decision-making, helps to develop an effective safety strategy, and reduces project risk from safety matters.

The ISA may also need to give advice where some part of the safety work is unacceptable—it is not particularly helpful if the ISA maintains this without saying why.

A strategic level of advice is reasonable, and is similar to the "assessment guidelines" produced by the statutory regulators. One possible criterion is that advice can be given when it is not specific to the project (e.g. advice on general safety argument structures) and facilitates the project's own decision-making.

A classic problem is that the contractor asks the ISA to revise portions of the safety documentation that they have found unsatisfactory. The ISA should not do this, as they would then take ownership of part of the safety argument. However, they can illustrate how such a revision should be performed, by reference to published standards, guidance or papers, or possibly by analogy with other, similar, projects.

3.2 Scrutiny of the Safety Argument

Many sectors in the UK, including defence and railways, are obliged by law to produce a written safety justification for their operations, which is normally known as a "safety case". The safety case for a system is based on a *safety argument*. Typically the overall, top-level argument is:

> The system is safe to use to provide the defined capability because:
> - The meaning of "safe" is defined and correctly captured in the safety requirements.
> - The system meets the safety requirements.
> - Safety will be maintained over the system's lifetime through a culture of safe working and safety management by the contractor and procurer/user organisations.
> - The assumptions and prerequisites on which the safety case depends are valid.

Safety cases are beginning to contain an explicit safety argument, in which case the ISA can base the safety audit around that. Many safety cases contain only an implicit safety argument, however, and in that case the ISA has to establish the argument as part of the audit activities.

The ISA's work then consists of examining each of the components of this safety argument and forming an opinion as to whether it is complete and correct. As an example, consider the first bullet point. This is often broken down as illustrated in Figure 1 below.

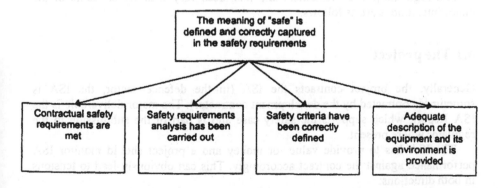

Figure 1. Safety argument tree for safety requirements definition

The ISA's checks of this part of the safety argument might include the following:

- *Contractual safety requirements*—review for correctness, completeness, consistency, achievability, conformance to standards and legislation; check that evidence likely to be needed for subsequent safety arguments is contracted for.
- *Safety requirements analysis*—check the analysis; review reports for correctness, completeness, consistency, achievability, conformance to standards and legislation; audit the analysis process for conformance to standards and safety management plan; attend analysis meetings to check conducted in accordance with standards and good practice.
- *Safety criteria*—review the report for conformance to standards and safety management plan; check against HSE guidelines such as R2P2 (HSE 2001) and sector-specific standards; check for agreement with criteria from similar projects.
- *System and operating environment description*—check that the description is sufficiently comprehensive for the reader to understand the safety argument.

Broadly speaking, this pattern of work is repeated throughout the lifecycle, but there are some differences. For example, in the design and manufacturing phases, the ISA may carry out diverse analyses to estimate software or hardware reliability by means of appropriate modelling techniques, in order to check the argument tree for the second bullet point in the safety argument above ("The system meets the safety requirements"). Human factors analysis is another diverse analysis often undertaken by the ISA at this phase in the lifecycle, in order to check the safety requirements are met with respect to the entire socio-technical system.

4 Interfaces and Customers

The ISA has a number of customers for their work. The major ones, and the ISA's interfaces to them, are illustrated generically in Figure 2.

Although the precise customers and interfaces vary with sector, some of the major interactions are as follows.

4.1 The project

Generally, the project contracts the ISA (in the defence sector, the ISA is sometimes contracted by the development contractor). The major deliverable is the ISA Report, which supports the safety case and is part of the submission to the regulator where present.

The ISA has to provide value for money and a project should monitor ISA performance against the contract accordingly. This can obviously lead to tensions in both directions:

- The ISA may feel inhibited about pursuing safety issues if they believe that the project has a negative view of the safety audit activities.

- The project may be reluctant to dismiss an ineffective ISA because of fears of being accused of compromising the ISA's independence.

These tensions can be avoided by monitoring the ISA's performance objectively, which is best done by checking their coverage of the safety argument as discussed in Section 3.2.

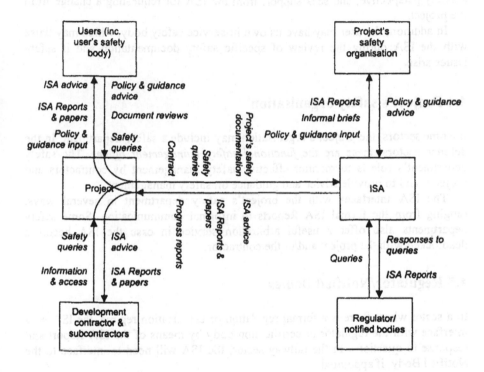

Figure 2. Typical ISA's customers and interfaces

4.2 The development contractor

It is essential that there is a spirit of co-operation between the contractor and the ISA, as otherwise the safety work will get bogged down with the danger to the project that the ISA will be unable to endorse the safety case.

The ISA should be acceptable to the contractor in terms of competence and scopes of work. The contractor can legitimately demand that the ISA safeguards their intellectual property and confidential information, and therefore may reasonably refuse to accept an ISA from a commercial rival. On the other hand, the contractor should provide access to the information that the ISA needs to form an independent opinion.

4.3 The user

Direct contact between the ISA and the user or end customer typically originates in safety committees.

However, it is possible that the user may raise safety concerns directly with the ISA where they are seeking a consensus on some safety issue. For example, user representatives may consider that certain functionality is implemented poorly from a safety perspective, and seek support from the ISA for requesting a change from the project.

In addition, the user may have its own in-service safety body, which may liaise with the ISA during the review of specific safety documentation and if safety issues arise.

4.4 Project's safety organisation

In some sectors, the project's organisation may include a safety department. In the defence sectors, these are the *functional safety management offices*. The safety department's role is to monitor effective safety management by contractors and projects, and to provide advice and guidance on safety management.

The ISA interfaces with the project's safety department in several ways, ranging from the formal ISA Reports to informal communication. Some safety departments also offer a useful arbitration service in case the ISA becomes deadlocked with the project and/or the contractor.

4.5 Regulator/Notified Bodies

In a sector where there is a formal regulation or certification regime, the ISA may interface with the regulator or certification body by means of the ISA Report and response to questions. In the railway sector, the ISA will need to interface to the Notified Body, if appointed.

5 Competence of ISAs

The ISA has to provide an authoritative, expert opinion on safety, and therefore has to be properly qualified. The qualifications required are not only technical, because the ISA also needs managerial and social skills in terms of safety audit planning, control of meetings, negotiating ability, and ability to defend their position in a firm but non-confrontational manner.

The author's approach is to prefer ISA teams for most projects, and this is also the position of the Yellow Book (Railtrack 2000). As well as enabling effective peer review of the assessment's outputs, teams and can provide specialist expertise in areas such as in human factors and software reliability modelling. Where a team is employed, it is the balance of skills that is important, and the team leader should demonstrate the ability to properly manage and co-ordinate the team. Individual team members should provide the in-depth knowledge that is required.

Competency requirements for ISAs are contained in sector-specific safety publications, and usually include Chartered Engineering status and several years' relevant experience. Formal competency assessment for ISAs has been discussed at length at the IEE/BCS ISA Working Group but there are difficulties with all schemes where competence is assessed by independent, third parties. In the absence of a completely satisfactory third-party scheme, this section discusses how ISA competence may be pragmatically assessed.

5.1 Competence criteria

There are three types of competence required for an ISA:
- *Technical competence*—safety and technical knowledge (of the application area and technology) required to support the activities of a safety audit.
- *Auditing competence*—skills necessary to perform the safety audit, i.e. to perform the activities that enable an expert, professional opinion to be reached on the safety of the system.
- *Behavioural competence*—qualities and attributes of behaviour and character needed to successfully perform the ISA role.

These are described in more detail in the following subsections.

5.1.1 Technical competence

Technical competence has two aspects:
- Technical competence in safety audit independent of the specific application and technology used. This includes knowledge and experience of the legal and safety regulatory framework, understanding the principles and concepts of safety management (e.g. ALARP, risk and safety requirements), and knowledge and experience of the standard safety analysis techniques such as Hazops and Fault Tree Analysis. It also includes the ability to estimate the necessary resources to perform such analyses and to judge the scope and depth of analyses carried out.
- Technical competence in the application domain, covering an understanding of the specific technologies used and their context in the particular domain. This includes safety engineering knowledge and experience appropriate to the application area and technology, including safety practices appropriate to the organisation and application area. It also includes engineering knowledge and experience appropriate to the application area (e.g. air traffic control) and technology (e.g. digital network communication). Experience of other systems engineering disciplines such as human factors may also be relevant.

5.1.2 Auditing competence

By contrast to technical competence, auditing competence considers the specific activities performed as part of a safety audit. This includes the ability to:
- Determine the scope and objectives of the safety audit and manage the auditing activities.

- Collect and analyse objective evidence to support the professional, expert opinion. As well as reviewing documents, this may include interviewing personnel at all levels and observing activities.
- Investigate evidence of possible problems.
- Carry out formal process audits against relevant standards, plans, etc.
- Make a judgement on the safety of a system.
- Document findings.

5.1.3 Behavioural competence

The ISA role can be stressful and demanding, particularly when the project under review is in trouble and time and money are in short supply. The ISA needs to have certain attributes of conduct and character in order to perform the role of ISA with efficacy. These include:
- Interpersonal skills.
- Competence in communicating at all levels of the organisation.
- Interviewing skills.
- Reporting and presentation skills.
- Integrity and trustworthiness.

5.2 Assessment of competence

The previous subsection lists the competence attributes that are expected of an ISA. Potential ISAs should be able to supply evidence of competence covering these attributes, supported by verifiable examples, as part of their proposal when bidding for an ISA role.

In principle, this evidence of competence could be of three types, according to who does the assessment:
- Self-assessment, i.e. the ISA presents evidence to demonstrate the competencies as part of their proposal. This will have to be assessed by the project on a case-by-case basis.
- Organisational assessment, i.e. the ISA is assessed by their organisation according to a scheme such as the IEE/BCS Competency Guidelines for Safety-Related System Practitioners (IEE 1999) or the Network Rail ISA Accreditation Scheme (NR 2003). The project should ask for any third-party audit of the scheme, which might be an ISO 9001 audit in the case of the IEE/BCS scheme, or Network Rail's audit in the case of their scheme.
- Assessment by a third-party independent organisation that designs a scheme and independently assesses the ISA. Currently the only third-party scheme in the UK is the CASS (Conformity Assessment of Safety-related Systems, see www.cass.uk.net) scheme, and there are very few registrants.

Given the limited extent of formal competency assessment of ISAs at the present time, projects will probably have to assess potential ISAs on the basis of organisational assessment where it has been carried out, supplemented by self-assessment to establish competence related to the specific programme.

6 Conclusions

The paper has described the ISA role as carried out at the present in the defence and other sectors in the UK. It has explained how the role arose in the defence and railway sectors in order to provide an expert, professional, independent opinion as part of the regulatory regime in those sectors. The balance of ISA activities between "traditional" audit and assessment is a source of confusion, but the paper has shown how the role can be defined in terms of the safety argument for the system that is the focus of the activities. The paper has also outlined the principal customers and interfaces for the ISA.

Clearly the ISA (whether an individual or a team) must be competent, but at present there is no established competency assessment scheme for ISAs. The paper has described the three types of competence required by ISAs (technical, auditing and behavioural), and discussed how ISA competence may be pragmatically assessed.

References

CAA (1999). CAP 670, Part B, SW01 (Requirements for Software in Safety Related ATS Systems), Civil Aviation Authority 1999
HSE (2001) Reducing Risks, Protecting People—the HSE's Decision-making process, HSMO, 2001
IEC (1998). IEC Functional safety of electrical/electronic/programmable electronic safety-related systems, IEC 61508 Parts 1–7
IEE (1999). *Safety, Competency and Commitment: Competency Guidelines for Safety-Related System Practitioners*, IEE, 1999. ISBN 0 85296 787 X
MoD (1991). Interim Def Stan 00-56, Safety Management of Defence Systems, 1991
MoD (1996). Def Stan 00-56 Issue 2, Safety Management Requirements for Defence Systems (Parts 1 and 2), 1996
MoD (2002a). JSP 430, MoD Ship Safety Management, Issue 2, May 2002
MoD (2002b). JSP 454, Procedures for Land Systems Equipment Safety Assurance, Issue 3, July 2002
MoD (2002c). JSP 520, Ordnance, Munitions and Explosives Safety Management System, February 2002
MoD (2003). JSP 553 (formerly JSP 318B), Military Airworthiness Regulations, 1st Edition, July 2003
MoD (2004). Def Stan 00-56 Issue 3, Safety Management Requirements for Defence Systems (Parts 1 and 2), to be published
NR (2003). Rail Corporate Independent Safety Assessor Accreditation, Crystal Blake, +44 (0) 20 7557 8513
Railtrack (2000). Engineering Safety Management, Issue 3 (Yellow Book 3), Railtrack, January 2000
RSSB (2003). Engineering Safety Management Yellow Book 3 Application Note 4, Independent Safety Assessment. Issue 1.0, Rail Safety and Standards Board

SAFETY AND SECURITY

Structuring a Safety Case for an Air Traffic Control Operations Room

Ron Pierce

CSE International Ltd, Glanford House, Bellwin Drive, Flixborough, Scunthorpe
DN15 8SN, UK

Herman Baret

EUROCONTROL Maastricht Upper Area Control Centre, Horsterweg 11, 6199
AC Maastricht Airport, The Netherlands

1 Introduction

Production of a formal safety case is a valuable part of the safety management of a safety related system. A safety case is a written justification that the given system will be tolerably safe during installation, commissioning and operation, and in some cases decommissioning. A well-written safety case will give all stakeholders (operating authority, members of staff and regulators) justifiable confidence that the system is safe to operate and to continue in operation. Although production of a safety case is now regarded as best practice in many quarters, there is still relatively little experience of writing safety cases and only a limited amount of literature on the topic. Many safety engineers find it a daunting task and some safety cases are still poorly structured, difficult to understand and less than compelling.

This paper describes the authors' approach to the development of the safety case, in the period between mid 2001 and mid 2003, for a major safety related system, namely a new air traffic control (ATC) operations room for the EUROCONTROL Maastricht Upper Area Control Centre (UAC). The Maastricht UAC controls all air traffic flying at over 24,500 feet over the Benelux countries and north-west Germany. It is a busy centre which handles over 1.2 million flights per year and the airspace is complicated by the presence of crossing air routes and by traffic climbing and descending from the many busy airports in the Maastricht UAC's area of responsibility or just outside it, such as Frankfurt, Paris, Amsterdam and London.

It is hoped that the experience related here will be helpful to other engineers who are faced with the task of constructing a safety case.

2 The New Operations Room

The New Operations Room (N-OR) is located in a new building adjacent to the old operations room and is equipped with a large suite of modern workstations for air traffic controllers, supervisors and flight data preparation staff.

The new equipment is collectively known as the New Operator Input and Display System or N-ODS. Each controller workstations (CWP) consists of a large (2K by 2K pixel) high resolution display screen for the advanced air traffic situation display, a screen for supporting information, mouse, keyboard and two touch input panels. Flight plan data is presented electronically, as was the case with the old equipment, and paper flight progress strips which are still used by many ATC centres are absent.

The Compaq computers which drive the display screens run Unix and X-Windows and are connected by a reliable multi-ring fibre optic (FDDI) LAN to the servers which provide flight data, radar data and other services. Workstations are grouped in sector suites as is normal practice in ATC. In addition to the controller workstations, there is an advanced recording and replay system which allows the air situation to be replayed exactly as it was presented to the air traffic controller at time of recording, including all the interactions with the machine. An operational monitoring system is used to display and control the status of all equipment and software.

In the event of failure of the radar surveillance data system, a fallback facility consisting of a diverse radar data processing system associated to a limited flight plan capability provides the radar picture to the CWP display screens via a video switch. An Ultimate Fallback Facility prints up to date flight plan information on high speed printers in case of loss of communication between the main flight data processing system and the CWP.

Procurement of the N-ODS system and the fallback facility pre-dated the need for a formal safety management regime and much of the safety evidence had to be constructed by retrospective analysis.

3 Arguments, Evidence and Goal Structuring Notation

A properly constructed safety case should consist, in essence, of arguments and evidence. The arguments provide the structure of the safety case, in terms of safety claims and explanations, while the evidence provides the facts to support the arguments.

The Use of Goal Structuring Notation (GSN) as a graphical means to express the essential argument and evidence structure of a safety case is becoming increasingly popular. GSN was used to develop the N-OR safety case and was found to be very useful both for thinking about the safety case when developing it, and for presenting it to others. Use of GSN is increasing, and other published examples of safety cases which use GSN are the RVSM Pre-Implementation Safety Case for Europe (EUROCONTROL 2001), the Merlin helicopter fly-by-wire control system (Chinneck et al 2004) and autonomous vehicle operation on an airport (Spriggs 2003).

The GSN diagrams in this paper are simplified in some cases from the originals for the sake of brevity. An introduction to the use of GSN can be found in Kelly (1997).

4 Overall Structure of the N-OR Safety Case

There has been a tendency in safety management generally to concentrate on physical and equipment aspects of a system, to which classical reliability, availability, maintainability and safety (RAMS) techniques such as fault tree analysis can be applied, and to pay less attention to human factors. In ATC, the human being provides the active control service with the equipment supplying information and communications facilities, and therefore the human and ergonomic aspects of the N-OR Safety Case were of great importance.

Figures 1 and 2 show the top-level structure of the safety case. It will be noted that there is no safety management plan mentioned in this structure. This is in contrast to the structure of a safety case as recommended in the railway standard CENELEC 50129 (BSI 2003) which has a whole section devoted to safety management. However, the results of the safety management activities were fully embodied in the arguments and supporting evidence for the safety case.

Another point that may seem unusual is that there is no mention of the use of a Hazard Log anywhere in the safety case structure. Since the safety case was only concerned with functional hazards, these were tracked by means of the Functional Hazard Assessment (FHA) report which contained the complete list of hazards and safety objectives (section 6). A separate hazard log was judged not to be necessary on the grounds that it would merely duplicate information in the FHA report. It is not unusual in the safety management of ATC systems to avoid the use of a hazard log when an FHA report is used.

As will be seen from Figure 1, the argument is divided into two areas (argument strategies ST1 and ST2): one demonstrates that the N-OR and its equipment are safe to enter service, and the other that the new equipment will be operated and maintained safely.

Figure 2 then decomposes the claim that the N-OR environment and equipment are tolerably safe into further arguments about human factors and equipment safety issues. A parallel argument that the existing ATS is tolerably safe is used at this point to establish that the new functionality is being added to a tolerably safe baseline; thus negating the need for extensive safety analysis of existing systems.

The choice of this particular structure was a matter of judgement by the authors that it presented the essential information in an appropriate, logical and understandable manner.

54

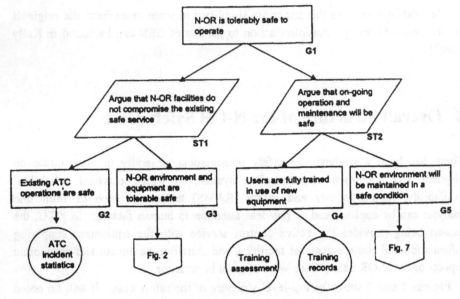

Figure 1. Overall argument structure

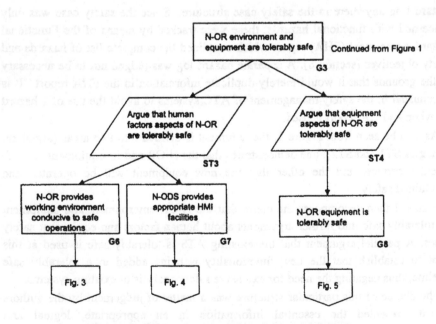

Figure 2. Human factors and equipment arguments

5 Human Factors Arguments

Many safety cases rightly concentrate on hazard identification and risk control. However, in the case of the N-OR it was felt to be necessary to show that, when the equipment is operating normally, it provides appropriate facilities to allow controllers to do their job of controlling traffic safely. Cases are known, although not at Maastricht, where ATC equipment has had to be withdrawn from service, or modified just prior to service, because the user interface did not allow safe operations.

The human factors argument (strategy ST3 on Figure 2) is decomposed into two goals, G6 on Figure 3 (which is concerned with the physical environment in which ATC staff work) and G7 on Figure 4 (which is concerned with the user interface of the new ODS).

There is an element of subjectivity about this part of the safety case since there is no ideal set of functions or ideal ergonomic design for ATC equipment and many compromises must be made (for example between the information content of a track label and the size and legibility of the label). It is not possible to say "here is the list of hazards which can be created by human error, and from this we can deduce that the following facilities are needed to mitigate these hazards". Different ATC centres have different approaches to specific aspects of the HMI although they do similar jobs.

The evidence that the user interface was appropriate was based largely on prototyping and evaluation exercises, rather than on a formal human factors assessment. If the screen display format had been radically different from that to which the controllers were accustomed, there would have been a greater need for a formal assessment of the interface (Kennedy et al, 2000). In addition, the overall ATC concept of operations and sectorisation of the airspace did not change with the activation of the N-OR, and it was not therefore necessary to provide any safety assessments for ATC procedural changes.

Goal G17 on Figure 4 is shown in italics since it did not form part of the first version of the safety case, but was added for the second version (see section 10) to allow confidential feedback from users to be captured. The great majority of users stated that the N-ODS was an improvement over the old system and would allow them to control more traffic without loss of safety.

6 Equipment Safety

This part of the safety case, shown in Figures 5 and 6, is concerned with the safety of the N-ODS. Note that this safety case is only concerned with functional safety; the occupational health and safety of controllers and other staff is not within its scope.

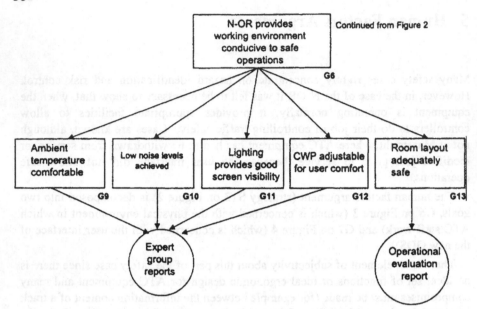

Continued from Figure 2

Figure 3. Arguments about working environment

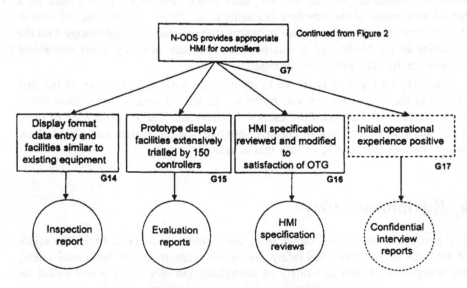

Continued from Figure 2

Figure 4. Arguments about HMI

Goal G18 on Figure 5 claims that that hazards which can arise from failures of the N-ODS and its supporting systems are tolerably unlikely (which is another way of saying that the risk associated with these hazards is tolerable). This claim is expanded in Figure 6.

The second claim (G19) is that all function and performance safety requirements have been met. The evidence for this claim is firstly the results of testing and performance (timing and capacity) analyses, and secondly an independent assessment of the validation tests (including the provision for non-regression testing of new software releases). In such a complex system, with over two million lines of code, it is inevitable that some defects would remain in the system at "O-date". The policy adopted was to classify known defects in terms of severity and only to allow the system to enter service with known defects of relatively low severity. Ultimately the operational users were in the best position to judge whether a particular failure would compromise their ability to deliver a safe service. There were no known defects which constituted an identified hazard.

The voice communications system (VCS) was largely outside the scope of this safety case, having been installed and commissioned several years earlier and was in use with the old operations room. However, it was necessary for completeness to mention the VCS and show that it had been reliable in service. This is addressed by goal G20 on Figure 5. It was also necessary to provide evidence that the New ODS would not compromise the safe operation of the VCS since both touch input panels (which were procured as part of the VCS) are connected to both systems and can be used either for control of voice communications or for input to the N-ODS. This technical aspect of the system is not mentioned in the GSN but is addressed in the SSA report.

Finally, goal G21 (Figure 5) refers to the presence of the fallback facilities which mitigate many of the hazards caused by failures of the N-ODS. As shown, the fallback facilities were the subject of a separate safety assessment.

6.1 Hazards and Safety Objectives

Figure 6 shows how the argument that hazards are tolerably unlikely is structured. The basis of the argument is that system safety objectives (requirements for control of hazard occurrence rate) have been correctly identified, and that all the safety objectives will be met. This is of course a common pattern seen in many safety cases.

A Functional Hazard Assessment (FHA) process was used to identify all the hazards which could arise from failures of the operator consoles, and to derive "safety objectives" (tolerable occurrence rates) for each hazard.

58

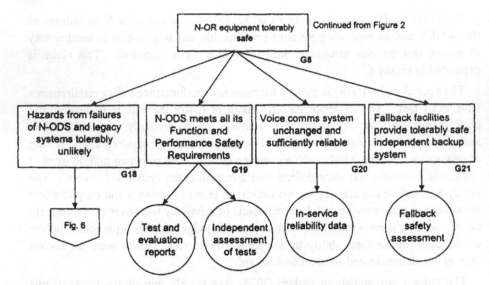

Figure 5. Arguments that N-OR equipment is tolerably safe

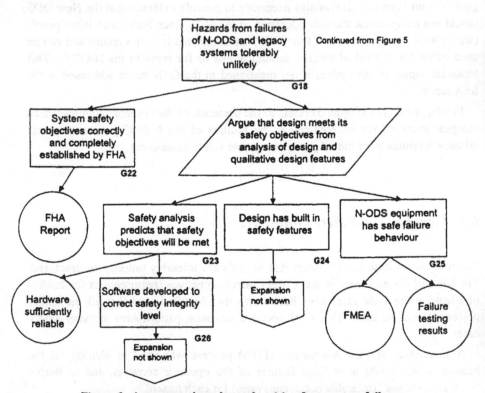

Figure 6. Argument about hazards arising from system failures

Note that in the air traffic management field the ALARP concept (that risk should be As Low as Reasonably Practicable) is not part of the regulatory framework. Risks only have to be tolerable (although some air traffic service providers do apply the ALARP principle on precautionary grounds). Having said that, the safety objectives were derived using a risk classification matrix based on the equipment failure severity classification given in the EUROCONTROL regulatory requirement ESARR 2 which is fairly conservative and the maximum tolerable risk from equipment failures of any kind is low.

Typical hazards (of which there are some 80) in this context include complete or partial loss of radar display information, loss of flight data, incorrect data, or loss of input or display control. The arguments that the hazard identification process was carried out correctly (with a competent HAZOP-style team, using a correct description of the equipment's intended behaviour) were largely contained in the FHA report, one of the items of supporting evidence as shown in Figure 6.

The FHA process also served to identify the safety functional and performance requirements and distinguish them from other system requirements which do not directly impact safety.

The argument structure in Fig 6 then shows how the claim that the equipment would meet its safety objectives was decomposed. Much of the detailed evidence was contained in the System Safety Assessment (SSA) report. New equipment reliability was addressed by fault tree analysis and reliability block diagrams for individual items of equipment, together with a Failure Modes and Effects Analysis (FMEA) to validate the base events in the fault trees. A common cause failure analysis was also undertaken. Reliability of legacy systems was established by examination of in-service reliability data.

All hazards were considered as a block – there was no attempt to argue over individual safety functions or hazards. Since all hazards were of a uniform (functional) type and all were controlled by building the system to the correct hardware reliability and software integrity level, this approach appeared to be the most appropriate.

6.2 Software Integrity

Although goal G26 is not expanded in a GSN diagram here, the software integrity of the N-ODS was argued by consideration of the software development process.

The software safety integrity level was determined by apportioning the top level safety objectives to hardware and software elements, and was SIL 2 in IEC 61508 terms.

Evidence that the software had been developed to SIL 2 was obtained by two independent software safety assessment reports. One of these reports, specifically against the requirements of IEC 61508 Part 3, was commissioned by the system supplier.

The other one (undertaken by CSE at the request of EUROCONTROL) used an evidence-based approach adapted from the requirements and guidelines given in section SW01 of CAP 670 (CAA 2003).

These complementary assessments both concluded, with minor reservations, that the software would reach its required SIL. Other arguments from field service experience were made for the legacy systems which support the N-ODS.

6.3 Qualitative Design Arguments

Arguments were also provided (goal G24, Figure 6) that the design had built in safety features and that it exhibited safety failure behaviour in defined circumstances. Although the contribution of the equipment safety features to system reliability is modelled in the fault tree analysis, it was felt to be important that this information should be presented explicitly in the safety case report rather than buried in the details of the sections of the SSA report which cover the fault tree analysis.

6.4 Failure behaviour

An important aspect of behaviour of a safety related system is its robustness, in other words its resilience to failures (or unexpected behaviour) of connected equipment and (where practicable) to failures of internal elements. Robustness contributes to system reliability and therefore to safety. The ability of the system to rapidly recover from a failure is also important for safety (a failure may not be hazardous if the duration of the failed state is sufficiently short). This is addressed by goal G25 with the supporting evidence being both the FMEA and the results of specific tests to ensure that the predicted failure behaviour was observed.

6.5 Safety Objectives Not Met

One safety objective clearly could not be met due to the presence of a legacy system whose historical failure rate had been higher than the tolerable occurrence rate for certain hazards. Since this equipment had been in use for many years with the old operations room, a special argument had to be made that the new situation would be no worse than the old in this respect, and if the old situation was acceptable (as clearly it was) then the new system would not make matters any worse.

In this case an ALARP argument was used to show that the cost of improving the old system would have been disproportionate to any safety benefit gained. A new system is currently being procured to replace the old one, and the new system is being developed to an appropriate integrity level.

7 Safe Transition, Operation and Maintenance

This aspect of the N-OR Safety Case is concerned with the arguments and evidence that the system will be operated safety and maintained in a safe state. The main arguments in this area are shown in Figure 7, with the arguments and evidence that the user community (operational and maintenance) had been properly trained in its use being shown on Figure 1.

Not shown in the GSN diagrams, but most importantly, the first version of the safety case provided arguments and evidence that the transition from the old to the new OR would be accomplished safely. The main evidence to support this claim was a formal assessment report on the hazards inherent in the transition process and the means by which they were mitigated. This formal assessment proved valuable and a number of changes were made to the transition plan as a result of the assessment.

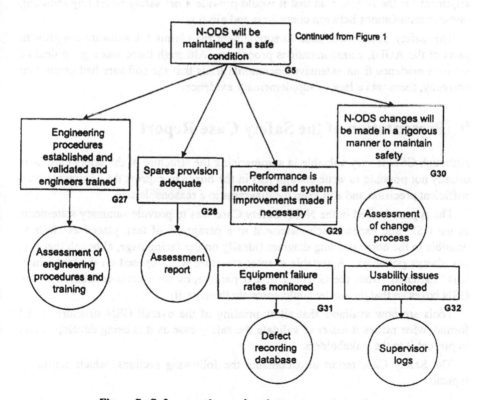

Figure 7. Safe operation and maintenance arguments

Figure 7 shows how the claim that the N-ODS will be maintained in a safe condition is decomposed.

The evidence to support goal G30, namely that changes will be made in a rigorous manner, was primarily that the software development process used for the initial development of the N-ODS software was transferred (including the software tools) to Maastricht UAC and maintenance is carried out by a joint team from the UAC and the system supplier.

Finally, goals G31 and G32 address the important aspect of safety performance monitoring which is an essential component of a safety management system. In this case both equipment performance and requests for improvements made by users (mostly HMI issues) are considered.

8 Looking on the positive side

There is a tendency in safety management to concentrate on hazards and failure rates, and ignore or place less emphasis on safety benefits that a new system can bring. The second version of the safety case to be issued covered the introduction of air-ground datalink (AGDL) operations, and an important element in the safety argument for the AGDL was that it would provide a net safety benefit by reducing mis-communications between controllers and aircrew.

This safety benefit was used to supplement the claims for software integrity in parts of the AGDL communications processors. Although there was a great deal of positive evidence from extensive operational trials that the software had performed correctly, there was a lack of supplementary evidence.

9 Presentation of the Safety Case Report

Although GSN is very valuable in summarising the structure of the safety case, it is usually not possible to write enough text in the boxes to express the arguments with sufficient precision and still keep the diagrams to a reasonable size.

The approach used in the N-OR Safety Case was to provide summary statements in the GSN and expand each statement in a paragraph of text, placed as close as possible to the corresponding diagram (ideally on the facing page, although that was not always possible). A suitable chapter structure was imposed on the text which was "flattened" from the GSN. The text paragraphs were cross-referenced to the GSN boxes so that the reader could correlate them easily.

Tools are now available that allow printing of the overall GSN structure in A0 format, what makes it easier to validate the safety case as it is being developed and to present it to the stakeholders.

The Safety Case report also contains the following sections, which are fairly typical:

- an introduction,
- a statement of scope and a system overview with suitable diagrams, a list of assumptions and dependencies,

- a list of safety objectives and with confirmation that they are either met or (as discussed above) not met,
- discussions of limitations and shortcomings and how they are mitigated,
- overall conclusions and recommendations.

These surround the central sections which present the structured arguments.

10 Maintaining the Safety Case

Following the opening of the N-OR for live ATC on 2nd November 2002, three new issues of the safety case were produced. The first of these was primarily to provide extra safety evidence from initial service experience and from a confidential opinion survey of the users.

The section of the safety case dealing with the safety of the transition process was deleted in this version since the transition had been accomplished.

The second post O-date issue contained a new section of the SSA report which covered the introduction of the limited AGDL service mentioned earlier. This required evidence that the AGDL functions had been implemented with sufficient integrity, that the new HMI was acceptable, that procedures for using the AGDL facilities had been developed and assessed, and that training of controllers in the use of AGDL had been adequate.

The third issue post O-date covered some new functions which were implemented in software and the corresponding software safety assessments were updated. At this point the N-OR and its systems were judged sufficiently mature and stable not to require any new issues of the safety case.

11 Conclusions

This paper has offered a brief tutorial in how one particular safety case was constructed. GSN was used to very good effect to define the arguments structure and corresponding safety evidence that would be needed, and allowed a rapid development of the safety management plan for the completion of the N-OR and its equipment. GSN also formed the central feature of the final safety case report and in presentations to the regulator.

It was found that very few changes needed to be made to the original argument structure as the N-OR approached completion.

The Safety Case was accepted by senior management and the regulator and the N-OR opened for operational use service on 2nd November 2002.

GSN is now either mandated or recommended for the construction of safety cases in many EUROCONTROL projects.

64

References

CAA (2003). SW01 – Regulatory Objectives for Software Safety Assurance, in Part B (Generic Requirements and Guidance) of CAP 670 Air Traffic Services Safety Requirements, Civil Aviation Authority, London.

BSI (2003). BS EN 50129: 2003. Railway applications – Communications, signalling and processing systems – Safety related electronic systems for signalling. (usually known as CENELEC 50129).

Chinneck P, Pumfrey D and Kelly T (2004). "Turning up the HEAT on Safety Case Construction". In F Redmill and T Anderson (Ed.): Practical Elements of Safety - Proceedings of the Twelfth Safety-critical Systems Symposium, Birmingham, UK, 17-19 February 2004. Springer, London.

EUROCONTROL (2001). RVSM Pre-Implementation Safety Case, http://www.ecacnav.com/rvsm/library.html.

Kelly 1997. "A Six Step Method for Developing Goal Structures", York Software Engineering Ltd, 1997.

Kennedy, R., Jones, H., Shorrock, S. and Kirwan, B. (2000). "A HAZOP analysis of a future ATM system" in P. T. McCabe, M. A. Hanson and S. A. Robertson (Eds), Contemporary Ergonomics 2000. London: Taylor and Francis.

Spriggs, J. "Developing a Safety Case for Autonomous Vehicle Operation on an Airport". In F Redmill and T Anderson (Ed.): Current Issues in Safety-critical Systems - Proceedings of the Eleventh Safety-critical Systems Symposium, Bristol, UK, 4-6 February 2003. Springer, London.

SafSec: Commonalities Between Safety and Security Assurance

Samantha Lautieri, David Cooper, and David Jackson

Praxis Critical Systems

Bath, England

www.praxis-cs.co.uk

www.safsec.com

Abstract

Many systems, particularly in the military domain, must be certified or accredited by both safety and security authorities. Current practice argues safety and security accreditations separately. A research project called SafSec has been investigating a combined approach to safety and security argumentation, and has shown that there can be practical benefits in performing a combined analysis and documenting a combined argument for both safety and security.

1 Introduction

Where a computer-based system is required to meet rigorous standards of dependability, certification and approval costs can form a substantial proportion of the overall development costs. When such a system is maintained in service for an extended period, the cost of maintaining these approvals through in-service modifications and changes in operating environment escalates this element of cost still further. In an effort to manage and reduce certification and approval costs, the Defence Procurement Agency sponsored the SafSec (Safety and Security) project, which aimed to support safety and security accreditation of complex computer-based systems, particularly those now being deployed as Integrated Modular Avionics (IMA) systems.

SafSec focussed on two major issues: identifying and exploiting commonalities between the various disparate certification processes that an IMA system may be subject to, and providing a framework for certification of *modular* systems – those composed of standard components which are re-used in different configurations by a variety of applications.

This paper illustrates how commonalities exist in safety and security certification. When the commonalities are exploited, the effort and cost involved will be reduced and, if undertaken through a modular approach, issues of obsolescence will also be minimised, and possibly removed.

The resulting approach is called the SafSec Methodology and is the result of two years of research and case studies, involving a large number of stakeholders from the development, procurement and approval communities.

2 Background and Motivation

The acceptance into service of an Integrated Modular Avionic (IMA) system (ARINC 1997) presents a number of challenges which are not unique but which are perhaps more stringent in the avionics domain than in many others. The primary challenge is the need to satisfy a number of different accreditation bodies that a system is fit-for-purpose before operational clearance will be granted – this will generally include both a *safety* certification and a *security* accreditation. The second major challenge is the need to support modular certification; where components are shared between applications, we wish to be able to re-use elements of the evidence offered to support their acceptance.

Defence Standard 00-56 (MoD 1996) is the key UK MoD requirement for safety management; security accreditation will typically require meeting an approved standard such as the Common Criteria (ISO 1999). Neither of these standards, as issued at the start of the SafSec project two years ago, was entirely suitable for dealing with modular certification[1]. Methods for certification need to support the certification of modules in isolation and support certification of combinations of such modules, rather than expecting certifiers to handle large complex systems as monolithic items for certification. This becomes a key issue in the on-going maintenance of certification – changing a single element in a modular system should be straightforward, and we do not wish to have to revisit the acceptance case for the whole system whenever a single substitution is made.

Although the detailed requirements of safety and security acceptance are often different, sufficient commonality is visible in the acceptance processes to encourage us to seek cost savings by eliminating duplicate effort. Certifiers need to be presented with convincing, objective arguments that the system has the safety and security properties that are required. The methodology therefore must be based on the presentation of direct arguments, and supporting evidence, that systems have the necessary properties and behaviour, and don't have any undesirable properties, to be safe and secure. Underlying acceptance by either community is a demand for good engineering practice in matters such as requirements traceability, verification and validation, configuration management and change control.

Note that although the SafSec project was initiated in the context of IMA systems, the challenges described here are generally applicable to a much wider domain, and we have already received substantial interest from other domains.

---

[1] The recent drafts of the new issue of DefStan 00-56 adopt a more flexible approach than the current issue, and are thus supportive of the goals of SafSec. The MoD team working on the new issue were included in the stakeholders consulted by the SafSec project.

3 The Goal of Common Certification

Conventional wisdom says that the safety and security domains have significant differences, and attempts to harmonise their work fail. Accreditation authorities demand different arguments, different evidence, presented differently, and focussed on different issues. Harmonisation is unattainable.

We think not.

Work we have carried out, supported by a range of stakeholders in the MoD, in military contractors and in the approval authorities, indicates that despite a number of differences between safety and security, there are still considerable benefits to be gained through a combined approach. Indeed, a case study currently underway is gaining these benefits and showing how safety and security can work together in a practical setting on a real project.

Our harmonisation is based on identifying common concepts between safety and security, and showing how the different analysis approaches can be seen as facets of a common, general analysis. This allows the different analyses to be documented in a way that highlights the common areas, and encourages the diverse teams to share information and insights. This common representation allows us to see overlap at four levels:

- system loss (e.g. death, security leak)
- cause
- mitigation
- evidence

The more the overlap, the greater the chance for re-use and savings between safety and security.

4 The SafSec Project

The results of the SafSec Project are captured in the Standard and Guidance Documents (Praxis 2004a, Praxis 2004b), which present an integrated methodology satisfying both safety and security certifiers.

The methodology illustrates a means for certification of both safety and security properties and is based on the identification of risks, and the justification that these risks have been adequately mitigated in the design and use of the system. Both safety and security fields require arguments and evidence to be provided that adequate measures have been taken to mitigate the risks, with the extent of the evidence required defined by the level of criticality of the mitigation measures. This commonality of approach provides an opportunity to apply a common method, and hence realise savings in effort and time.

One of the advantages of new modular approaches to system architecture, where properties as well as functions of modules are defined, is the feasibility of evolving systems, as technologies or requirements change, with limited impact on the design or implementation of systems or modules. If these benefits are to be realised for critical systems, then a way of structuring the process of certification, to minimise the need for re-certification when evolution occurs, is required.

One of the SafSec Methodology principles came from the realisation that both fields work from a base concept of *Risk* assessment and management. Identifying and mitigating risk is an essential driver for development processes. However, this concept is rarely given a central role in current certification approaches based on procedural frameworks.

Another emerging principle was the need to consider *Properties* of systems alongside the functions they perform, if safety and security are of concern. This leads to the idea that properties (expressed as objectives and assurance requirements (Hawes and Steinacker 1997)) should be central to the design process as well as function. Although this approach of focusing on properties can be applied to other non-functional aspects of design, SafSec has restricted its attention to just safety and security aspects.

The three technical areas which are central to the Methodology are those concerned with the processes of risk management, argument and evidence production during development, and modular certification. The three components of the Methodology combine as illustrated in Figure 1, and fit into a wider framework.

The Unified Risk Management Process takes account of safety hazards and security threats, together with the operational requirements of the target system, to produce a risk model alongside the architectural model of the system.

The Risk Directed Design Process uses the risk model, together with the architectural model of the system, to define the dependability properties of all the system modules in parallel with their functional properties, and produce the arguments supporting traceability of this process.

The Modular Certification Process takes the module's functional and dependability properties, and uses supporting arguments and evidence to justify certification of a module. As modules can be composed from collections of other modules, multiple applications of this process contribute to system certification. The result of the process is a set of safety and security certificates, and information that can support operational acceptance.

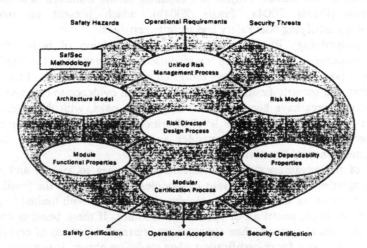

Figure 1: The SafSec Methodology

These three components of the methodology fit together, as indicated in Figure 1, and provide a core set of methods that support the key processes of requirements identification, modular design, and modular certification, based on a common understanding of the need to use dependability properties as one of the prime structuring principles.

5 Illustrating the Commonalities in Safety and Security Assurance

In this section we consider a simple example showing how safety and security analysis can be viewed in a common way, and hence overlaps and areas for re-use can be identified.

We will look at a (simplified) safety analysis, presented reasonably traditionally, together with an equally simplified security analysis. From these analyses we shall consider the likely mitigations that may be put forward, one set derived from the safety analysis and one set from the security analysis. We shall then view these analyses in a common SafSec framework, and suggest how common elements may be identified, leading to improved mitigations and re-use of arguments and evidence.

5.1 Introducing the Example

The example we will consider is derived from the Allied Standard Avionics Architecture Council (ASAAC) designs for modular avionics systems. The system consists of a variety of (safety and security related) software tasks running on a networked collection of identical processing elements. The distribution of tasks among processors, and the configuration of input-output and communications links, is controlled by an *Application Manager* process. The Application Manager configures the system according to one of several pre-defined *blueprints*, which are stored in a database. The Application Manager can reconfigure the system dynamically to take account of changes in hardware availability (e.g. if a processor fails).

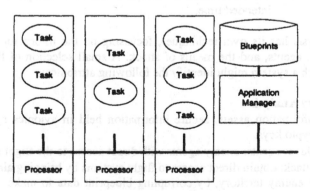

Figure 2: Example Architecture

Our illustration will focus on the *re-configurability* of the system. In order to cope with system failure or damage, the aircraft avionics are designed to allow tasks to run on different processors with different communication paths, and to allow the distribution to change dynamically during flight. If, for example, one processor were to be damaged in flight, then the tasks running on it would be migrated to other processors and the communications re-routed. We shall consider only the case of a pre-determined set of allowed configurations, called *blueprints*. If one blueprint becomes inappropriate, a different blueprint may be called up, leading to a different configuration of tasks, processors and resources.

We shall consider the safety and security analyses centred on the difficulties encountered in invoking a change of blueprint in flight. The boundary of the system being analysed is that of the *avionics system*, within the overall aircraft.

5.2 Conventional Analysis

Conventionally, a safety analysis would involve Hazard Analysis, workshops, Fault Tree analysis, FMEAs, etc. A fragment of the safety analysis for an IMA-supported aircraft might identify the following:

Safety Analysis
- Accident: Death of aircrew.
- Hazard: avionics and flight control systems catastrophically mis-configured.
- Cause/Consequence: Hazard leads to inoperable avionics, including flight control, which leads to an inoperable aircraft, which leads to total loss of aircraft and hence death (if ejection and recovery systems fail).
- Causes of Hazard (derived from FTA):
  o blueprint data as read corrupted or otherwise incorrect (and hence does not work safely).
  o Or: inability to read blueprint data successfully during system reconfiguration.
  o Or: installation of blueprint does not complete within the intended time.

Security analysis has its own techniques, focussing on the information assets at risk, the threat agents, and the means of attack. A small selection of the security analysis of such a system might identify the following attributes:

Security Analysis
- Information assets: secure information held in avionics system, e.g. crypto keys.
- Threat agents: enemy agents with direct access to the flight systems.
- Attack: obtain direct access to flight systems by bringing aircraft down in enemy territory, by corrupting blueprint data to make aircraft un-flyable on re-configuration.

Clearly these two analyses have produced different outputs and have brought different expertise to bear on the problem. However, in amongst the genuine differences there are hidden commonalities that may be hard to detect. If left to work in isolation, the safety and security teams may move on to propose the following mitigations:

Safety Mitigations
1) Include some form of checksum on the data to ensure that the read was successful.
2) Ensure that the blueprint data is read successfully before the old configuration is removed.
3) Carry out timing analysis to demonstrate that the worst-case execution time for each blueprint is within the allowed time window. Rely on the blueprint manager to install only blueprints that have been successfully analysed for timing behaviour.

Security Mitigations
1) Cryptographically sign the blueprint data at source.
2) Ensure that the blueprint data is read successfully before the old configuration is removed.
3) On read, check that the signature is still valid, and has been signed by an authorised source. This ensures that the read was successful, and that no accidental or malicious corruption has occurred.

We can see the overlap in these two analyses, but they each come from a slightly different angle and propose slightly different mitigations. The analyses are hard to compare, and we are in danger of implementing two overlapping mitigations, such as implementing both a checksum and a cryptographic signature, when one would do. Of course, in this simple example one would expect this overlap to be spotted. But in real systems, with hundreds of safety and security risks and multiple independent teams such confusions are more likely to arise and pass unnoticed.

5.3 Combined Analysis

Consider instead a combined analysis derived from inputs from both safety and security.

Combined Analysis
- Loss: Death of aircrew
     Or: Loss of secure information to enemy troops.
- Caused by: aircraft crashes in enemy territory.
- Caused by: aircraft inoperable.
- Caused by: avionics and flight control systems catastrophically mis-configured.

- Caused by: blueprint data as read has been corrupted (by accident or maliciously) or otherwise incorrect (and hence does not work correctly).

  Or: inability to read blueprint data successfully during system reconfiguration.

  Or: installation of blueprint does not complete within the intended time.

This demonstrates clearly that the two potential losses: of aircrew and of sensitive information, are both due to the same underlying risk: loss of aircraft. This loss of aircraft in turn is caused by the same issues and risks with dynamic reconfiguration. When we get down to the level of technical problems like data corruption we can see that safety and security look at the same basic issues with slightly different emphasis. For example, safety considers first and foremost the risk of accidental corruption of data, whereas security focuses on malicious attacks. Both result in corrupted data, and a single mitigation, if selected correctly, can be used to address both aspects. If safety and security are considered jointly, we can derive the following combined mitigations.

Combined Mitigations
1) Cryptographically sign the blueprint data at source.
2) Ensure that the blueprint data is read successfully before the old configuration is removed.
3) Carry out timing analysis to demonstrate that the worst-case execution time for each blueprint is within the allowed time window. Rely on the source of the blueprints to sign only blueprints that have been successfully analysed for timing behaviour.
4) On read, check that the signature is still valid, and has been signed by an authorised source. This ensures that the read was successful, that no accidental or malicious corruption has occurred, and that the blueprints are certified as having successfully passed a timing analysis.

5.4 Re-use

During development, both safety and security authorities need evidence to support the arguments relating to the losses and mitigations, and evidence that the system development has followed required development standards. By combining the safety and security analysis it will be possible to re-use the same evidence for both authorities – within limits. For example, there is a reasonably complex argument that needs to be made to show that timing constraints are met from the combination of timing analysis at source, cryptographic signing at source, and signature checking at configuration time. Such an argument can be constructed and documented in, say, a GSN form (Goal Structuring Notation, Kelly 1999). The argument will be supported by evidence that demonstrates its validity. This will include, for example, contractual conditions to ensure that blueprint developers will perform timing analysis; technical evidence demonstrating the effectiveness of such an analysis, and design information relating to the management of the cryptographic keys used for signature and verification. The whole argument and its supporting evidence will be of interest to both security and safety authorities.

There will, of course, be cases where one authority is not interested in some of the arguments, or possibly needs the arguments presented in a certain, specific way. In these cases there will need to be specific safety or specific security arguments presented. Does this conflict with our claim that finding the commonalities is cost effective? Does the occasional need to pull safety and security apart negate the benefits of merging them together?

We believe not.

Experience on a case study currently running with an MoD contractor suggests that the benefits of merging safety and security in the analysis phase greatly compensates for later having to present the same information in different styles. In fact, by concentrating first on the task of analysis, divorced from the idiosyncrasies of individual authorities' needs for presentation of evidence, we have achieved more effective analysis and clearer internal project documentation.

6 Revisiting the Goal of Common Certification

This example indicates how searching for the commonalities between safety and security can lead to a common presentation of information, despite safety and security focussing on different issues and using different analysis technique to arrive at the information. A single "cause-effect chain" presentation can capture both security- and safety-relevant information.

In this example there is no overlap in terms of the system loss: the accident identified as death of crew is different from the asset compromise identified as information leakage. But following down the cause-effect chain there is a lot of overlap. Indeed, the underlying causes of accidental and malicious alteration to data apply to both safety and security, although they tend to be given different weight by the two disciplines. Note that the notion of a combined analysis is independent of the manner in which the analysis is carried out – it applies equally to 'top-down' analysis (eg using fault- or attack-trees) and to bottom-up analysis (eg using event trees).

There is overlap of mitigation, too, and the system design may be simpler because the overlap has been identified.

For certification, the safety and security authorities may demand different types of evidence. But within the common framework it is easier to see how evidence can be re-used, and may even lead to certification authorities converging on their demands.

6.1 Implementing Common Certification

To facilitate realising the possible benefits of common certification, the SafSec standard and guidance documents provide a framework for planning development and assurance activities so as to meet the requirements of both assessment communities. The approach taken is objective-based: the SafSec documentation identifies targets that a developer should satisfy rather than specific processes to be followed. The targets address four main areas:

- identification of losses and the causal relationships between them;
- definition of protection and mitigation measures and the associated assurance requirements;
- implementation and maintenance of systems which meet the identified requirements; and
- verification that the requirements are satisfied to the necessary assurance levels.

In some areas, the SafSec standard defines objectives at several levels – in deciding to implement the standard, we may choose to address a high-level objective directly, or to accept the breakdown proposed by the SafSec standard and meet a number of more detailed lower-level objectives.

The SafSec guidance supports assessment by both safety and security communities by providing a mapping between the SafSec objectives and their respective domain standards.

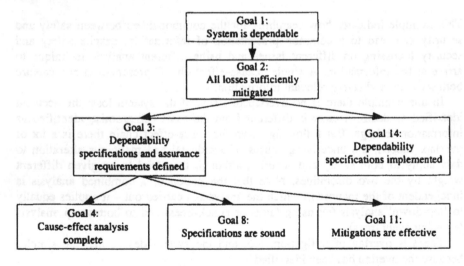

Figure 3: Simplified top-level goal structure for the SafSec Standard

The common framework provided by this argument structure also provides an important support for the certification of modular systems.

The process of identifying unified and explicit dependability properties can be carried out at component level. Extending the analysis of cause and effect relationships across modules allows safety and security properties to be expressed as *contracts* between components. Decomposition of safety arguments in this way has already been studied (Kelly 2001) – the SafSec framework allows this approach to be extended to exploit commonality between safety and security properties.

7 Conclusions

This paper has provided an overview of the work of the SafSec project, which has derived a new approach to the certification of highly modular safe or secure systems, such as proposed for advanced avionic architectures, based on the construction of safety and security arguments and the collection of evidence supporting those arguments.

Investigations into the opportunities and problems presented by modular architectures, and into the potential for the exploitation of commonality between the safety and security certification processes, have resulted in the definition of a framework and methodology which should provide scope for reducing the effort, cost and timescales associated with certification of a wide range of modular systems, including those that are safety- or security-critical.

The project has defined the SafSec Methodology, which combines:

- a unified approach to risk assessment for safety and security,
- a risk directed design process, which includes risk mitigation decisions in the design process and produces substantiated arguments to support them,
- a process supporting certification of modules within a modular architecture.

This paper presents the primary arguments for the usefulness and utility of this methodology, as a means of exploiting the inherent commonality between safety and security certification processes, and through modular certification realises the potential presented by modular architectural approaches.

References

ARINC (1997). ARINC 651-1 Design Guidance for Integrated Modular Avionics, ARINC Incorporated, Annapolis, November 1997.

Hawes and Steinacker (1997). Combining Assessment Techniques from Security and Safety to Assure IT System Dependability—The SQUALE Approach, VIS97 security conference, Freiburg, Germany.

ISO (1999). ISO 15408, Common Criteria for Information Technology Security Evaluation. International Standardisation Organisation August 1999 (Version 2.1).

Kelly, T P (1999). Arguing Safety – A Systematic Approach to Safety Case Management, DPhil Thesis, York University, Department of Computer Science Report YCST 99/05.

Kelly, T P (2001). Concepts and Principles of Compositional Safety Case Construction, University of York, COSMA/2001/1/1, May 2001.

MoD (1996). UK Ministry of Defence, Defence Standard 00-56, Safety Management Requirements for Defence Systems, Parts 1 and 2, Issue 2.

Praxis (2004a). SafSec Standard Material S.P1199.50.2, Issue 2.6, May 2004.

Praxis (2004b). SafSec Guidance Material S.P1199.50.3, Issue 2.6, May 2004.

Acknowledgement

We are grateful to Mark Suitters FBG Strike (4) DPA, for his support and funding for this work, and all the SafSec stakeholders for their invaluable contributions.

ACCIDENT INVESTIGATION

Learning from a Train Derailment

Kevin Payne

London Underground

Abstract

This paper discusses wider engineering lessons that may be drawn from the investigation of a train derailment that occurred on the Northern Line of London Underground on 19 October 2003 at Camden Town. It summarises the accident investigation process followed and the main findings and discusses: the management of "legacy" systems; maintaining the links between design intent and maintenance practice; the concept of insidious criticality; and the use of standards to control interactions.

1 Introduction

This paper briefly describes the investigation into a passenger train derailment and some of the key findings of the investigation into its causes, and discusses some wider lessons that may be drawn from both the investigation findings and the investigation processes used.

2 The derailment

At 10:01hrs, on Sunday 19th October 2003, a northbound train derailed on the approach to Platform 3 at Camden Town station on the Northern Line of London Underground while travelling at approximately 20mph. Seven people attended hospital as a result; two of the injuries were serious, one a broken femur and the other a head injury.

The derailment occurred as the train traversed a junction in a tube tunnel. The track sustained damage, the rear two cars of the train were damaged, severe damage occurred to line-side cabling and some slight damage occurred to the iron lining of the tunnel.

3 The investigation into the derailment

The investigation into the derailment was conducted in accordance with the relevant London Underground procedures and the main steps are summarised in Figures 1 and 2. The practices and processes used have been compared with various models of good practice, the comparison is being reported in-full elsewhere[1], but some aspects are discussed later in this paper.

4 The main findings of the accident investigation

The derailment occurred as the leading axle of the rear car of a six car train traversed the switchblade of a set of facing points. The points were correctly set and locked. It was established that the train had been travelling at a speed consistent with the designated limit, and had been driven in accordance with recommended practice. Although the track and its lubrication displayed a number of unusual features, there was no apparent fault that could explain the derailment; likewise, there was no immediately apparent fault on the train.

It was found that the design of the point switchblade was such that it predisposed wheels to derail when:

1. the switchblade formed part of a facing point; and
2. that the track leading into the point was curved below a critical radius in the same direction as the turnout; and
3. that the switchblade had not experienced significant amounts of wear; and
4. that high levels of friction existed between the wheels and the rails.

All of these conditions existed at the derailment site. Conditions (1) and (2) were functions of the design configuration of the track and, as such, had existed since 1986. Conditions (3) and (4) were set-up the night prior to the derailment, when the left-hand switchblade was renewed. It was found that the design weakness n the switchblade had existed since it was adopted as an industry standard item in 1968, but had never before manifested itself by causing a derailment on a "main line".

One key question that the investigation attempted to answer was: why had the particular wheel, as opposed to any other, derailed? Twelve trains of the same kind, and five cars of the train that derailed, had passed over the site without incident since the switchblade had been replaced. When the bogie that first derailed was examined after the accident, it was found to be more prone to wheel unloading (a reduction in downward forces on the wheels) than was expected. Subsequent analysis showed that the way that the suspension had been set-up reduced the margin of tolerance that prevented serious wheel unloading. There was still a good margin of tolerance to cope with the normal range of track conditions, but possibly not enough to cope with the conditions at the site of the derailment. The Northern Line trains were, at the time, approximately five years old and it had recently become necessary to re-profile the wheels on some cars to compensate for wear. This re-profiling had reduced the diameter of the wheels, so shims had been fitted above the primary suspension to re-set ride height and level. It was found that the procedures governing suspension shimming could lead to vehicles being set-up in a way not envisaged by the designers. It was found that eighteen cars had been set-up in a way not intended by the designers and that the vehicle that derailed was furthest from the designed condition.

The Final Report of the investigation is available from the internet[2] and provides more detail of the above and of a number of other matters that came to light during the investigation.

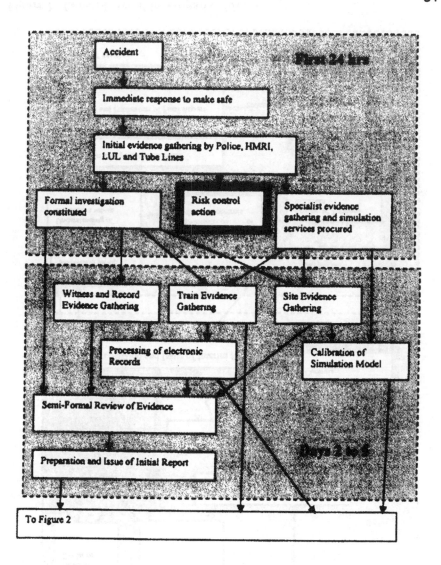

Figure 1 - Early phases of investigation process

82

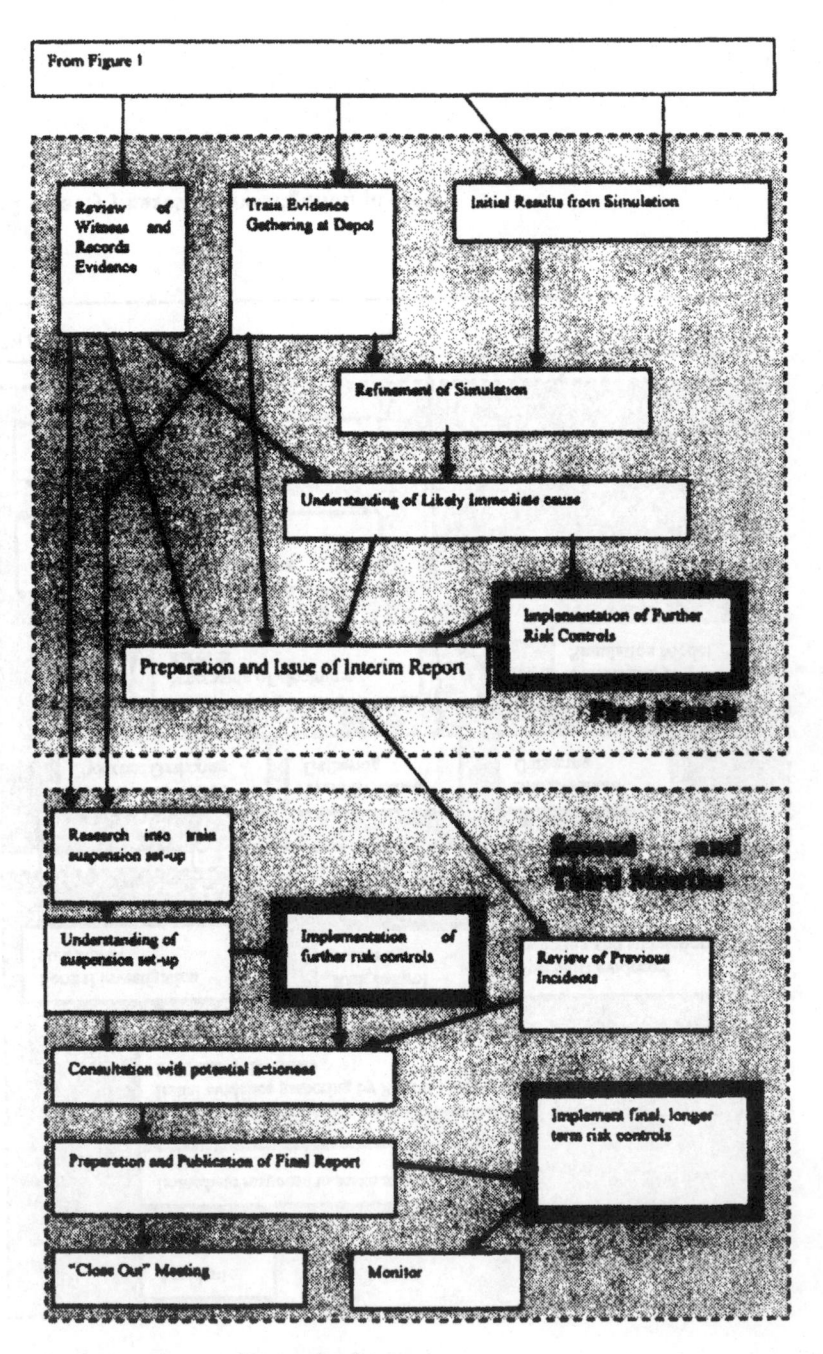

Figure 2 - Later phases of investigation process

5 Legacy systems and designs

The derailment was explained by a hitherto unrecognised weakness in the design of a legacy system, i.e. one that was inherited by the current generation of engineers responsible for it. There are huge numbers of such systems in use and any engineer taking up new responsibilities is likely to "inherit" many such items. Such systems are often said to have acquired "Grandfather Rights" and are frequently accepted, without question on the basis of a track record of good performance. The pressure to continue to use such systems without question is great, because the costs of reviewing them all, let alone carrying out any remedial actions, are likely to be immense and, given a history of satisfactory performance, it is not easy to understand what benefit it might bring. In outlining his "resident pathogen" metaphor, which states that: *"...at any one time, each complex system will have within it a certain number of latent failures, whose effects are not immediately apparent, but that can serve to both promote unsafe acts and to weaken its defence mechanism."* , Reason[3] recognises the potential problem. In summary, systems that have acquired "Grandfather Rights" are very likely to have hidden "Grandfather Frailties" too. It is notable that Reason uses the term "latent failures", rather than "latent defects", making the point that the system does not need to be defective in the sense of having departed from its intended condition, in order to be frail.

An exhaustive search for latent failure modes is likely to involve very careful examination of the system to characterise its current state or condition, followed by extensive testing of the behaviour of the system over the range of foreseeable operating scenarios, probably by use of models or simulations. For anything other than a very simple hardware system, this is likely to be extremely time-consuming and costly, and for complex systems, especially those incorporating software, it may be completely impractical, and it is suggested that some form of criticality focussed approach is likely to be more appropriate than exhaustive review. In identifying criticality, it may be necessary to take a slightly unusual perspective and rank on the basis solely of consequence, rather than the more usual approach of ranking by risk, i.e. some function of both probability and consequence, simply because the probability of unrecognised latent failures cannot be known.

Although the accident described in this paper has primarily "hard engineering" causes, the search for latent failures may well need to look into systems that incorporate a large human element, as described in the examples given by Simpson et al[4].

London Underground has some experience of reviewing legacy systems. At the broadest level, the company's Corporate Quantified Risk Assessment model[5] began as a way of representing the risks inherent in a very complex legacy system, an entire railway and its operating arrangements and external interfaces, which was then used as a way of carrying out a criticality focussed search for latent failure modes. At a more detailed level was the "Critical Asset Failure" initiative, which searched for single-point failure modes in a number of legacy systems such as train fleets and classes of escalators. Having identified potential failure modes, this work went on to examine the nature and effectiveness on the preventive measures already in place and to add further controls. The changes initiated by this work ranged from alterations to equipment, designed to obviate the identified modes, through changes to inspection and maintenance practices, to actions to improve the competence profiles of personnel looking after equipment.

6 Maintaining the link between system design intent and maintenance practice

The train suspension set-up problems revealed by the Camden Town derailment appear to have at their root a disconnection between what the people who codified the maintenance practice knew and the behaviour of the system as designed. When suspension was set-up during manufacture, the work was done without the anti-roll bars fitted to the bogies; when the suspension was reset, following wheel profiling, the work was done with the anti-roll bars in place. The presence of the anti-roll bars caused uneven wheel loading to be locked into the system. Whether the designers themselves realised the potential for a problem is not known, the fact that suspension set-up during manufacture took place before the anti-roll bars were fitted to the suspension may have been intentional, based on such understanding, or purely fortuitous, driven by convenience of the assembly sequence.

The lesson appears to be that a member of the design team should be involved in the preparation and "field testing" of maintenance procedures, because they are very likely to detect departures from design intent. Kletz[6] highlights a very similar lesson when discussing pipe failures in chemical process plants; a member of the design team should be involved in the inspection of construction work, because they will notice departures from design intent.

7 Insidious criticality

As noted in the description of the findings of the accident investigation, one of the factors that had to be present to predispose derailment was high friction between the wheel of the train and the switchblade. It was found that the gauge face of the new switchblade still carried surface rust, and that it had not been deliberately lubricated; it bore only a few dry lumps of grease that had been carried onto it by wheel flanges. This was not expected; senior engineers considered manual lubrication of the gauge faces of newly installed switch blades to be good practice and believed that it was being undertaken as a matter of normal practice. It became apparent during the investigation that this was not the case. Understanding of whether or not it was good practice differed, even among very experienced operatives, and it was not mentioned in standards, work instructions or training.

In normal circumstances, track lubrication does not perform an immediate safety function. It is used to control wear rates and, in some cases, noise production, and any safety function is both secondary (by controlling wear, it controls the rate of deterioration that could, if left unchecked progress to create danger) and extremely long removed in time. In this particular case, the absence of this lubrication effectively became a "hinge factor" in the accident sequence, because the switch blade design weakness made the whole system unstable in its absence.

The train suspension set-up problems may also have been driven as much by an unrecognised change in the criticality of the process as by any disconnection between design intent and maintenance practice. In earlier train designs, the bogie and suspension systems were only loosely coupled to the car body, permitting significant body roll. In more recent designs, a tighter coupling has been created between the suspension system, bogie and car body in order to control body roll, thereby permitting higher speeds within the tight confines of tube tunnels. This coupling has been carefully designed, so as to optimise against wheel unloading when everything is set correctly. A possibly unlooked for side-effect is that maintenance activities affecting the relationship between suspension and car body have become much more critical to the control of wheel unloading, and hence, derailment risk, than was the case for earlier designs.

If this change has not been fully recognised by maintainers, and the author has no evidence as to whether it has or has not, this may affect perceptions of the criticality of suspension set-up. If this is the case, the lesson is that changes in criticality should be made overt, be explained, to all of those who might be affected.

8 Using standards to control complex interactions

The interactions between train and track that were at the heart of the derailment investigation were intended to be controlled by adherence to standards. It is a basic tenet of engineering that the behaviour of complicated systems can be controlled if the components are built to fixed standards and that those standards are compatible at their interfaces, a frequently cited example being the international telephone system, see, for instance Boardman[7]. In examining failures at the interfaces between sub-systems controlled by separate standards, it can be useful to consider three possibilities:

- **Non-compliance with standard(s)**, the condition where one or more sub-systems are non-compliant with the interface standard;
- **Incompatibility between standards**, a condition where unacceptable outcomes can result from the interactions between the sub-systems even when all are in compliance with the interface standards; and,
- **Fragile compatibility**, a condition where incompatibility between systems, and unacceptable outcomes, is likely to arise because, although the standards are compatible, it is extremely difficult to ensure compliance, i..e. the margin for error is too small.

In this case, the problem was one of unrecognised incompatibility between standards; the new switch blade component was in accordance with standards, yet it disposed trains to derail. Kuhlmann[8] discusses the difficulties that such incompatibilities pose for the accident investigator, the key problem being that there is a heavy presumption that parts in accordance with standards are appropriate, and that failures will occur as a result of non-compliance with standards.

"The change-based analysis is established on the precept that the program and the program standards are adequate and that a problem is caused by a change of some kind which consequently causes a deviation from the standard. Institute research has, in point of fact, shown that the majority of programs are out of control .... from lack of compliance with standards."

Fragile compatibility can result from the inappropriate setting of standards, for example taking insufficient account of the difficulty that may face field-operatives when attempting to achieve a stated finish or dimension under foreseeable levels of stress, but it may also result from unrecognised changes in the demands made on the sub-system, resulting in a gradual tightening of coupling, effectively an example of insidious criticality.

In the UK railway environment, both National Rail and London Underground, there are particular challenges to the management of interactions through the use of standards because the changes to the structures of the industry over the past ten years have been accompanied by a strong tendency to move from prescriptive standards, which define interfaces very tightly, to performance standards, i.e. standards that define required outcomes, avoiding prescription of method or solution. Such standards operate well where they define outcomes from relatively closed systems under the control of a single integrator, but may not be well suited to the definition of components within tightly coupled systems. In order for standards to retain their effectiveness as risk controls, it may be necessary to either adjust their "field of view", replacing individual standards covering traditional discipline activities or sub-systems, which often have their boundaries where coupling is very tight, with standards that span more widely, with the interfaces between standards being set where coupling is loose. It may also be necessary to overlay sub-system standards with others that define systems engineering process or practice requirements.

9   Investigation process representations and models

The comparison of the investigation with models of good practice included consideration of:

- Investigation process representations, i.e. generalised ways of illustrating the process of undertaking an investigation; and;
- Investigation process models, i.e. generalised ways of representing the often complex findings of investigations as both an aid to the conduct of the investigation and a way of making the findings more easily comprehensible.

The process of incident or accident investigation is often represented by a simple serial listing or a diagram of the kind shown in Figure 3, see for instance HSG65[9]. As Figures 1 and 2 illustrate, the actual process of investigation, other than of a very simple incident, can be much more complex. Kuhlmann provides a representation that better expresses the reality that the phases of an investigation usually overlap. For example, evidence gathering often commences before the decision as to exact level and nature of the investigation is made; indeed the nature of the early evidence often helps determine the form of investigation. Figure 4 provides an expansion of Kuhlmann's representation, and it will be seen that it fits closely the actual processes used in this case.

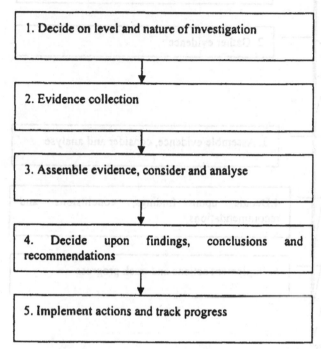

Figure 3 - Basic representation of investigation processes

Investigation process models range from simple tools, such as checklists, through a range of software tools that permit the representation of complex relationships and/or uncertainties. These packages generally include means to create an incident specific model, providing prompt questions that help direct evidence gathering, and act as a repository for evidence or links to evidence stores. Benner[10] identified 14 accident models and 17 different accident investigation methodologies in 1985, and more have become available since, see for instance the range of techniques discussed at The Third Bieleschweig Workshop on System Engineering[11].

The purposes of the various models are essentially similar:

- To aid critical thinking:
- To ensure a comprehensive identification of possible causes;
- To clearly identify the actual, from the field of possible, causes;
- To ensure that interactive causes are properly understood; and,
- To avoid the need to invent new processes for each separate investigation.

Choice of model can have a significant impact on the findings of the investigation, as analysed in a case study [12]showing how widely differing findings resulted from

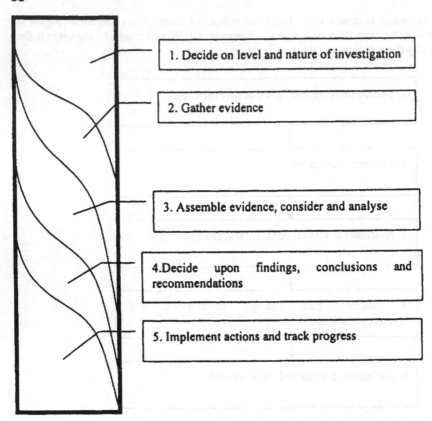

1. Decide on level and nature of investigation

2. Gather evidence

3. Assemble evidence, consider and analyse

4. Decide upon findings, conclusions and recommendations

5. Implement actions and track progress

Figure 4 – Developed investigation process representation (after Kuhlmann)

the application of three different models to the investigation of a single fire. Researchers are now attempting to form meta-models or a universal model, which are intended to overcome the problems of diversity and, particularly, to draw on ideas from diverse disciplines, e.g. medicine and engineering, see, e.g. McClay[13].

During the investigation reported in this paper, only simple representations were used. A simple cause/consequence diagram, based on experience of fault and event tree representations was created, the objective being to fully identify the range of possible causes and then to eliminate or confirm each in turn. A summarised version of the diagram is given in Figure 5; and, a detailed multi-linear chronology, tracing the history of all of the relevant "actors", people and pieces of equipment, back as far as was necessary before the derailment and forward from the derailment, through at least the initial response phase. A key purpose was to search for any times at which the configuration of the signalling, track and/or the train had been changed. At the outset, it was far from clear exactly how many "actors" needed to be studied, over what periods and to what degree of resolution, but it was possible to make some initial assumptions based on a

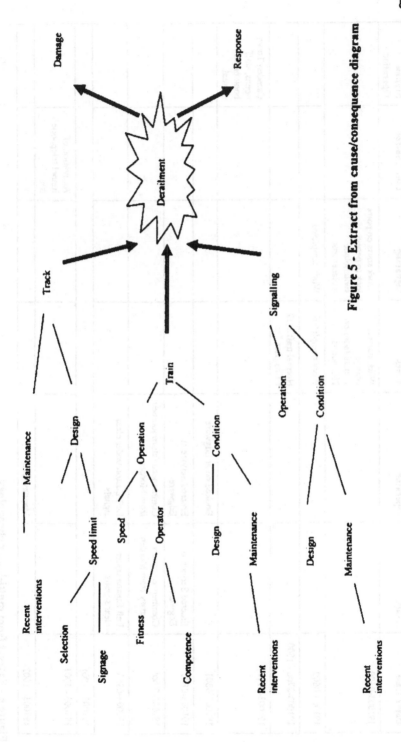

Figure 5 - Extract from cause/consequence diagram

Date / Time	Train	Operator	Track	Signalling	Line Control	Station Operation
191003-0300			Work starts to change switchblades on 20B points	Work starts on point lock to permit switchblade replacement		
191003-0600			Work completed	Work completed		
191003-0700 - 1000			Normal traffic; 12 trains pass			
191003-0710						Camden Town opens, staff book on as normal
191003-0801		Booked on at Edgware				
191003-0805	Entered Service at Edgware	Entered Service at Edgware				
191003-09xx	Commenced return journey from Morden	Commenced return journey from Morden				
191003-0958	Left Euston under clear signals	Left Euston under clear signals				
191003 - 1001						
191003 - 1001					Activation of tunnel telephone trip	
191003 - 1002		Mayday Call				

Figure 6 - Extract from multi-linear chronology

knowledge of operating conventions and the typical rates of change applicable to track, trains and signalling. Figure 6 gives an outline of the form of chronology that was being sought.

In later phases, it became apparent that the chronological representation was not adding great value to the understanding of engineering matters, although it was very useful in other respects, e.g. understanding the operational response to the incident. Its lack of value in the engineering arena may have been because it was used at the wrong level of resolution; "train" and "track and signalling" were too large as "actors" to be useful. For example, to have studied the suspension set-up question using this method would have required consideration of "actors" such as:

- Author of procedure
- Wheelset
- Shim (packing piece)
- Primary suspension
- Wheel lathe operative
- Bogie fitting operative

Using such an approach may have been a helpful way of representing the actions *after* understanding how the chain of events occurred, but it is very questionable whether it could have been used to *lead* to an understanding.

At one level, the representation was even less suitable to help gain an understanding of the switchblade design weakness. The design decisions had been taken so long before the incident and, as a result, were so difficult to fathom, that they could not have been represented effectively. At another level, the representation did have the ability to display the key change to the switchblade, from "worn" (and, therefore, tolerable) to "new" (and, therefore, intolerable), but it is debatable whether it alone would have been sufficient to highlight the *importance* of the change.

10 Conclusions

This paper has used the investigation of a train derailment as a case example through which to explore some aspects of investigation processes and a number of aspects of the control of safety in complex systems.

It can be concluded from this exploration that:

- Systems that have acquired "Grandfather Rights" may contain hidden "Grandfather Frailties"; although they have established a record of satisfactory performance, they may contain latent failure modes;

- Consequence focussed reviews of legacy, safety related systems, in an attempt to identify and deal with latent failure modes, are likely to be worthwhile;

- A thorough understanding of design intent is essential to the preparation or amendment of system maintenance procedures; ideally, members of the design team should participate in both the drawing-up and "field testing" of such procedures;

- The criticality of components of a system, whether they be items of hardware, software, processes, procedures, or people, and of the relationships between them, can change insidiously;

- Engineering standards that define required outcomes, avoiding prescription of method or construction, operate well where they govern relatively closed systems under the control of a single integrator, but my not be appropriate to govern the relationships between tightly coupled sub-systems in the absence of a single, active integrator; and,

- The use of one or more process models can materially improve the quality of incident investigation, but the choice of model has the potential to affect the findings, as has the level of resolution at which the model is applied.

References

[1] Payne, K.G. "The Investigation of an underground train derailment". Dissertation prepared in connection with MSc studies, Lancaster University Engineering Department, 2004.

[2] http://tube.tfl.gov.uk/content/pressreleases/0402/02.asp

[3] Reason, J. "Human Error", Cambridge University Press, 1990.

[4] G C Simpson, A M Rushworth, F H von Glehn and R H Lomas. "Investigation of the causes of transport and tramming accidents on mines other than coal, gold and platinum", Safety in Mines Research Advisory Committee Report, 1996.

[5] See details within London Underground's Railway safety Case, posted in full at http://tube.tfl.gov.uk/content/about/report/sqe/

[6] Ketz, T. "Learning from Accidents", Third Edition, Gulf Professional Publishing, 2003.

[7] Boardman, J. "Systems Engineering, An Introduction", Perntice Hall, 1990.

[8] Kuhlmann, R L. "Professional Accident Investigation", Loss Control Institute, 1977.

[9] "Successful Health and Safety Management", HSE Books, 1997.

[10] Benner Jr, L. "Rating Accident Models and Investigation Methodologies", Journal of Safety Research, Vol. 16, pp. 105–126, 1985.

[11] http://www.rvs.uni-bielefeld.de/Bieleschweig/B3/#content, website of The Third Bieleschweig Workshop on System Engineering, 12-13 February 2004, Center of Interdiciplinary Research (ZiF), University of Bielefeld.

[12] "The Warwick Explosion; a case study", Investigation Process Research Roundtable and Library website, http://www.iprr.org/COMPS/WRWENG.html

[13] McClay, R E. "Using the Universal model in Accident Investigation", Professional Development Conference Proceedings, East Carolina University, 2003.

Accident Investigations - Meeting the challenge of new technology

Established methods challenged by uncertain safety concepts and failure behaviour in new technology

Knut Rygh
kr@aibn.no
Chief engineer system safety
Accident Investigation Board Norway

Keywords: Safety, Accident investigation, Transport system, Digital system, STAMP, Barrier, Safety concept, Root causes, Safety constraints, Accident causation

Abstract New technology and new organisational concepts are being introduced at a pace that does not allow enough time to demonstrate control of possible residual risk by means of technical design and human performance. One area where this is becoming increasingly noticeable is the transport sector. Through identification of causal factors resulting from accident investigations, it may seem for digital systems that some transport sectors are facing challenges when ensuring documentation of safe operations. Operators and approval authorities are also facing a challenge in understanding the safe limitations and risk aspects involved when introducing new technology to transport systems The purpose of this paper is to demonstrate through lessons learned from accident investigations in the transport sector:

1) Why applied safety techniques to prevent accidents sometimes fail to show preventive effect in modern systems

2) Why a system for understanding the safety concept needed to investigate these transport systems has not been established.

It is becoming increasingly important to speed up the efforts to modernise techniques for accident prevention as these have been lagging behind the use of new technology in several sectors. Furthermore, this paper wishes to bring focus on the fact that the pace of introduction of digital automation systems to certain parts of modern transport systems during the last 15-20 years seems to have outstripped one's ability to assure and document safe operations. The fact that the safety of such systems cannot be assured in accordance with established and traditional methods and safety principles, combined with the fact that replacements are immature and unproven, calls for a more cautious and conservative approach with regard to how this technology should be applied to safety- critical systems/operations.

1)   Introduction

Innovation and new technology are found to provide a positive increase in wealth and way of living. The basis for accepting new technology into our lives lies in the fact that the risks are known and under control. Standards and established methods for engineering safety features into systems to prevent accidents are predominately based on handling failure of simple systems and physical components in chain or sequential events.

Digital technology has created a revolution in most fields of engineering, but system engineering and system safety engineering have not kept pace. One example among others is the introduction of a new safety system on board aeroplanes, Traffic Alert and Collision Avoidance System (TCAS), to give the pilot a warning and recommended action when two planes are on a collision course. This system operates isolated from air traffic controllers on the ground, which gives us two entities controlling the same airspace without communicating with each other. The extreme consequence of this was demonstrated in the Ueberlingen accident in Germany on 1st. July 2002 when a Tupolev TU 154M passenger aircraft had an in-flight collision with a Boeing B757-200 transport aircraft that resulted in 71 fatalities. The root cause, seen from a system perspective, was a severely deficient safety system where the airborne technical safety concept to avoid collisions did not correspond with the human ground-based air traffic controllers' collision avoidance system. (#1)

Digital systems introduce new "failure modes" that are changing the nature of accidents. Several approaches that worked on electromechanical components – such as replication of components to protect against individual component failure (i.e., redundancy) – are ineffective in controlling accidents that arise from the use of digital systems and software. Redundancy may even increase risk by adding complexity. (#2)

2)   The safety concept – investigating the built-in safety features

Findings on the accident scene are usually a manifestation of a result that has its origin in systemic weakness and a failure, which symptoms ought to have been noticeable for some time. It is an accepted fact that a transport system's level of safety is determined by the safety concept for that transport system, which includes all safety features for prevention of any serious incident or an accident. It is also a proven fact that it is a weakness in one or more of these or the lack of safety features that allows an accident/incident to occur.

It is also an established practise, and therefore a continuing challenge for the accident investigation boards of the transport sectors, to document that investigations have systematically identified the missing, maladaptive, failure in, or the operational ineffectiveness of, these same safety features. To achieve this would call for a change of paradigm in accident investigation with respect to digital systems.

The law, regulations, certifications and permits to operate put strict safety constraints on transport systems and their operators to safeguard operations from accidents. Bridging the gap between fulfilling the regulation requirements of bookshelf obligations and the real safety conditions of practical performance in traffic operations (i.e. the real status of all technical, human performance and systemic controls), to avoid accidents seams to be an unresolved grey zone in the effort of accident prevention. An example here is the Alaska Airlines 261-accident where a MD-80 experienced an in-flight failure of the screw-jack (single point failure to catastrophic consequences) holding the horizontal stabiliser, killing 88 passengers + crew. The investigation uncovered a systemic history of incrementally extended lubrication intervals from every 300-flight hour to 2550 hours of the nut, which drives up and down a vertical jackscrew pushing the front end of the horizontal stabilizer up or down. The jackscrew recovered from the seabed however, showed that it might have been more than 5000 flight hours since last received a coat of fresh grease. Without enough grease, the constant grinding will wear out the thread on either the nut or the screw. Furthermore, the investigation could reveal more drift into failure: the endplay check interval (which gauges thread wear on the jackscrew-nut assembly) was stretched from 3600 to 9550 flight hours. The extended intervals were only an incremental away from the previously established norm. No rules were violated, no laws broken. This maintenance history of the screw jack teaches something about "systemic accidents". (#3)

3)   Understanding the safety concept for identifying the causal factors

A transport system of any kind does have, through concept and layout selection, detailed engineering, production and qualification testing, identified what kind of built-in safety features the technical systems need to have in order to prevent accidents. Furthermore, when the transport system becomes operational, a new set of operational safety requirements (constraints) ought to be identified based on the aforementioned for the entire socio-technical system design that bridges the gap between:

1)   What the systems of built–in safety features technically can cover of the established risk picture

and

2)   Extra operational and system related safety constraints that have to be covered by the pilots, train driver and others to safeguard all (residual hazards) invitations to accidents.

All necessary safety features and operational safety constraints for a dedicated transport system is what constitute the safety concept for that particular transportation system. Experience from accident investigations often reveals that neither the safety professionals in the operating companies nor the surrounding socio-technical system had the overview and control over the accident's causal factors.

> *It is an established fact that a systematic safety assessment is an accident investigation before the accident occurs.*
> *Therefore, incident and accident investigations should be regarded as safety assessments. It is a challenge in accidents investigations to use the same safety principles in an assessment as those that were applied as system safety features in the detailed design, operation and assurance system of the transportation system as a safety fundament for the investigation.*

It seems obvious to expect, but not normal to find evidence of this in reports from accident investigations. Causal factors for accidents are often referred to as broken bolts, missing brackets, human factors or inadequate adherence to a procedure. Experience shows, however, that these elements are symptoms (direct cause) and not the root cause of an accident. Consequently, safety recommendations are often addressed to symptoms and not to the root cause and therefore the preventive effect for avoiding reoccurrences are limited.

It is proven that best effect of accident investigations is obtained when the identification process of root causes and issuing safety recommendations to prevent reoccurrences are based on thorough knowledge of the difference between:

1) <u>The safety base line</u>

   The complete safety concept that was or should have been established based on law, regulation, certification and authority approval

   <u>and</u>

2) <u>The actual safety status during the accident</u>

   The safety concept that was physically in place immediately before and at the time of the accident.

It is this difference that normally constitutes the accident's causal factors.

Experience tells us that identifying the above differences in the safety concept cannot be based on random guess work or what we believe it to be, but requires a systematic safety assessment (gap analysis) of all technical, operational and system safety features of the transport system. For certain investigations in complex transport systems a thorough knowledge of applied safety principles during the detail engineering phase would be required and the investigation team would need to be supported by a member with a professional background in system safety.

4)   The advantages of digital systems can be disadvantageous for safety

The development of digital systems has left the methodology for engineering safety features into the design far behind. It does not help the situation that authority certification and approval of new transport systems face a challenge in gaining sufficient knowledge and expertise to understand the failure behaviour of this new technology. The continuous strive for faster, more reliable and comfortable means of travel in today's competitive transport market challenges all aspects of ensuring a system design that rests on sound safety principle development in new technology.

Before software was introduced to safety critical functions, these were easy to inspect and often controlled by conventional (non-programmable) mechanical and electronic devices. We have entered the digital world where software technology is applied that allows us to construct systems with a level of complexity and couplings that is beyond our ability to control; in fact, we are building systems where the interactions among components cannot be planned, understood, anticipated, or guarded against by manual means. This change is not solely the result of using digital components, but is also made possible due of the flexibility of software. (#2)

A software program of only a few hundred lines may contain any number of decisions, allowing for thousands of alternative paths of execution. Programs for fairly critical applications vary between ten and millions of lines of code. Despite rigorous and systematic testing, most large programs contain some residual bugs when delivered. (#4)

Modern transportation like; aviation and high speed trains, utilises various approaches to safety engineering, mathematical sciences/quantitative methods for risk assessment and quantifying the probability of human failure behaviour in critical operations. Digital system concepts that utilise handling of massive information combined with the possibility of creating unlimited numbers of interactions, open up for a myriad of system complexity and unintended functional paths in built-in software and operating systems in modern transportation. The failure history of digital systems reveals operation of complex transport systems with incomplete information about its behaviour in a failure or maladaptive situation. Considering all the effort invested in and priority given to safety, it is a paradox that accident investigations in the transport industry often reveal a practise of utilising digital systems in safety critical functions without developing necessary safety documentation. An example of lack of a system level approach in building software-controlled systems:

A tram's inoperable door opening system in emergency opening mode kept the passengers trapped inside when the tram experienced a failure situation in the brake system when standing still at a tram stop. This happened because the emergency opening modes of the doors could only be executed if the tram braking system with speed sensors allowed door opening. The tram experienced a failure of the speed sensor that sensed a train motion of 12 km/hr when the tram stood still. This resulted in an operation mode of the tram which was in contradiction to the fundamentals in the safety design philosophy of free, independent and uninterrupted operating mode of emergency escape doors ensuring passenger exit at any time during danger. This escape possibility ought to be independent of the operating state of the train and/or driver. The operating company, the driver and approving authorities were not aware that a digital system in the brakes determined successful operation of tram doors during an emergency opening mode.

Established methods for safety analysis and systematic implementation of safety engineering principles and accepted protocol for documenting risks and their means of control are based on event chain models. These methods are not easy adaptable to new technology characterized by failure behaviour that is not event sequential in its nature, and is therefore not suitable for documenting failure characteristics in digital systems.

Approving authorities and inspectorates for transportation sectors constitute "a bench marking" entity with regards to what level of acceptable risk exposure shall be allowed when issuing "permit to use" for transport systems. Today, it is a challenge for the approval authorities to judge the operators' effectiveness proactively in accident prevention when digital systems are used in safety-critical applications without sufficient and formalised format of documentation available to systematically demonstrate a safe system.

5)   Facing the consequences of automating the pilot function

The use of digital systems, specifically on aviation flight deck, changes the safety concept of safeguarding the operation of the plane.

The system operator role	☞ to ☞	System monitoring
role		(fly-by-wire)
The pilot relies completely on own performance		The pilot must share reliance between automation and own performance

The increasing level of automation in pilots' performance and overall safety has for years been assessed with regards to how it changes the system operator role. The first effect of automation is the nature of the pilot's role on the flight deck. On modern aircrafts the pilots have become supervisors who, during predominant parts of the flight, monitor aircraft systems in normal situations and intervene only when unanticipated events occur. Instead of "hand flying" the airplane, pilots contribute to the control of the aircraft by acting as mediators, instructions being given to the automation. (#5)

By eliminating the need for manual control of normal situations has reduced the opportunities for the pilot to acquire experience and skills necessary to safely cope with abnormal events. (#6)

Difficulties in assessing the state and behaviour of automation arise mainly from four factors (#5):

- The complexity of current systems (#7) and consequent mode-related problems (#8)

- The intrinsic autonomy of automation which is able to fire mode transitions without explicit commands from the pilots (#9)

- The bad quality of feed-back from the control system's displays and interfaces to the pilots (#10) and

- The fact that the automation usually lacks explicit representation of the pilots' intention and strategy (#11)

The conjunction of the above induces a large set of crew-automation interaction problems that pose questions to the current research: difficulties in anticipating computer-generated mode changes, difficulties assessing the implications of changes to previously given instructions, difficulties in reacting to unanticipated events and in commanding changes, difficulties in finding, integrating and interpreting relevant data for situation assessment and difficulties in building extended and refined mental models of how automation is working and how instructions have to be put in. (#9) For pilots, the consequences of these difficulties are an increase in cognitive workload and the development of "unofficial" strategies to override or "hijack" the automation, in an attempt to satisfy "official" goals. (#12)

One example to illustrate the above is:

> A Boeing 757-200 with 75 passengers during the landing phase at Oslo Airport Gardermoen in Norway 22nd January 2002 was 1 second from in-flight crash with ground due to the automated go-around system that lured the crew into an "automatic trap", thereby losing control of the aircraft.

The descent and approach to Oslo Airport Gardermoen was made in strong tailwind and with the auto throttle engaged, the plane was too high on the glide path down to the runway, the correct flap setting was not made, the approach speed was too high, and the pilot in command did not have vital data on the Instrument Landing System (ILS) showing how the plane was positioned on the glide path down to the runway. The crew cooperation and crew resource management (CRM) during this phase broke down.

Since the pilots did not manage to stabilize the plane with low enough height when the plane reached final approach (the entrance of the runway), the commander, in a mental overload status with loss of situational awareness discontinued the unstable approach and initiated auto "go-around". In such a setting, where the implementation of sequential checklist actions during the approach was interrupted and not completed for this phase of flying, it resulted in an unplanned, unprepared transition phase to automatic "go-around" and correct settings of vital flight control data like flaps settings etc. was not implemented. The commander had an inadequate mental model of what an initiation of automatic go-around would represent. With the plane still not under his control, climbing with full automatic power setting at an angle of 21deg. to 2895 feet, he was more than occupied just hanging on to the ride.

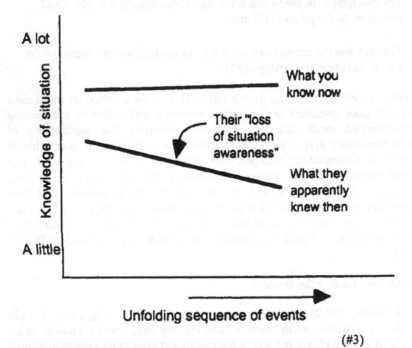

(#3)

The power was then automatically reduced when levelling off the plane into a cloud at a rate that the commander feared would cause the plane to stall. By reflex he initiated a full stick forward motion and the plane experienced an over-the-top manoeuvre with negative G-force and entered into a nose dive of extreme 49 degrees before pulling out at 321 feet above ground with both pilots pulling back the control stick, exposing the passengers to a new G-force of nearly +4 before the crew eventually gained control of the plane.

For the passengers the movement of the plane, with negative and positive G-forces, was extremely uncomfortable and frightening. Some passengers were "screaming and others were praying to God". It led to chaos in the cabin and all loose articles in the passenger compartment was thrown around and water "geysered" from the toilets. The stewardess afterwards compared the motion to "a brutal facelift".

The pilot's human reflexes for manual flight fought the manoeuvre resulting from the automated throttle mode, thereby causing the event above. The automation of the pilot's task of "auto go-around" was disrupted by a commander with loss of situational awareness influenced by the pilots 8034 hours of flying experience. (#13)

This example coincides with current problems encountered with the "technology-centred automation" (#14) and corresponds to the most common questions asked by pilots in glass cockpits that are: "What is it doing?" "Why did it do that?" and "What will it do next?" to which Sarter and Woods (1993) add (#8): "how in the world did I ever get into that mode?"

6)   A change of paradigm in system safety and accident investigations

The drive for new technology in transport systems seems to be much stronger than the effort to ensure that all failure mechanisms that could be a threat to passenger safety are well understood and adequately controlled. The accident models based on system theory consider accidents arising from interaction between system components and do not usually specify single causal variables or factors (#15). The nature of accidents, however, is changing due to use of digital systems. Investigation models use chain of failure events and failure in human functions causing accidents that are limited in their ability to handle system accidents arising from dysfunctional interactions between components and not just component failures.

A new accident model Systems- Theoretic Accident Model and Processes (STAMP) based on system theory has been developed where events are substituted with constraints. Safety is viewed as a control problem: accidents occur when component failures, external disturbances, and/or dysfunctional interactions among system components are not adequately handled. This model provides a much better description of how software affects accidents than a failure mode. The primary safety problem in computer-controlled systems is not software "failure", but the lack of appropriate constraints on software behaviour, and the solution is to identify the required constraints and enforce them in the software and overall design. System engineers must identify the constraints necessary to ensure safe system behaviour and effectively communicate these behavioural constraints to the software engineers who, in turn, must enforce them in their software. (#16)

In system theory and control theory, systems are viewed as hierarchical structures where each level imposes constraints on the activity on the level below – that is, constraint or lack of constraint at a higher level allows or controls lower-level behaviour (#17). Safety-related constraints like system variables are specified and constitute the non-hazardous or safe states – for example:

The Traffic Alert and Collision Avoidance System (TCAS) should in real time give a down link message to the air traffic controller of any "Collision Avoidance Command" given for the airspace under his control; The activation of an automatic train stop system should only be able to be reset by clearance from the traffic controller; the control of a catastrophic failure should have a redundant dissimilar barrier independent of the digital system.

From a system perspective results from accident investigations often show why a change of paradigm in system safety and accident investigations is necessary. Two types of mechanisms that often constitute the causal system factors of an accident can illustrate this;

- **Unknown failure behaviour and characteristics**

  The operator of an aeroplane or a high-speed train was not aware of the weakness, failure behaviour or mechanism causing a serious incident/accident. What is worrying here is that this category is increasing in numbers with the magnitude of new technology being applied without knowledge of subsequent failure behaviour and characteristics. This is caused by insufficient methods and practise in performing safety analysis and identifying failure propagation to hazardous effect in digital systems

- **Violation of the safety-related constraints**

  These constraints were often overlooked by the developer in the system-engineering phase or were not communicated to the operating organisation in the form needed for operating limitations or system barriers.

The basis of safe operation of a transport system rests on the assurance that failure mechanisms, their behaviour and operating limitations that represent a threat to passengers and/or cargo, are identified, and that control of residual risk by means of technical, human and system barriers is implemented. Furthermore, investigations often reveal that it is important that this is documented in a way that is easily communicated in the form of safety constraints to operational personnel.

This identification and control can hardly be achieved in digital systems by means of established safety techniques. What makes digital systems, with their unique operating characteristics and innate features a major advantage for the industry are the same characteristics that create difficulties when applying established regulations, standards for safety engineering and applied safety principles on the same systems with the purpose of preventing accidents.

The regulating authorities and research organisations need to focus on the abovementioned contradiction of digital system characteristics to improve accident prevention methods and techniques for transport operations when using digital systems in safety critical applications.

7)   Lessons learned – what do results from accident investigation tell us?

A traditional accident investigation follows a systematic approach of collecting information, answering what, when, where, by whom and how the accident could occur. Since an accident investigation actually is a safety assessment, the investigation also focuses with a systemic perspective on "why" the system allowed the accident to take place. The sole purpose of the investigation is, by finding and understanding all mechanisms that caused the accident to happen, to develop safety recommendations aimed at preventing reoccurrence of the accident, without apportioning blame or liability. What do results from accident investigations tell us?

7.1   Recurrence of accidents

A review of several accident reports for one transport sector often draws a pattern of the same failure mechanism causing the same category of serious incident or accident. A closer scrutiny of causal factors reveals that common trends and recurring causes have resulted due to not addressing the systemic side of preventive measures. This frequently results in safety recommendations from accident investigations being addressed towards treating symptoms rather than the root causes.

7.2   How to qualify humans as a safety critical barrier?

The various transport modes depend heavily on humans for controlling residual hazards in the operation of technical transport systems. From a safety perspective it is usually advantageous at the beginning of an investigation to view the transport system as unmanned and from this position ask which premises and specified qualifications were given to humans, the lay-out of the cockpit and to the organisation to enable control of residual hazards during operation of the transport system.

It is an established fact that safety-critical functions executed by technical systems normally have higher degree of functional reliability compared to execution by man.

- What premises are necessary to improve reliability of the human function?

- What is needed to qualify man as a safety-critical barrier?

Human error is often expressed as a causal factor of an accident and it is easier and more convenient for the Prosecuting Authority to blame the driver or the pilot than to investigate the system for potential weakness to prevent accidents.

> *The point of an investigation is not to find where people went wrong; it is to understand why their assessments and actions made sense at the time. (#3)*

It is only when the human function is described as part of the safety concept that it is possible to understand:

- Under what operational circumstances shall a human constitute a safety barrier?

- What kind of selection process of candidates was used, what kind of man-machine interface adaptation of the workplace/cockpit was made to humans and what kind of training was given to ensure that the candidate had the innate human resources and premises needed to constitute a safety barrier?

Accident investigations have revealed on numerous occasions that the causal factor leading to an accident was human error. It is a paradox, seen from a safety concept perspective, that it is so easy to address the causal factor only to human performance when the premises necessary to qualify the same human as a safety-critical barrier normally are not specified, identified by the investigation or discussed in the accident report. Furthermore, experience from investigations indicates, when issuing safety recommendations to improve the human function to qualify as a safety-critical barrier, it is imperative that this assessment should not be done in isolation in the human factors domain, but should be analysed and recommended developed as part of the total safety concept.

7.3   Deficiencies in Safety Management Systems

The law and regulations for the various transport sectors set strict requirements for a functional safety management system. The purpose of this is to ensure that all hazards associated with the transport operation in question are identified and those that are not eliminated shall always be under adequate and documented control.

Accident investigations for railway accidents often find that safety organisations in operating companies organise themselves away from the task of identifying, implementing and monitoring the operational safety status on barriers. Although they follow the regulation requirement of employing safety professionals with higher technical and safety education in order to ensure in-depth knowledge of complex technical and operational transport systems, they often position this type of personnel only in higher positions far away from complex technical systems and practical operations. Paradoxically, the same companies often place the actual responsibility for traffic safety in the line organisation, in actual fact often at the lowest level of operations, with personnel with no professional safety qualifications to ensure in-depth knowledge of safety principles applied and updated operational status of the safety barriers. The result is of course that it is difficult for the investigation team to find who within the company had the necessary insight to assure that the right safety principles were employed, and at any time could assure an adequate operational status of the built-in safety features (barriers) to prevent a technical or operational failure from propagating to hazardous effect. Investigations of train accidents often show this as a root cause of avoidable accidents.

7.4   Accident investigation from a system safety perspective

Traditionally, accident investigations have been performed with the aim to improve safety without apportioning any blame or liability. The changing world and concepts of transport systems calls for a need to introduce new elements in models for accident causation. The challenge today is to document if and how the systematic analysis and investigation work is anchored in a system safety approach and how application of new technology in transport systems with abnormalities and failure behaviour in digital systems can be investigated based on a non-event-chain model (non-sequential) mode. Accident investigations experience a change of paradigm in response to the introduction of new technology in transport systems with resulting new behaviour of failure propagation mechanisms that require tailor made processes in investigation work. Accident investigations face a challenge in documenting the safety concept of specific objects under investigation. Accident reports need to supply a clearer picture of where for example a missing bolt or broken bracket is placed within the safety concept of the failed system, thereby illuminating the built-in safety feature that was meant to prevent a failure from propagating to hazardous effect.

One of the underlying reasons why this is seen as a challenge for some accident investigations could be that not all commissions are staffed with professional system safety engineers. Another reason could be that accident investigations and their resulting reports not always have been able to document how and to what degree the investigation has been based on the safety concept of the transport operation in question.

8)   Conclusion

This paper has illuminated the need to flag an increasing concern for the widening gap between safety assurances based on traditional technology used in transportation systems and how safety is assured when based on new unproven digital systems used in safety critical applications.

Furthermore, the increasing use of digital systems in automation of pilot functions reveals that automation is accepted as a safety critical function operating alongside humans, but seemingly without a system safety perspective that includes the inherent characteristics (subconscious reflections) in humans as part of the design premises of this technology. Examples in this paper show what can happen when a conflict occurs in this area.

The fact that the safety of such systems cannot be assured according to established and traditional methods and safety principles combined with the fact that replacements are immature and unproven, calls for a more cautious and conservative approach with regard to how this technology should be applied to safety critical systems/operations.

In addition, lessons learned show that established methods in accident investigation are being challenged by uncertain safety concepts and failure behaviour in new technology. The insufficiency of traditional safety principles and methods for safety assurance when dealing with modern transportation is a known fact, and serious effort has been made since early 80's and 90's to improve knowledge in this area. In the mean time, however, transport systems have continued to introduce more new technology, seemingly without considering the increasing grey area of unknown safety implications. It is time yet again to focus on the need for a change of paradigm in system safety and accident investigations, a need that should be viewed as serious, but also as a positive challenge to our system safety community.

> *The human mind cannot grasp the causes of phenomena in the aggregate. But the need to find these causes is inherent in man's soul. And the human intellect, without investigating the multiplicity and complexity of the conditions of phenomena, any one of which taken separately may seem to be the cause, snatches at first, the most intelligible approximation to a cause, and says: "This is the cause!"*
>
> *Leo Tolstoy*
> *War and Peace*

9)   References:

#1)   Investigation report AX001-1-2/02 May 2004, German Federal Bureau of Aircraft Accident Investigation

#2)   Nancy G. Leveson, Ph.D., 14.Feb. 2004 MIT.; " The Role of software in Recent Aerospace Accidents". This research was partially supported by grant from the NASA Ames Design for Safety Program, and by the NASA IV & V Center Software Initiative Program

#3)   Sidney Dekker 2004, Ten questions about human error. A new view of human factors and system safety

#4)   Bev Littlewood and Lorenzo Sterigini: Nov. 1992, Scientific American, Software "glitches" that endanger public safety

#5)   Denis Javaux, Michel Masson, & Véronique De Keyser, 1995; Beware of agents when flying aircraft: Basic principles behind a generic methodology for the evaluation and certification of advanced aviation systems. University of Liége. N95-34787

#6)   Bainbridge L. (1987). Ironies of automation. In J. Rasmussen, K. Duncan, & J. Leplat (eds.), New technology and human error. United Kingdom: John Wiley and Sons Ltd.

#7)   Billings, C.E. (1991). Human-Centred Aircraft automation. NASA Tech. memo No. 103885. Moffett Field, CA: NASA-Ames Research Center

#8)   Sarter, N. B., & Woods, D.D. (1993). "How did I ever get into that mode?" Mode Error and awareness in supervisory control. CSEL Technical report. Submitted for publication

#9)   Sarter, N. B., & Woods, D.D. (1992). Pilot interaction with cockpit automation: Operational experiences with the Flight Management system. The international Journal of Aviation Psychology, 2 (4), 303-321. Lawrence Erlbaum Associates, Inc.

#10)   Norman, D. A. (1990). The "problem" with automation: Inappropriate feedback and interaction, not "over-automation." Philosophical Transaction of the Royal Society of London, B327.and Sarter, N. B., & Woods, D.D. (1992). Pilot interaction with cockpit automation: Operational experiences with the Flight Management system. The international Journal of Aviation Psychology, 2 (4), 303-321. Lawrence Erlbaum Associates, Inc.

#11)   Onken, R. (1992a) New developments in aerospace Guidance and Control: Knowledge-based pilot assistance. IFAC Symposium on automatic control in aerospace. 8-11 Sept. 1992, München

#12)   Amalberti, R. (1992). Safety in process-control: An operator-centred point of view. Reliability Engineering and System Safety, 38 (313), 99-108

#13)   Report on the serious incident to Boeing 757-200 at Oslo airport Gardermoen Norway 22. Januar 2002. Aircraft Accident Investigation Board Norway.

#14)   Wiener, E. (1989). Human factors of advanced technology. ("glass cockpit") transport aircraft (NASA Contract Rep. No. 177528). Moffett Field, CA: NASA-Ames Research Centre

#15)   Leplat, Jacques (1987) Occupational Accident Research and System Approaches, in Jens Rasmussen, Keith Duncan, and Jacques Leplat (eds.) New Technology and Human Error, John Wiley & Sons, New York, pp. 181-191

#16)   Nancy G. Leveson, Ph.D.; Applying STAMP in Accident Analysis. Research partially supported by NASA grant NAG2-1843 and NSF ITR grant CCR-0085829. And A new accident model for engineering safer systems. Safety Science, vol. 42 No. 4. April 2004. pp 237-270

#17)   Checkland, Peter (1981) Systems Thinking, System Practice, John Wiley & Sons, New York

RISK AND ITS TOLERABILITY

Identification of Time At Risk Periods of Significance to ALARP Justifications

Mark George

Devonport Management Limited (DML),

Plymouth, PL1 4SG, UK

Abstract

Behind the simplicity of the ALARP Principle – which requires that all reasonably practicable risk reduction measures should be taken – lies a great deal of complexity. One of the difficult areas is Time At Risk, when risks are above the mean value for a period of time. In this paper, three methods are developed as an aid to the process of agreeing what constitutes a significant period of increased risk that may possibly be worthy of separate ALARP consideration.

Disclaimer: The work discussed in this paper has been developed from an MSc dissertation by the author (George 2003) and is a personal view.

1. Introduction

UK Health and Safety legislation can be considered as consisting of two types: Prescriptive, where precise and specific requirements are laid down, and Goal-setting, which requires judgements to be made on how well safety goals have been met. The trend in recent years has been towards reducing prescription in favour of a goal-setting approach. The main embodiment of this is the 1974 Health and Safety At Work Act which requires protection of health, safety and welfare of employees and the public *"so far as is reasonably practicable"*. This philosophy is perhaps better known through the ALARP Principle: the requirement for risks to be As Low As Reasonably Practicable.

The subjectivity associated with the Goal-setting approach has created many areas of debate. It is on one of these – periods of elevated risks (or "Time At Risk" (TAR) periods) - that this paper is focused; specifically, it proposes ways to identify whether or not a particular TAR period is significant enough to warrant a separate ALARP justification. It is anticipated that this will be of most benefit when handling large numbers of risk profiles and/or large quantities of data.

The proposals presented in this paper have developed from consideration of nuclear-related risk, where there is the potential for accidents to lead to large and widespread consequences. The methods are sufficiently general that they might, with suitable adjustment, form the basis of applications in other sectors where the consequences may be of lesser magnitude and/or more localised.

1.1 The ALARP Principle

The ALARP Principle is an essential part of an overall decision-making process in which potential risk-reducing measures are identified, assessed and the most Reasonably Practicable solution chosen. The benchmark definition of Reasonable Practicability was set by Lord Justice Asquith in 1949 when he described it as a comparison between risk and the *"sacrifice involved in ... averting the risk (whether in time, money or trouble)"*. In order to claim that risks are ALARP, the sacrifice must be shown to be very much greater than (in Gross Disproportion to) the amount of risk averted. The Gross Disproportion varies with risk: the higher the risk, the more effort is expected to be spent on each quantum of risk reduction.

The ALARP Principle is often illustrated through the ALARP "Carrot" shown in Figure 1. The varying width is depicts this increased effort at higher risks.

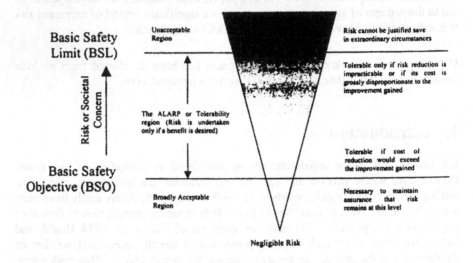

Figure 1: ALARP Carrot

1.2 Regulatory Guidance on ALARP

The ALARP Principle is simple in concept but can be very difficult to apply. The most recent general guidance from the Health and Safety Executive (HSE) is contained in the document commonly known as R2P2 (HSE 2001) and is expanded in the "ALARP Suite" of three other documents (HSE 2001A, B & C). A number of divisions within the HSE have followed by providing more specific guidance for their own areas – for example, the Nuclear Installations Inspectorate (NII) published their Technical Assessment Guide (TAG) in 2002 (NII 2002). Outside the HSE, other regulatory bodies have also produced ALARP guidance, and these include the Ministry of Defence (MoD) nuclear plant regulator, the Naval Nuclear Regulatory Panel, in JSP518 (MoD 2003).

The various guidance documents recognise that there are a number of outstanding issues with ALARP. In some cases, it is likely to be a considerable time before a solution is found, however an improved common understanding should be achievable in the shorter term. The latter group includes TAR periods and these are discussed below.

2. Time At Risk

Risk assessments and ALARP justifications are usually considered in terms of time-averaged values, generally producing annualised risk figures for comparison against annualised criteria. This both provides a natural timeframe on which to examine other parameters (e.g. cost), and allows smoothing to recognise that risks will generally fluctuate – perhaps with the different phases of a process, with maintenance routines or worker shift patterns. A disadvantage of time-averaging is that it can mask periods of elevated risk when more detailed investigation would be beneficial. These TAR periods will often be associated with a particular activity or set of circumstances that exists only for a relatively short period.

2.1   The Need to Consider Time At Risk Periods

In the nuclear industry, both the TAG and JSP518 make particular mention of the potential need for a separate ALARP consideration of significant TAR periods. There are two issues to address for such periods:

- how they are identified
- how they are then treated.

The first of these issues is considered in this paper. The question of how to treat these periods is outside the scope of this current paper, although brief comments are made in Section 5.

TAR Periods have been separated into two types for the purposes of this paper. The first is "Sustained Elevated Risks" and relates to periods when the risk remains above its mean value for a substantial amount of time. Even though the risk level at any one time may not be sufficient to cause concern, the fact that this is a long-term condition may be important. The second type - "Highly Elevated Risks" - relates to periods when the risk is much higher than the mean. In this case, the key parameter is the magnitude of the risk, irrespective of its duration.

2.2   Specific Aim of this Paper

The TAG and JSP518 guidance documents do not specifically define the conditions under which a TAR period should be given more detailed consideration. The aim of this paper is to propose ways to more easily identify and agree what constitutes a "significant" period of above-average risk. This is not an attempt to replace the subjectivity that is inherent in the Goal-setting approach: instead this initial filtering of TAR periods would allow subsequent assessment effort to be more efficiently directed. The benefit might be relatively small for an individual risk profile, but would be greater for larger amounts of data – e.g. groups of profiles, or very long or detailed profiles.

3. "Significant" TAR Periods - Identification Methods

3.1   Assumptions

Three main assumptions have been made in developing the identification methods described below and in presenting their results. The appropriateness and validity of these assumptions are discussed in detail in Section 5.

Assumption 1

The TAR periods that might require a more detailed or separate ALARP justification are only those deemed "significant". This means that other periods of increased risks can be screened out. (The criteria for identifying such periods are discussed within this paper.)

Assumption 2

The annualised BSL may be subdivided on a pro-rata basis for the purposes of presenting a "Daily BSL". In the graphs presented in Section 4, the Daily BSL is shown as $1/365^{th}$ of 10^{-4} (i.e. 2.7×10^{-7}).[1]

Assumption 3

The calculated instantaneous risk (the Point in Time risk) is permitted to exceed the annualised BSL.

3.2   Identification Methods for Sustained Elevated Risks

Two methods are developed below for identifying "significant" instances of this type of risk period, where risks are above-average for a sustained period.

3.2.1   Simple Percentage Method (SPM)

The Simple Percentage Method (SPM) proposes that any risk period should be considered for more detailed examination if the risk remains more than a certain amount (say 10%) above the annualised mean value for a certain proportion (say 10% or more) of the total duration of the risk profile. Other combinations of risk level and duration are also considered, and give rise to the criteria in Table 1.

---

[1] 10^{-4} is the annualised BSL stated in R2P2 for the death of a member of the public as the result of the normal operation of a plant or process.

Degree of Elevated Risk (% above mean value)	Duration of Elevated Risk (% of overall risk period)
Sustained ≥10	10
Sustained ≥20	5
Sustained ≥25	4
Sustained ≥33	3
Sustained ≥40	2.5
Sustained ≥50	2
Sustained ≥60	1.5
Sustained ≥75	1
Sustained ≥100	0.5

Table 1: SPM Criteria for Identifying Periods Requiring Examination

The product of the elevation and the duration is 100 for most of the rows, particularly the ones relating to smaller risk increases. As the level of elevated risk rises, it becomes more important to trigger early identification of the period for a more detailed analysis: the product has therefore been reduced for larger risks.

The method naturally assumes that risks are known or estimated to a level of accuracy that is compatible with the above elevated risk bands. This is discussed further in Section 5.

3.2.2   Integrated Elevated Risk Method

The SPM is limited in two main respects: firstly, in merely requiring that the risk is above a certain threshold value for a sustained period, the method does not distinguish between those periods that barely pass the criterion and those where the risks are substantially higher than the threshold. Secondly, risk periods might fail to be identified if the risk falls below the threshold for a single day. These suggest that account ought to be taken of the magnitude of the risk. The Integrated Elevated Risk (IER) Method does this by calculating the area above the annualised mean value of the risk.

The following descriptions of the IER Method assume that the risk profile is defined in terms of one value per day for an entire year. The method could easily be adapted for a different frequency of data or profile duration.

Consider a time-varying risk profile r(t). The total risk over the year – i.e. the summation of r(t) – is divided into 365 equal parts to give an averaged daily risk of A. In the time interval between days d1 and d2, the IER is:

$$IER = \sum_{t=d1}^{d2}(r(t) - A) \qquad \ldots\ldots\ldots\ldots\ldots\ldots\ldots\ldots(1)$$

The value calculated for IER could be used in a number of ways. The most useful of these is likely to be comparing it with the risk that would have resulted if the annualised mean value had instead been experienced over that period. In other words, the ratio

$$F_1 = IER/\{A \times (d2-d1)\} \dots\dots\dots(2)$$

could be calculated. If F_1 is high (and "high" would need to be defined), it would suggest that the period might warrant additional examination. This approach could, however, identify TAR periods that are not significant in comparison to the annual risk – i.e. the following ratio is small:

$$F_2 = IER/\{365 \times A\} \dots\dots\dots(3)$$

The following criteria for F_1 and F_2 have been used for the test profiles:

- Periods should be identified for further consideration if the IER over that period is ≥50% higher than the integrated mean over that period – i.e. if $F_1 \geq 0.5$.
- Periods should be identified for further consideration if the IER over the period is ≥10% of the overall annual risk – i.e. if $F_2 \geq 0.1$.

It is suggested that a period should be considered in more detail if either of these criteria are met. Further, the amount of effort appropriate for any in-depth ALARP review could be gauged by using both criteria: e.g. if $F_1 \geq 0.5$, the amount of effort could be scaled in accordance with the value calculated for F_2.

These criteria have been chosen according to what the author considers to be a reasonable starting point for further discussion, at least for the test risk profiles. The choice of F_1 and F_2 is discussed further in Section 5.

3.3   Identification Method for Significantly Elevated Risks

This type of period relates to risks that are significantly above the annualised mean. The identification method proposed for these periods adds a Trigger Factor (TF) to the annualised mean risk in order to define a trigger level such that risks at or above this level are then identified as being "significantly" above the mean value. A key factor in choosing how to define TF is that it should be reasonably easy to apply: it has therefore been set in terms of a multiple of the Root Mean Square Difference (RMSD) of the whole risk profile. This can be easily calculated for any frequency of data or duration, and is a property that is specific to the profile rather than being an arbitrary generic value.

Assuming daily data points and a year-long risk profile, the TF is therefore:

$$TF = S_p \times \left(\frac{\sum_{t=1}^{365} (r(t) - A)^2}{365} \right)^{1/2} \dots\dots\dots(4)$$

where S_P is a Scaling Parameter to be determined.

The value of S_P should be set such that the risk periods identified by this method are recognisably different from the minor fluctuations that will be present in a risk profile (hence values of $S_P<1.0$ may be too low for many profiles). On the other hand, the value must not be set too high (say, $S_P>3$) that it identifies only the extreme peaks (since these could be easily identified by simple visual inspection). A value of $S_P = 1.5$ has been used for the test assessments. The choice of S_P is discussed further in Section 5.

4. Application of the Methods – Illustrative Results

4.1 Risk Profiles

A total of 9 artificial Risk Profiles have been generated specifically to test the proposed methods. The main reasons for using artificial profiles are that genuine profiles were not available in sufficient quantity, and some of those that were available have commercial or political sensitivity. The use of artificial data is not crucial in the context of this study as the purpose is merely to illustrate the principles of the identification methods.

The intention has been to represent a plant/process where there is an inherent feature that provides a continual level of background risk. Examples include a shut down nuclear reactor, and the storage of hazardous chemicals at a chemical plant during maintenance outages when the plant itself is not operational. Risks associated with regular activities such as maintenance routines have then been added. These are assumed to occur weekly, monthly, 3-monthly, 6-monthly and annually. Different durations and associated risk levels have been set for each type of activity. Finally, a time-dependent component has been added – comprising sine and cosine terms – to represent a general variability of risk. This component is different in each of the 9 profiles.

The total risk for each day is then calculated by summing the contributions from the inherent, regular and cyclic risks. After experimentation with parameters, a final set of profiles was chosen on the basis that they all:

- Have an annualised mean risk that is lower than the BSL (in order to ensure the risk is not intolerable)
- Produce "interesting" but discernible profiles rather than relatively flat or wildly fluctuating ones. (The subjectivity involved in this choice is not important since this exercise is merely a demonstration of the methods.)

4.2 Application of the Methods

The results from Cases 2, 4 and 7 are presented below. For reasons of space, the other cases are not presented explicitly in this paper, but the overall performance of the methods is summarised in Section 5.3.

Each graph shows the risk profile and the levels corresponding to: the annualised mean risk, the "Daily BSL" (see Section 3.1), and the TF trigger level. The horizontal bars towards the top of each graph indicate the results from applying the three identification methods: each period spanned by a horizontal bar has been identified as being potentially worthy of further consideration.

The SPM and TF methods have both been fully implemented. The IER Method comprises two parts, one being a comparison against the annualised mean risk, and the other comparing the integrated risks against the overall annual level of risk. Only the first of these has been examined in this present study.

The details of how the IER Method was applied are worth noting. The method is based around risks integrated over periods of time, hence these periods must first be selected. As a first pass, the method was applied in a systematic manner by examining each day in turn and summing the risk associated with that day, the three preceding days and the three following days: the day being examined thus becomes the central day of a week. The summed figure was then compared with a week's worth of annualised risk. The central day was identified as worthy of further consideration if the F_1 criterion was met.

4.2.1 Results from Case 2

The results from Case 2 are shown in Figure 2.

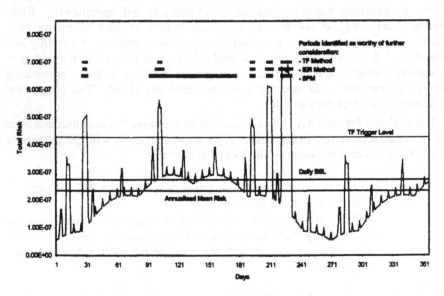

Figure 2 – Analysed Risk Profile for Case 2

<u>Simple Percentage Method</u>

The period between days ~90 and ~180 was identified almost entirely on the basis of the first criterion in Table 1 – i.e. a long period where the risk was always above the annualised mean value, albeit only slightly at times. Without this criterion, two smaller periods of ~25 days would have been identified instead, mainly based on the next criterion (20% above the mean for 5% of the time). It is plausible that this risk profile could be reasonably realistic, with a substantial cycle (perhaps associated with a lengthy batch process) and a long period for which the risks remain above the mean value. The entire process would require an ALARP justification, hence identification of this 90-day particular period for separate assessment would not appear to be necessary.

Apart from the long period, the identified periods appear to be in fairly consistent with what would be expected to be identified by visual inspection.

Integrated Elevated Risk Method

Instead of identifying the whole of the period from ~90 to ~180 days, this method identified one short period centred on the peak at around 100 days. Otherwise, the results were broadly similar to the SPM results.

Elevated Risks: Trigger Factor Method

The periods when the Trigger Level is exceeded are generally very similar to those identified by the IER Method, although the durations of the identified periods sometimes differ by a day or two.

4.2.2 Results from Case 4

The results from Case 4 are shown below in Figure 3.

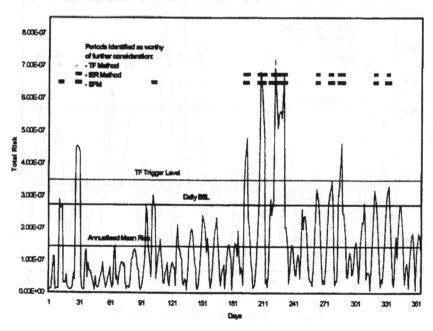

Figure 3 - Analysed Risk Profile for Case 4

Simple Percentage Method

The results from the SPM approach appear to be broadly consistent with those that would be identified from visual inspection, although the periods sometimes extend for longer than might have been expected.

Integrated Elevated Risk Method

Again, the results appear reasonable. The results illustrate the sensitivity to the choice of method since the peak at around day 260 is identified by both the SPM and IER approaches, but the IER method does not identify the slightly lower peak at around day 100. This type of difference will often be seen when numerical criteria are used: one peak does just meet the IER criterion, while the other is just below the identification value.

Elevated Risks: Trigger Factor Method

Insofar as the TF method identifies fewer periods that the other two methods, its results are in line with expectation for a first pass, however it fails to identify some potentially important peaks – e.g. that at around day 275.

4.2.3   Results from Case 7

The results from Case 7 are shown below in Figure 4.

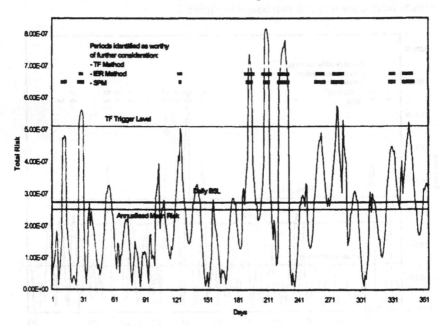

Figure 4 - Analysed Risk Profile for Case 7

Simple Percentage Method

In this case, there were no periods which satisfied the first three criteria in Table 1 (i.e. the long-term, slightly or moderately increased risk periods). All of the other SPM criteria were met at some time during the year. The method has successfully highlighted the main periods that would be identified by visual inspection.

Integrated Elevated Risk Method

The method has generally identified similar periods to the SPM method, although the IER Method does not identify the first peak (around day 15) and perhaps extends too far the flagged period for the first two major peaks around mid-year.

Elevated Risks: Trigger Factor Method

The use of the Trigger Factor identifies fewer periods for further consideration than the other two methods. In particular, potentially important peaks at around days 15, 120, 260 and 330 were not identified.

5. Discussion

5.1 Usefulness of Purpose of the Methods

The inherent subjectivity associated with the ALARP Principle can be labour intensive. An experienced analyst or assessor will generally be able to determine fairly quickly which elevated risk periods are significant enough to require further investigation, nevertheless this still requires effort and carries with it the potential for prolonged debate. While this might not be too onerous a task for a fairly simple risk profile, it will not necessarily be so for a complex profile or when a large number of profiles have to be processed. (A particular example of the latter might be where multiple investigations are carried out of the effect of parameter/scheduling changes on risk profiles.)

This paper suggests that it would be useful to have guidelines to aid (and perhaps automate) a "first cut" decision. This would allow resources to be focused on the less clear-cut situations.

This is not an attempt to undermine the analyst or the assessor, but should improve efficiency and focus. There will be a number of "grey" areas for debate as to whether or not they warrant consideration, however these are likely to be much less than the unfiltered total.

It is important that any method for determining these periods should be validated: the method should, at the least, identify those periods that would be highlighted during visual inspection. In examining sustained risks, it is likely that the SPM and IER methods might also identify additional periods that might not be so clear-cut from visual inspection. In order to facilitate validation, tuning factors have been incorporated into the methods and adjusted accordingly for the test cases. These factors are discussed later.

5.2 Appropriateness of Assumptions

The main assumptions within the identification methods are discussed below.

5.2.1 The Need to Identify Only "Significant" Time At Risk Periods

Both JSP518 and the TAG recognise the variability of risks, JSP518 noting that:

> "In practice, the risks from any activities are very rarely constant or regular. They are far more likely to be highly variable over the course of a year, with occasional peaks of risk superimposed on an uneven continuum of lower level risk."

It then goes on to stipulate that:

> "The periods where the risks are high should be assessed and the risks shown to be tolerable and ALARP."

Neither "high" nor "tolerable" are explicitly defined in this context.

The TAG states, in Annex 2, that: "Any period in which the risk exceeds the normal level of risk" must have a specific ALARP demonstration, with the degree of robustness of the argument depending on "both the normal risk and extent of the temporary increase in risk". This could be interpreted as an unnecessarily strict requirement, given that there may be very many periods of above-average risk. The author considers that, in practice, little if any separate argument will be required for most periods, and that the main focus will be driven by the guidance in the main part of the TAG (Paragraph 7.3):

> "... brief periods of substantially higher risk than average should be separately reviewed against ALARP requirements".

The identification of what is meant by "high" or "substantially higher than average" levels of risk is the key to this, hence has been the focus of this paper.

5.2.2 Use of a "Daily" BSL

The TAG does not explicitly discuss short-term BSLs, although it does recognise the "need to interpret the concepts and criteria for shorter periods". The use of pro-rata limits is discussed in Appendix K to Annex A of JSP 518 where they are considered to be somewhat inadequate. The document states that:

> "The BSOs and BSLs do not reflect this variability [in risk]. For safety criteria, risk limits and objectives should not be divided to derive acceptance criteria for shorter periods, as such subdivision can produce distortions in the safety case which are not warranted."

This implies that the use of a pro-rata BSL would be expected to produce results that are conservative, possibly overly so. This will only be the case if the pro-rata BSL is actually used for a purpose such as defining Point in Time tolerability. This is discussed further below. Nevertheless, the pro-rata BSL has been a useful reference level when presenting the results in Section 4.

It should be noted that the use of a Daily criterion is somewhat arbitrary and that other apportioned BSLs – weekly, monthly, even hourly – might have been chosen instead. Certainly, the shorter the period, the more likelihood of falling foul of the JSP518 warning of unwarranted distortions in the safety case.

5.2.3   Exceeding the "Daily" BSL

Several sections within the TAG and JSP518 suggest that operation of a facility and/or process with an associated risk that is intolerable – even if only for a very short period – would either not be permitted or would require there to be exceptional circumstances. The difficulty is that the boundary between Tolerable and Intolerable is not well defined in the context of short-duration risks. As discussed above, and it would appear inappropriate to simply use a pro-rata BSL to determine this boundary.

Much the same conclusion is also reached by considering relatively high risk plant and processes – for example, those for which the annualised risk is close to the BSL. Such risks are, by definition, tolerable and, provided a case can be made, can be shown to be ALARP overall. Since risks fluctuate, this annualised figure (which may be as high as 99% of the BSL) will almost certainly contain periods when the Point in Time risk would exceed the annualised BSL. It therefore appears that explicit acceptance of the plant/process carries an implicit recognition and acceptance that the Point in Time risk may exceed the BSL. This is equivalent to saying that, on a particular day, the risk is permitted to exceed the Daily BSL.

It is therefore not clear what numerical criterion should be used to gauge tolerability for short-term risks, and the derivation of potential candidates is outside the scope of this current paper. The key point for this paper is to note that the "Daily BSL", if calculated on a purely pro-rata basis, may be useful as an indicator of risk when considering Time At Risk periods, but should not be seen as a limit on the allowable daily risk.

5.3   Performance of the Identification Methods

The three methods have been used to assess all of the 9 risk profiles, although only 3 profiles are shown in this paper for reasons of brevity. The performance of the methods is obviously linked to the artificial risk profiles, however they nevertheless form a reasonable starting point for developing approaches that will be applicable for real-life profiles. Overall, the methods have generally been successful in identifying the important areas of the profiles.

5.3.1   SPM Approach

Use of the SPM approach is a straightforward way of identifying most of the main periods of interest in relation to sustained periods of elevated risks,. The results have generally been good. The method did however identify periods in Cases 1, 4 and 6 (not shown in this paper) which would perhaps not be chosen by an assessor. The need to review the inclusion of long-term, moderately increased risks within the SPM is particularly highlighted by the results from Case 2 (see Section 4.2.1) where a long period was identified as warranting further consideration, probably incorrectly. The SPM has further slight weaknesses in that it does not take account of the magnitude of the risks, and may fail to identify periods which include a short time at lower risk.

5.3.2   IER Method

The IER Method does allow account to be taken of the risk magnitude for sustained elevated risks. It was successful in identifying most of the periods that would be identified from visual inspection but also identified a number of additional periods, some of which need not have been identified. Many of the periods were extended too far: this is a function of the time segments used in the method (where each day is linked to the three preceding and three following days). It is suggested that the sensitivity of the results to the choice of time segment should be examined if this approach is developed further. The choice of week-long segments was arbitrary: as will be seen, the results are potentially sensitive to the segment length and this should be examined if the method is to be used further. It is possible that improved results might be generated by undertaking a number of passes with various segment lengths and combining or contrasting the results.

5.3.3   TF Method

The TF Method identifies only the larger peaks hence can sometimes neglect lesser, but still potentially important ones (as seen in Profile No. 7). On the whole, the method performed satisfactorily, however further investigations are required in order to identify appropriate values for S_P for realistic risk profiles. This is discussed further in Section 5.4.

5.4   General Application of the Methods

The identification methods described in this paper are deliberately fairly simple. This is because they are guidelines aiming to aid and support the judgement of the risk assessor. Complex methods, as well as being harder to understand and apply, might generate a temptation to place more value on the results than is warranted. Furthermore, the risk profiles may have substantial uncertainties associated with them: the identification methods must therefore convey an appropriate degree of accuracy, and detailed methods might imply an undue and unwarranted precision. In any case, as the TAG implies, good safety and ALARP practice should not be "... an exercise in playing with numbers".

It is suggested that all three methods should be used together to identify periods potentially worth more detailed assessment. It must be emphasised that:

- the identified periods are not necessarily the complete set of significant periods nor will every identified period necessarily require detailed examination. The analyst/assessor will be able to use the methods to speed up the identification process but must not rely on the results exclusively. (The level of result checking might reduce as the validity of the methods becomes more proven.)

- the methods do not absolve the owner of the risk from the responsibility of ensuring that an overall ALARP argument is made.

It is expected that any formal use of these methods would require debate about the type and depth of further consideration to which the identified periods are subjected. This would vary according to the details of the TAR Period. As discussed, the IER Method may provide a guide for sustained risks in that the level of scrutiny could be guided by the importance in terms of the annual risk (i.e. F_2).

5.4.1 The Use of Adjustment Factors

The three identification methods have a general applicability, although each may require a degree of tailoring depending on the risk profile to which they are applied. For a profile with a very low mean risk, it might prove justifiable and more illuminating to use a fairly high value for S_P in the TF Method; for a profile where the mean risks are close to the BSL, much tighter control would be expected and a lower value preferred for S_P. This is exemplified by Case 7 (see Section 4.2.3). In addition, the values might be affected by context: the more sensitive the issue (or the higher the consequences), the tighter the expected control hence a more stringent identification criterion might be used. This is particularly true for applications such as the nuclear industry where the potential consequences of accidents are very high and the industry itself has a high public profile.

The TF Method might also benefit from using a range of values for S_P rather than a distinct level which means that slightly lower – but perhaps still important – peaks are missed. This could be linked to assessment guidelines: for example, a clear S_P value could be set for the risk level at which further analysis of the period was required under Company procedures; a lower threshold might also be set where further analysis might be recommended, but was not mandatory.

In a similar way, the values chosen for the F_1 and F_2 parameters used in the IER Method appear generally appropriate for the test profiles but may need to be adjusted for other profiles or sensitivity of application.

An adjustment parameter (F_0) could also be added to the SPM approach and would allow the level of elevated risk within a particular band to be scaled: for example, the first band would become $\geq(F_0 \times 10\%)$ of the mean risk. As above, this would allow larger values of F_0 to be used for low risks, if appropriate and justifiable. This could also allow account to be taken of uncertainties in the risk profile, since risk bands of 10% may be too refined hence values of $F_0 >> 1$ may be more appropriate.

5.4.2 Derivation of Adjustment Factors

While it would be desirable to have provided more definitive values for the various factors (F_0, F_1, F_2 and S_P), that is not possible at this time for three main reasons.

Firstly, the analyses within this paper are based on a small set of artificial profiles: the factors should instead be set and/or validated on realistic data. Secondly, the factors may vary between applications and between organisations, depending on a number of issues such as sensitivity and overall level of risk. Thirdly, the setting of any firm criteria may require negotiation with the appropriate authorities (primarily the regulatory bodies).

5.5 TAR Periods – Wider Issues

The methods discussed above will allow the identification of "significant" TAR periods for further consideration. They do not, however, answer the more difficult question of what form and extent this should take. This is outside the scope of the current paper, although a comment is offered below.

ALARP is based around the principle of the sacrifice needing to be grossly disproportionate to the benefit before further risk reduction can be claimed to be impracticable. The TAG suggests that the gross disproportion factors should be 10 or more *"in the vicinity of the intolerable region"*, but potentially larger still for hazards that could have large associated consequences. This could have important implications in terms of making ALARP justifications for Significantly Elevated TAR periods since, as discussed in Section 5.2, "tolerable" is not well defined in this context and the Daily BSL could be exceeded.

This reinforces the need for such a definition or, alternatively, an acceptance that estimates of sacrifice (including from methods such as Cost Benefit Analysis) are only to be used on annualised figures. As described earlier, the IER Method may provide a way of gauging the amount of reasonable effort that should be invested for significant sustained risks.

6. Conclusions

There is a need to identify TAR periods where the risk is "significant" in comparison to the mean, since regulatory guidance – at least in the nuclear industry - indicates that further ALARP consideration of that period might be required. In most cases, this will be clear, however this paper suggests that it might be useful to develop an agreed framework by which these periods can be identified. The aim is not to replace subjective judgement, but to provide an initial agreed filter that will allow resources to be more efficiently focused on periods of potential importance. This may become particularly useful when dealing with large numbers of and/or complex risk profiles.

Three identification methods have been developed as an initial investigation into this subject. Tested against artificial risk profiles, the results appear promising. Further work is required to derive the appropriate scaling factors necessary to adapt the methods for realistic risk profiles. Between them, the methods are capable of addressing both sustained elevated risks and shorter-term high risks. The methods are intentionally fairly simple so that they might be easily and widely applied, and because they are only intended as an aid to analysts and assessors.

The work has emphasised the fact that criteria – particularly definitions such as "tolerable" – usually relate to annualised risks and do not exist for shorter periods. The assumption has been made that pro-rata apportioned BSLs are not valid as definitions of short-term tolerability, and an argument for this has been presented.

This paper does not directly address the more difficult issue of the treatment of these identified "significant" periods. This is expected to vary considerably according to factors such as the sensitivity of the situation and the magnitude of the potential consequences. For some situations, the identification methods might provide a starting point for gauging the amount of effort that should be expended on ALARP measures.

References

George MA (2003). Issues Associated with the Application of the ALARP Principle in the Nuclear Industry. MSc Dissertation. Lancaster University. 2003.

HSE (2001). Reducing Risks, Protecting People. HSE. 2001.

HSE (2001A). Principles and guidelines to assist HSE in its judgements that duty-holders have reduced risk as low as reasonably practicable. Published on the HSE website 13 December 2001. www.hse.gov.uk/dst/alarp1.htm

HSE (2001B). Assessing compliance with the law in individual cases and the use of good practice. Published on the HSE website 13 December 2001. (Updated May 2003). www.hse.gov.uk/dst/alarp2.htm

HSE (2001C). Policy and Guidance on reducing risks as low as reasonably practicable in design. Published on the HSE website 13 December 2001. www.hse.gov.uk/dst/alarp3.htm

MoD (2003). Regulation of the Naval Nuclear Propulsion Programme. MoD Joint Services Publication. JSP 518, Issue 1.2. 2003.

NII (2002). Technical Assessment Guide – Demonstration of ALARP. HSE Nuclear Safety Directorate. T/AST/005, Issue 001. 2002.

Developing and Using Risk Matrices

Michael Prince

Atkins Consultants Ltd

Introduction

Risk Matrices have long been adopted in parts of the systems safety community as a simple means of categorisation of risk, yet they are often developed and used incorrectly leading to confusion and poor safety management.

This paper seeks to cut through to the essential elements and help the reader avoid the common pitfalls. It focuses on system safety risks to people, but could be similarly applied to environmental safety assessment too.

Throughout this paper the term "Equipment" will be used to mean some item of plant, platform, process, system or indeed equipment within the boundary of study.

The experiences recounted in this paper relate primarily to the application of risk matrices in the Defence industry but have, I believe, a wider relevance.

The treatment of topics surrounding risk matrices in the paper are not intended to be comprehensive; simply sufficient to keep the central subject matter of risk matrix development in context.

Risk Matrices - Overview

Risk, as a combined measure of severity and likelihood, is an established concept, which I am taking the readers fore-knowledge of for-granted. The concept of a risk matrix can therefore be immediately introduced:

Severity

		High	Low
Likelihood	High	1	2
	Low	2	3

Table 1: Sample Risk Matrix

Each cell in the 2x2 matrix of Table 1 represents a level of risk. For simplicity we might say that:

- The (High, High) cell represents High Risk, marked "1" in Table 1;
- The (Low, High) and the (High, Low) cells represent Medium Risk, marked "2" in Table 1;
- The (Low, Low) cell represents Low Risk, marked "3" in Table 1.

A series of risks identified can each be placed by some means (judgement, estimation, formal assessment) in one of Table 1's cells, but not before some definition of what "High" and "Low" Severity and Likelihood mean.

For example, in an assessment of business (rather than safety) risks we might say that High Severity means "a cost to the business above £10,000". We might say that High Likelihood means "expected to happen in the next 12 months". Because the above matrix is only a 2x2 matrix the definitions of "Low" are obvious; in this instance everything that isn't "High".

To establish some formality however we draw up tables of likelihood and severity definition:

Likelihood Category	Likelihood Definition
High	Expected to happen in the next 12 months
Low	Not expected to happen in the next 12 months

Table 2: Sample Likelihood Category Definitions

Severity Category	Severity Definition
High	A cost to the business greater or equal to £10,000
Low	A cost to the business less than £10,000

Table 3: Sample Severity Category Definitions

Any business risk can now have its likelihood and severity assessed against these criteria, be placed in the matrix, and by so-doing be categorised for action. We might even formalise what level of action is merited in each case, as in Table 4.

Risk Category	Priority of Action	Level of action
1	Tackle first	Senior management sanction
2	Tackle next	Local management sanction
3	Tackle last (if at all)	No sanction required

Table 4: Sample Risk Category Definitions

Tables 1 to 4 form a simple example of the construction and use of a risk matrix, used to introduce this paper with familiar concepts, but which nonetheless demonstrate an important point:

A risk matrix is of some help with the management of risk even when the overall acceptability of any particular level of risk has not been defined.

However, to use risk matrices without considering levels of acceptability / tolerability is not recommended since to do so is to risk disproportionate and inappropriate action. Get it wrong in the example and "Senior Management" may either end up wasting their time on trivial matters or at the other extreme, not be consulted for action on serious matters when they should have been.

We might therefore revise Table 4 to incorporate a view on acceptability. For instance if we feel that a £10,000 impact to the business is unacceptable under any circumstances then we extend Table 4 to record that:

Risk Category	Priority of Action	Level of action	Acceptability
1	Tackle first	Senior management sanction	*Unacceptable. Risk must be eliminated.*
2	Tackle next	Local management sanction	
3	Tackle last (if at all)	No sanction required	

Table 5: Sample Risk Category Definitions - Extended

and in a similar vein we complete Table 5 as shown in Table 6:

Risk Category	Priority of Action	Level of action	Acceptability
1	Tackle first	Senior management sanction	Unacceptable. Risk must be eliminated.
2	Tackle next	Local management sanction	*Make reasonable effort to reduce risk*
3	Tackle last (if at all)	No sanction required	*No action required. Will accept risk.*

Table 6: Sample Risk Category Definitions – Extended and Completed

The importance of calibrating the matrix to reflect the known levels of risk acceptance becomes clearer if we now turn our attention to the main focus of this paper: Safety risks.

In the field of safety (of people and of the environment) there are some levels of risk which society may not be prepared to accept, whatever the circumstances. How do we recognise those on our matrix? It becomes clear that to use the matrix in a context where there is an overall view on the acceptability of risk, we must align the matrix with that threshold level in some way.

Levels of Risk Acceptability - Risk Assessment Criteria, Limits and Targets.

Generally equipment is developed and put into service with the expectation that it will yield some benefit, either directly to the user community or to society at large. These stakeholders have an expectation that the safety risks to people and the environment presented by the employment of that equipment are low overall in proportion to the benefits to be gained and in all cases those risks are well managed and reduced to the lowest practical level.

As soon as the capability requirement is acknowledged and as soon as a concept for the equipment is identified, it is possible and necessary to determine risk limits and targets, against which the development and acceptance of the equipment can be performed and judged. These limits and targets are what the risk matrix needs to be calibrated against.

In practice it is useful to set an upper level, above which the risks associated with the equipment are deemed unacceptable and a lower level, below which the equipment's safety performance is deemed broadly acceptable. Such an approach is well described in UK Health and Safety Executive literature (HSE, 2001).

For the purposes of this paper, the upper level will be termed a Risk Limit and the lower level a Risk Target. Other terms abound, for example 'Basic Safety

Limit' and 'Basic Safety Objective' respectively are the common terms used in the UK Nuclear Industry.

We can therefore redraw Table 6 and superimpose our Risk Limit and Risk Target as follows:

Risk Category	Priority of Action	Acceptability	Risk Limit (RL) and Risk Target (RT) Boundaries
1	Tackle first	Unacceptable. Risk must be eliminated.	
			RL
2	Tackle next	Make reasonable effort to reduce risk	
			RT
3	Tackle last (if at all)	No action required. Will accept risk.	

Table 7: Safety Risk Categories

In other words we have extended our definitions in Table 6 to give more meaning to terms such as "Category 1 risk" and "Category 3 risk": In Table 7, Category 1 risks lie above the Risk Limit and are unacceptable and Category 3 risks lie below the Risk Target and are broadly acceptable.

Remember that our labels are self-selected. We could have more categories if we like (by sub-dividing the existing ones) and apply different labels if we like; we could just as easily talk about "Category A risks" through to Category "D" risks for example (MoD, 1996), as long as we say what they each mean in relation to the Risk Limit and Risk Target.

"Calibration"

To introduce the mechanics of calibrating a safety risk matrix for an equipment, to the Risk Limit and Target for that equipment, we will perform the act in stages:

Firstly we select a Risk Limit and a Risk Target. There is some brief guidance on this later in the paper, although for detailed discussion the reader is referred elsewhere (HSE, 2001). For our example we choose:

RL = Individual risk of fatality of 1 in 1000 per year from interaction with the equipment

RT = Individual risk of fatality of 1 in 100,000 per year from interaction with the equipment

We draw up our likelihood category definitions (Table 8) to span RL and RT.

Likelihood Category	Likelihood Definition
High Likelihood	An individual can expect to be affected more than once in 1000 years from being exposed to / interacting with the equipment
Medium Likelihood	An individual can expect to be affected between once in 1000 years and once in 100,000 years from being exposed to / interacting with the equipment
Low Likelihood	An individual can expect to be affected less than once in 100,000 years from being exposed to / interacting with the equipment

Table 8: Likelihood Categories

Because the typical human life span is only of the order of 100 years (rather than 1000's or 100,000's!), such definitions as found in Table 8 can at first sight appear absurd. But to take the "High Likelihood" definition from Table 8, it is really equivalent to saying that if the individual were to be exposed to / interact with the equipment along with 999 of his colleagues for a single year (1000 years of experience in total), then he/she could reasonably expect that at least one member of the total group would be affected by a "high likelihood" risk during that year.

The risk to an individual in that group is 1 in 1000 per year (which can also be written 10^{-3} per year).

For this example we will not draw up a severity table. We shall limit our attention to fatal accidents only, (noting that accidents are risks that have manifested themselves).

The resulting risk matrix (Table 9 - not really a matrix – but it illustrates the point) is shown below. For clarity I have included the full likelihood definitions:

		Likelihood Definition	Likelihood Boundary	Severity – Single Fatality
	High Likelihood	An individual can expect to be affected more than once in 1000 years		Cat 1 Risks
			RL	
Likelihood	Medium Likelihood	An individual can expect to be affected between once in 1000 years and once in 100,000 years		Cat 2 Risks
			RT	
	Low Likelihood	An individual can expect to be affected less than once in 100,000 years		Cat 3 Risks

Table 9: Risk Table – Not Quite a Risk Matrix

Inspecting Table 9, it can be clearly seen that since our likelihood definitions are expressed in the same units (individual annual risk of fatality) as RL and RT, it is a simple matter to place RL and RT.

Table 9 can be said to be calibrated since each Risk Category cell has a definition (its severity in combination with its likelihood) which is consistent with its placement in relation to RL and RT and their definitions.

This whole exercise serves to show that:

- The use of consistent units of measure throughout (in this case, individual annual risk of fatality) is essential for clarity and simplicity.

- A one-dimensional matrix serves no purpose as a prioritisation tool: If the only type of accident being identified is a fatality, then it's already obvious that you tackle the high-likelihood causes first and work down the list in decreasing order of likelihood.

- Using such a scheme, each fatal accident identified is individually addressed with a priority and effort commensurate with its categorisation

While working with this one-dimensional example, it is also opportune to note the following additional points:

- Just as with the risk categories, we are at liberty to define as many likelihood and severity groups as we wish and to label them as we wish.

  Hence instead of "High Likelihood", "Medium Likelihood", etc, we might prefer to use labels such as "Frequent", "Occasional", etc for likelihood and "Catastrophic", "Critical", etc for severity.

  The danger with such labels is that they carry a certain amount of presumed meaning because of their typical use in our daily language. Even labels like 'high" likelihood" or "high severity" contain a certain linguistic bias. Impartial terms like "Likelihood Band 1", "Severity Band 1" are arguably superior for the purpose, although perhaps more cumbersome.

  To illustrate the point I have re-cast Table 9 by refining and re-labelling the likelihood bands, (Table 10).

Severity

	Likelihood Definition	Likelihood Boundary	Single Fatality
Likelihood Band 1	An individual can expect to be affected more than once in 10 years		Cat 1 Risks
Likelihood Band 2	An individual can expect to be affected between once in 10 years and once in 100 years		Cat 1 Risks
Likelihood Band 3	An individual can expect to be affected between once in 100 years and once in 1000 years		Cat 1 Risks
Likelihood Band 4	An individual can expect to be affected between once in 1000 years and once in 10,000 years		Cat 2 Risks
Likelihood Band 5	An individual can expect to be affected between once in 10,000 years and once in 100,000 years		Cat 2 Risks
Likelihood Band 6	An individual can expect to be affected less than once in 100,000 years		Cat 3 Risks

Likelihood

Table 10: Re-Cast Risk Table

- Whatever label system is adopted the essential point is that the definitions accorded to the each band should be unambiguous and have some relevant meaning in relation to the equipment, its usage style and pattern and to those persons from whom risk estimates are being sought.

So, while we have defined likelihood in terms of the experience of an individual, (so as to be consistent with the chosen definitions of RL and RT), it is also useful to provide relevant conversion factors. E.g. if we know that each individual equipment has a "user" population of 10 persons (the term "user" here meaning the totality of persons having a planned interaction with the equipment) and that there are 100 such equipments in service, then Table 8 can be expanded as shown in Table 11):

Likelihood Category	Definition for individual persons	Definition for individual equipments	Definition for the total population of equipments
High Likelihood	An individual can expect to be affected more than once in 1000 years from being exposed to the equipment	The equipment is expected to cause an accident more than once in 100 years	Across the total population of equipments, an accident can be expected more than once per year
Medium Likelihood	An individual can expect to be affected between once in 1000 years and once in 100,000 years from being exposed to the equipment	The equipment is expected to cause an accident between once in 100 years and once in 10,000 years	Across the total population of equipments, an accident can be expected between once a year and once in 100 years
Low Likelihood	An individual can expect to be affected less than once in 100,000 years from being exposed to the equipment	The equipment is expected to cause an accident less than once in 10,000 years	Across the total population of equipments, an accident can be expected less than once in 100 years

Table 11: Equivalent Likelihood Definitions

The definitions in the "individual equipment" column are 10 times more frequent than in the "individual person" column, because each equipment is associated with a population of 10 users to each of whom it presents an individual risk.

Similarly the definitions in the "population of equipments" column are 100 times more frequent than in the "individual equipment" column, because there are 100 such equipments each posing a risk.

Providing a likelihood category table with such conversions shown in it is useful when we seek risk estimates from the equipment operator (whose experience relates to a single equipment) and from the equipment maintainer (whose experience stems from looking after a population of equipments); they each have a meaningful definition to work with and even from their apparently different perceptual starting points are likely to reach consensus.

Full Risk Matrix Development

Putting the above issues to one side, let us now look at the more complicated matrix that is derived when a whole spectrum of accident severities is accommodated.

Firstly we have to define our severity categories. We start with the perspective of an individual worker / "user":

Severity Category	Severity Definition for an Individual Worker
Severity Band 1	Death
Severity Band 2	Injury resulting in work absence for 3 or more days
Severity Band 3	Injury resulting in less than 3 days of work absence

Table 12: Severity Category Definitions

The definitions are our own choice, but importantly, fulfil the criteria of being unambiguous and being easy and meaningful to relate to. (I have selected these definitions because relevant UK Health and Safety statistics are collected in broadly these same groupings).

The underlying premise for risk assessment is that, in general, an overall level of risk is tolerated in exchange for the realisation of an overall level of benefit. Not unreasonably, we can conclude that a higher likelihood of occurrence is acceptable for an accident with consequences in our Severity Band 2 than for an accident whose consequences fall within our Severity Band 1. Likewise we conclude that a higher likelihood of occurrence will be acceptable for an accident with consequences in Severity Band 3 than for an accident whose consequences fall within Severity Band 2.

Again rather than directing the reader to any specific values, to construct our risk matrix we will simply confirm that having selected a value of RL for individual annual risk of fatality (10^{-3} per year in our previous example), then we would almost certainly have selected a higher (more frequent) RL for injuries in Severity Band 2 and a higher value still for injuries in Severity Band 3. E.g:

Severity Category	Severity Definition for an individual with planned interaction / use of the equipment	RL	RT
Severity Band 1	Death	10^{-3} per year	10^{-5} per year
Severity Band 2	Injury resulting in work absence for 3 or more days	10^{-2} per year	10^{-4} per year
Severity Band 3	Injury resulting in less than 3 days of work absence	10^{-1} per year	10^{-3} per year

Table 13: Extended Severity Category Definitions

Using Table 13 we can now extend Table 10 (which dealt only in fatal risks to the individual worker / "user") to produce a risk matrix which recognises a spectrum of severity outcomes. The process of construction is the same as we went through for Table 10, simply placing the appropriate values of RL and RT for each Severity category against the corresponding Likelihood category. The result is Table 14.

Severity

	Likelihood Boundary	Severity Band 1	Severity Band 2	Severity Band 3
Likelihood Band 1		Cat 1	Cat 1	Cat 1
				RL
Likelihood Band 2		Cat 1	Cat 1	Cat 2
			RL	
Likelihood Band 3		Cat 1	Cat 2	Cat 2
		RL		RT
Likelihood Band 4		Cat 2	Cat 2	Cat 3
			RT	
Likelihood Band 5		Cat 2	Cat 3	Cat 3
		RT		
Likelihood Band 6		Cat 3	Cat 3	Cat 3

(Likelihood — vertical axis label on left)

Table 14: Risk Matrix for Harm to an Individual

Harm to Several Individuals at Once

Because our current definitions of Severity all relate to harm to a single individual worker, so does the matrix we have developed in Table 14. It is a straightforward matter however to extend the severity definitions and hence the risk matrix to cover instances of harm to several individuals at once.

For example, a new Severity Band 0 could be added to reflect multiple deaths (with RL and RT scaled according to the number of persons affected, such that the individual risk figure remains broadly constant) as in Table 15.

Severity

	Likelihood Boundary	Severity Band 0	Severity Band 1	Severity Band 2	Severity Band 3
Likelihood Band 1		Cat 1	Cat 1	Cat 1	Cat 1
					RL
Likelihood Band 2		Cat 1	Cat 1	Cat 1	Cat 2
				RL	
Likelihood Band 3		Cat 1	Cat 1	Cat 2	Cat 2
			RL		RL
Likelihood Band 4		Cat 1	Cat 2	Cat 2	Cat 3
			RL		RL
Likelihood Band 5		Cat 2	Cat 2	Cat 3	Cat 3
				RL	
Likelihood Band 6		Cat 2	Cat 3	Cat 3	Cat 3

Table 15: General Risk Matrix for Worker Population

In Table 15, "Severity Band 0" has been given the definition "between 2 and 10 fatalities.

On the assumption that an individual will wish his risk of fatality to be treated equally seriously whether he is 'set' to die alone or simultaneously with his colleagues, it is understandable that we should not seek to alter the individual risk of fatality. The determination of RL for multiple fatalities is therefore a straight factor of the RL we have previously selected for a single fatality. In the above example, we adopt the premise that it is ten times less acceptable for 10 times as many people to die; then the individual risk of fatality is unchanged (which is what we are seeking).

To address the non-fatal accidents involving harm to multiple persons, the existing severity band definitions (Bands 1 to 3) can be revised. E.g. "Severity Band 1" definition could be extended to encompass "Single Fatality or Multiple 3-Day Lost Time accidents".

Harm to the Public

The other way in which the matrix can be extended is to cover not just workers who have an expectation of interaction with the equipment, but also those who don't (both workers who aren't directly involved and also the public – from hereon collectively referred to as simply "The Public".). As discussed in "Reducing Risks, Protecting People", (HSE, 2001) there is a societal expectation that such persons should be exposed to a lower level of risk than the direct workers, an order of magnitude reduction being cited in this case.

Having selected values for RL and RT relating to the public on this (or some other justifiable basis), a separate risk matrix can be developed (in the same manner as previously demonstrated) and used for the categorisation of those risks.

Using a separate matrix for public risk is a simpler approach than trying to re-scale the worker's matrix to accommodate risks to the public. The reason this is true, is that from the point of view of trying to manage safety, it is less complicated to have a system where a "Category 1 Risk" is always treated as "Unacceptable" and therefore receives the same amount of risk reduction effort, irrespective of whether worker or public risks are being discussed.

Selection of RL and RT

While this paper opened with a simple example that showed that a risk matrix can be used to prioritise risk reduction effort, (even when the matrix is not anchored to any particular scale of acceptance or tolerability), it was emphasised that the real value of the risk matrix is realised only when it is aligned to an objective scale of acceptability / tolerability of risk. Selecting values for RL and RT at each level of severity is therefore understandably an important part of the process.

The selection of RL and RT values is purposefully not covered in this paper, a superficial treatment of this complex topic not being appropriate, and a detailed treatment of the issues already being available elsewhere (HSE, 2001). What the paper concentrates on is the demonstration of how to develop and calibrate a risk matrix for whatever values or RL and RT are selected.

It should also be emphasised that the units of measure used in this paper (individual annual risk of fatality / injury) are not the only possibilities. For example, in the Nuclear Industry, levels of annual radiation dose to workers (measured in Sievert) are used to express accident severity. The Risk Limit and Risk Target (Basic Safety Limit and Basic Safety Objective in Nuclear speak) are therefore also expressed in those units.

Common Confusions and Errors

A risk matrix provides a succinct mechanism for sentencing and managing individual risks. Confusion and error often ensue when it is used in other ways, without appropriate understanding of the limitations:

- It is a temptation to perform some kind or numeric risk assessment of the whole equipment, by summation of the individual risks in accordance with the risk matrix estimates. This process should be used only in full cognisance of its limitations and with only very limited expectations of accuracy – in other words it will yield no more than a ball-park assessment of system risk and is not a substitute for formal probabilistic risk assessment, which recognises such issues as common-cause failure in a way that the simple summation of a risk matrix does not.

- It is also a temptation in developing the matrix to try and factor usage patterns for the equipment into the definitions of likelihood themselves, rather than factoring the usage pattern in to the estimation process when sentencing each individual risk. This again causes unnecessary (and often unsustainable) complication and errors.

- If the selected bands of likelihood do not span fully across RL and RT, then the matrix will be incomplete and the categorisation process unsatisfactory as a result.

- While the matrix developed in this paper follows a symmetric and logarithmic pattern, this is not an automatic (or necessary) outcome. Indeed in defining severity categories, it is certainly not necessary and user groups / equipment populations will seldom be factors of 10 as in the examples in this paper.

- Having gained an understanding of how the risk matrix is developed, it should be obvious that inspecting a matrix to assess its "harshness" based on the number of "Category 1" cells it has, (or Category A, or whatever label has been used), is a nonsensical activity, just as comparing matrices developed for different equipments as a means to judge which equipment is "higher risk" is also flawed.

Defence Standard 00-56

The UK Defence Standard, No. 00-56 (MoD, 1996) gives an example risk matrix In the Defence Standard example, the likelihood bands are given labels

("Frequent" through to "Incredible") and the severity bands are given labels ("Catastrophic" through to "Negligible"). The risk categories themselves are labelled "A" through to "D".

In developing this paper I have deliberately eschewed using the Defence Standard notations; to provide a fresh presentation of the issues for those readers who are familiar with the Defence Standard and equally to avoid imposing unnecessary perceptual constraints on those who are not.

The significant point I wish to emphasise is that the risk matrix, the definitions of likelihood and severity, and the risk categorisations themselves, are included in the Defence Standard as examples only. I therefore encourage the reader to consider the needs of their own specific projects first and foremost and to at least check that their proposed risk matrix is calibrated to the risk limits and targets before use.

Conclusions

This paper has sought to introduce the subject of risk matrices, to demonstrate how they can be simply developed, and to discuss the factors influencing their development.

It has sought to help the reader avoid common pitfalls and to impress upon the reader that the selection of Risk Limits and Targets is important to the process. I have tried to convey to the reader some of the complexity and indeed subjectivity of that selection process and to point to the UK Health and Safety Executive for additional guidance and assistance in this respect.

Finally, this paper has been prepared in response to numerous requests for guidance from persons in the UK defence industry. I hope it has been at least partially successful in that respect.

References

HSE (2001). Reducing Risks, Protecting People. HSE Books. ISBN 0 7176 2151 0

MoD (1996). Defence Standard 00-56 (Part 1). Safety Management Requirements for Defence Systems. Issue 2, UK Ministry of Defence.

ACHIEVING AND ARGUING THE SAFETY
OF MODULAR SYSTEMS

Health Monitoring for
Reconfigurable Integrated Control Systems

Dr Mark Nicholson
Department of Computer Science, University of York
York, England

Abstract

The next generation of control systems are likely to be characterised by much higher integration, where common / shared computer resources perform multiple system functions. It is possible to reconfigure such systems to provide continued functionality when an element of the system fails. To achieve this aim a number of pre-requisites must be in-place: the ability to determine when a failure has occurred, the appropriate configuration to move to and the ability to safely transfer from one configuration to another. This paper concentrates on the first of these in the form of health monitoring systems for IMS. The approach takes into account the potentially safety critical nature of the applications and the nature of these computer systems.

1. Introduction

Most current control system architectures, such as avionics systems, are federated systems with each function located within its own processor and connected to each other by a data bus. Integrated Modular Avionics (IMA) (EUROCAE 2004) is a term to describe a distributed real-time computer network aboard an aircraft. This network consists of a number of computing modules capable of supporting many applications, which in turn may have different safety criticality levels. One possible IMA architecture is presented in Figure 1 (ASAAC 2002). Each module contains an application that 'services' either a sensor or output or both. A common shared bus network connects the sensors, modules and outputs. Other domains, such as the automotive sector, have also looked at the concept of IMA. Thus, in this paper the more general term Integrated Modular System (IMS) is employed.

Reconfiguration is the capability of a system to adapt its functionality to the changing conditions of its environment (Trapp and Schurmann 2002). One such event could be a change in the mode of operation of the system, such as a move from the initialisation mode to the running mode. Another event that may be addressed via reconfiguration is a failure of one or more elements of the system. This could be a hardware, software or logical failure. This implies that the system has the ability to adapt its behaviour in the presence of faults to achieve continued safe operation and graceful degradation. Limited reconfiguration capability already exists in federated systems but the potential is much greater in IMS. Thus one of the benefits of moving to IMS is the ability to reconfigure the system in response to a range of triggering events.

One current approach to failure management in a federated system is to employ redundancy; that is to employ multiple copies of a system element. In the long term it may be possible to trade-off the level of redundancy employed in a safety related control system with the ability to provide "reconfiguration on failure".

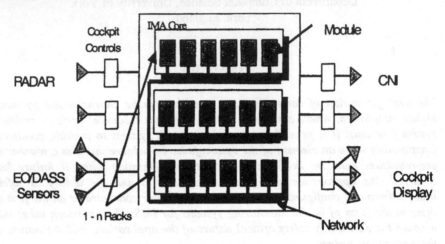

Figure 1: ASAAC Architecture for an IMA radar system

If "reconfiguration on failure" is to provide effective fault-management the ability to determine when a reconfiguration should take place is required. To accomplish this the concept of health monitoring needs to be adapted and extended to take into account the potentially safety critical nature of the applications placed on the IMS platform and the characteristics of IMS computer systems. Health monitoring (HM) is the ability to identify the failure of one or more system elements. Historically, health monitoring has been used to provide maintenance-related failure data for mainly mechanical systems. For instance the F22 flight critical systems have extensive self-diagnostics and built-in testing capability for the various subsystems (Globalsecurity 2004). There are more than 15,000 fault reports available for the avionics systems. Most of these are low-level fault reports that do not result in warnings or degrade the operation of the aircraft.

In IMS health monitoring could be the function responsible for monitoring the system to detect, and report hardware and software (application and operating system) faults and failures. The fault management part of the IMS then uses this information to determine the appropriate system level response, such as reconfiguration. Thus, an ability to detect, and handle failures in such systems become requirements that the system must comply with in order to meet safety objectives. One of the decisions that must be made for instance is which combinations of failure reports will lead to a reconfiguration. Furthermore a decision must then be made as to how extensive the reconfiguration will be. Safety implications accrue if either of these decisions is incorrect.

In Section 2 the concept of a configuration of the elements of an IMS is introduced. Reconfiguration mechanisms are then discussed with reference to the requirement to be able to safely reconfigure a system on failure. The elements of a health monitoring system for IMS are presented in Section 3. The paper then introduces possible safety analysis of a proposed reconfiguration on failure mechanism for IMS in Section 4. Finally, the work still needs to be undertaken to extend and validate the approach, for instance to provide safety argument and evidence is presented.

2. IMS System Blueprints

2.1 Configurations

A configuration of a system consists of a set of hardware elements (sensors, actuators, processors, communication buses, etc) and software elements (applications, operating systems, device drivers, embedded software in the sensors, etc). The configuration is set up to meet a given set of system level requirements such as timing, functionality, computing resource usage and fault tolerance requirements. In an IMS each function capable of being run as software can be mapped to any of a number of processors. Thus, a mapping of the software to the hardware is required (Nicholson, Hollow and McDermid 2000) for a given set of applications to be run on the IMS platform. In some standards, for example ASAAC, this mapping is referred to as a system configuration or "System Blueprint".

Blueprints can take many forms. Each is a generic template for that part of the system, with its own constraints (e.g. hardware performance limitations). The 'best' bits are taken from each blueprint to create the System Blueprint that can then be loaded on to the relevant IMS platform. This will depend upon a set of constraints or 'rules'. Figure 2 below shows how this is designed to work conceptually.

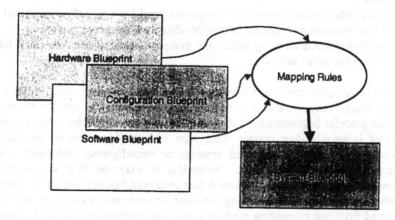

Figure 2: Elements of a System Blueprint (Joliffe 2004)

The elements in Figure 2 are:

Software Blueprint – contains a description of each software application in terms of memory, scheduling and communications requirements.

Hardware Blueprint – contains a description of each type of hardware employed (sensors, actuators, processors, communication buses, etc). For the computer modules for example this blueprint will contain data on the available memory, processor type and speed, and available communications.

Configuration Blueprint – contains a description of how the hardware and applications can be physically and logically connected together e.g. bandwidth, maximum number of connections, etc.

Mapping Rules – optimise the Software, Hardware and Configuration blueprints against a set of constraints.

System Blueprint – also known as a Run-time Blueprint, is the output from the application of the mapping rules, and can be implemented on a target system or platform.

A number of projects have been working on this issue. The VICTORIA (VICTORIA 2001) project looks at mappings / blueprints for civil aerospace IMS and the ASAAC standards look at blueprints for IMS in the military domain.

2.2 Reconfiguration Mechanisms

A single system blueprint can be produced for a system and several methods exist to do this (Bates et al 2003). There are a number of reasons however, why it may be desirable to change the system blueprint at run-time. A change from one system blueprint to another one is known as a *reconfiguration*. Three steps have to take place for a successful reconfiguration:

1. Determine a set of possible system blueprints that can be employed for reconfiguration on failure by defining a set of mapping rules to determine a set of blueprints that can be used when a set of particular component failures occur.
2. Determine the events that will trigger the need for a reconfiguration and select the appropriate new system blueprint when each trigger occurs
3. Employ a mechanism by which the system transfers from the old to the new system blueprint safely.

System reconfiguration can take many forms. For instance, it may be that a smart sensor design may be able to undertake a reconfiguration activity to mask, or provide graceful degradation, of the sensing services it provides when a particular class of internal failure occurs. This type of reconfiguration comes under the heading of "adaptive embedded systems or reconfiguring embedded systems" (Trapp and Schumann, 2002). Secondly, it may be that a processor or communication bus failure is reported thus requiring functionality to be reallocated to other computing modules during run-time. In other words software functionality is moved from one computing module to another. Furthermore, it may be necessary to reduce the amount of low safety criticality functionality to allow the critical functionality to be preserved. IMS is much more flexible than existing federated systems in this respect and this type of reconfiguration is emphasised in this paper.

Ultimately, in IMS the intention is for a platform to be capable of reconfiguring its system blueprint whilst operational. The simplest approach to this is to produce a set of system blueprints and have them available in the form of look-up tables to be used if a given trigger events occur (Nicholson, Hollow and McDermid 2000). One possible mechanism for transferring from one configuration to another is to employ an intermediate mapping that only has the processes in the old mapping that remain in the new mapping in the intermediate mapping and then to add in the new / changed processes to form the new configuration. There is a significant number of safety related issues that still need to be addressed (Jolliffe 2004) with this approach, this is an area of potential future research, but let us assume for the purposes of this paper that a set of system blueprints can be determined and that a reconfiguration mechanism can be developed.

In the discussion above it is implicit that reconfiguration can take place at a number of different levels in the system. The concept of a hierarchical reconfiguration system based on local and global reconfiguration mechanisms is relevant. The impact of a reconfiguration can therefore be very localised or extensive dependent on the nature of the event that triggers the reconfiguration. The safety argument for the reconfiguration system employed will need to be based on the properties of the reconfiguration system at the overall platform level.

The remainder of this paper focuses on step two, that is identifying a failure via health monitoring and triggering the appropriate reconfiguration process. The failure that has occurred must be identified by the appropriate part of the IMS. Recovery from this failure may involve changes to multiple elements of the IMS The need to correctly identify faults, and which system element should be responsible for doing so, is therefore paramount to the overall effectiveness and accompanying safety argument for reconfiguration on failure. An extension to the concept of HM offers the best chance of providing the trigger for reconfiguration on failure in an IMS at an appropriate level of safety integrity.

3. Health monitoring

3.1 Current Practices

Health Monitoring (HM) is a broad term used to mean a wide range of maintenance related activities including condition-based maintenance, condition monitoring, fault management and life usage monitoring of electro-mechanical components in a system. It is therefore essentially an extension to system failure diagnostics. A vast amount of work has been directed towards developing reliable and state of the art HM related techniques (Kacprzynski and Hess 2002). However, explicit HM systems have only been applied in a limited manner, for example to helicopter systems. The HM systems in helicopters, also known as Health and Usage Monitoring System (HUMS), are intended to monitor the health of helicopter rotor and rotor drive system components which are primarily concerned with mechanical parameters. They are also intended for off-line data processing for maintenance purposes.

Tanner and Crawford (Tanner and Crawford 2003) have developed an Integrated Engine Health Monitoring System for Rolls-Royce gas turbine aero-engines. They claim that as long as no other component is dispatch-critical the system brings at least two benefits:

- Reduction of operational n-service disruption by the avoidance of "surprise" failures
- Improved maintenance process resulting from greater in-service knowledge and failure identification, leading to a more selective and cost effective engine strip procedure and piece part replacement

The majority of this work has been undertaken in the aerospace domain. However the automotive industry are also interested in diagnostics for drive by wire systems. In (You and Jalics 2004) a generalised diagnostics component (GDC) and a modular hierarchical fault diagnostic strategy is developed. One advantage of the approach they recommend is that

"The architecture can be quickly and gracefully updated to a new By-wire diagnostic model on the reconfiguration of GDC's to adapt to the changed environment."

This reduces the overhead associated with updating the diagnostic system when the system is changed. The overhead associated with the HM system and the effort required to change and recertify the HM system when a change is made to the system will have a major impact on the viability of the reconfiguration approach to failure management. This is considered further in the future work section of this paper.

If reconfiguration is to be triggered by the results of a HM system then authority must be given to some system element to initiate the reconfiguration. This element may, or may not, be the HM system. Four levels of authority for a HM system can be envisaged (see Table 1). The current generation of HM systems can be characterised as level 3 or level 4 systems. For dynamic reconfiguration on failure to occur at run-time, that is while the system is operational, level 1 or level 2 HM is required. If reconfiguration is to take place when the system is not operational then approaches using any of the different levels of HM can be envisaged. However, if level 3 or level 4 HM systems are employed support personnel or another system would be required to make the decision to reconfigure, or not, based on the data from the HM system.

3.2 Health monitoring for IMS

Computer based systems such as IMS pose particular problems for HM and the concept of reconfiguration on failure. The sensors and actuators attached to the IMS are amenable to the current generation of HM systems. However, for reconfiguration on failure a high level of authority to initiate reconfiguration would be required, which is beyond the current state of the art.

The hardware employed within an IMS such as processors and communication buses may be amenable to current HM techniques if failure is gradual, indicated by parameter deviations. However, electronic components are often subject to instantaneous failures, which poses more of a challenge for HM systems designers. Thus an extension to current HM systems is required to enhance the capabilities of

HM systems so that they can be applied to identifying failures in IMS computer based hardware. Furthermore, hardware failures in the IMS may impact on the ability of the HM system to identify failures and to reconfigure the system as the IMS also hosts the HM system. Suitable partitioning of the HM system will be required to overcome this issue.

1. Full authority	HM carries out health monitoring such as fault detection and fault analysis (i.e. extent of failure) and reports any failure or degradation in operation. It has authority to shut down equipment, applications, etc and to initiate software / hardware reconfiguration when required.
2. Semi authority	HM carries out health monitoring such as fault detection and fault analysis in operation but has no authority to shut down equipment, applications, etc. It reports any failure or degradation and recommends actions to be performed, by the operators, such as shutting down failed components, requesting immediate maintenance actions at destination or software / hardware reconfiguration.
3. Maintenance	HM carries out health monitoring such as fault detection and fault analysis and reports any failure or degradation in operation for maintenance purposes only.
4. No authority	HM carries out health monitoring such as fault detection for later analysis.

Table 1: Levels of Health Monitoring

IMS employs a layered approach with an operating system and separated application software. These layers are connected via an interface layer, such as that provided by ARINC 653 (ARINC 2003). It is therefore necessary to identify the types of failure that can occur in the software logic of the IMS and to identify such failures at appropriate levels in the HM system.

Failures in a component, such as a communication bus failing silent, are propagated through the IMS and may be transformed by it into other forms of failure, or may indeed be masked by the system. This propagation and transformation (Lisagor et al 2004) of a failure needs to be studied by the system designer to determine the appropriate level to place the authority to decide to initiate a reconfiguration on failure. Furthermore, the nature of this propagation and transformation may determine the form of the reconfiguration required. A technique to consider the safety implications of reconfiguration is presented in Section 4.

Thus a number of questions remain to be answered with respect to the use of HM in an IMS. Does a computer system failure such as computing component burnt-out show gradual deterioration? Are there correlations between component failures and system crashes? If so, what are they? Can failures during execution be correlated to failures in a hardware component or flaws in software logic? The first steps towards answering these issues are presented in this section.

For HM of an IMS a distinction should be made between deviation due to malfunction of computer hardware / software and deviation due to malfunction of electro-mechanical components, such as sensors. HM for failures within an IMS should be designed following the principles adopted for IMS, which are open system principles conforming to an Application Programming Interface (API) standard. Thus, IMS health monitoring could be the function responsible for monitoring the system to detect, and report hardware (sensors, actuators, buses, processors, etc), software application and operating system faults and failures. The complexity of IMS will require a high degree of capability and authority to be invested in the HM system if reconfiguration on failure is to take place.

Standards such as ARINC 653 discuss HM as an integrated part of an IMS operating system based on various levels determined by where a fault / failure arises. ARINC 653 does not explicitly address reconfiguration on failure issues. It does however provide a good starting point. It classifies errors within an IMS according to the location of their causes: module level errors, partition / application level errors and process level errors. Module level errors include module configuration errors during initialisation, errors during partition switching and power failure. Partition level errors encompass partition configuration error during initialisation, error during process management, error during an error handler process. Examples of process level errors are memory violation and illegal operating system request. From this classification ARINC 653 defines three levels of health monitoring:

- Module level health monitoring (MHM)
- Partition / application level health monitoring (PHM)
- Global level health monitoring (GHM).

MHM provides means for detection of hardware errors in a hardware module, which are non-function related errors such as violation of partition boundary and timing overrun. PHM supports detection of specific functional application errors as well as some external hardware failures such as monitoring data from sensor. GHM provides error logging from the other HM levels and passes on information to particular modules.

ARINC 653 fails to address many important issues that should be defined for a health monitoring system of an IMS, especially those that are potentially essential for safety and certification if the HM system is to be employed as part of a reconfiguration on failure approach to fault tolerance. Examples are a definition of the roles/authority in monitoring and management of failures and responsibilities of health monitoring.

HM for reconfigurable IMS will need to be either level 1, with full authority to initiate a reconfiguration, or level 2, with operator assisted authority to reconfigure the system. In fact different failure modes will require different levels of authority. Determining this authority for each potential reconfiguration becomes an activity as part of the design of the fault tolerance aspects of the applications hosted by the IMS. The mechanism to undertake the commanded reconfiguration would be controlled by the operating system of the IMS.

For systems that employ reconfiguration on failure controlled by the operating system in response to a trigger event four levels of health monitoring would seem to be more appropriate than the three proposed in ARINC 653. These four levels are:

- Software process / hardware component monitoring (CHM)
- Module / application level health monitoring (MHM)
- Partition /application level health monitoring (PHM)
- Global level health monitoring (GHM).

There is a strong need to define clearly the scope of each level of the HM system for reconfigurable IMS. For instance, what failures are to be identified and addressed by reconfiguration? This is known as the reconfiguration coverage of the system. An unclear definition will lead to great difficulty in certifying the IMS because reconfiguration coverage is one of the most crucial aspects for the performance of an IMS under failure. This definition of responsibility should be incorporated into a regulatory standard to assure compliance. The following scope in monitoring a reconfigurable IMS are proposed based on where a failure can arise:

- **CHM**: responsible for monitoring the health at software process / component level such as the presence of a violation, deviation of particular parameters (data from a sensor). At the component level, HM reports the status of that component. This includes deviation of values, no values, persistency of faults, and response. This is similar to built-in-test. At the software process level, HM reports violation / exception.
- **PHM**: covers violations at the partition / application level, deviations in function performance, etc.
- **MHM**: is responsible for monitoring communication, data flow between modules, etc.
- **GHM**: monitors performance related parameters, performance trends, etc.

There is a clear link between the level of authority and the scope of a HM. For instance, it may be reasonable to give full authority to a CHM to shut down a faulty piece of hardware or software process given certain failure modes of the system. It is unlikely that a CHM will also be given the authority to order a reconfiguration of the system. Reconfiguration on failure is likely to be a function of MHM or GHM depending on the architecture of the IMS. There is also a link between the propagation and transformation path of a failure and the level of authority of a particular HM to initiate reconfiguration. Work is continuing into guiding the ability to decide on the scope and authority of each level of HM within an IMS.

In this section the issues surrounding the use of HM as part of a reconfiguration on failure approach to fault tolerance for IMS have been introduced. These issues can be summarised as which failures should be identified by the HM system for reconfiguration and where in the HM system hierarchy should the decision to undertake reconfiguration in response to a given failure event reside. In section 4 the safety and certification issues of a reconfiguration on failure approach are addressed.

4. Safety and Certification of HM for Reconfigurable IMS

4.1 Safety aspects of HM for Reconfigurable IMS

The ability to reconfigure on failure clearly has safety implications. If the health monitor system does not identify a failure that should be addressed via a reconfiguration activity then the system may be put into a potentially hazardous state. Alternatively, if the health monitor incorrectly initiates a reconfiguration this may also have safety implications. A safety argument will need to be developed for the HM system used as part of the deployment of the reconfiguration on failure approach. This is beyond the scope of this paper but the framework of such an argument can be found in (Jolliffe 2004).

Two safety analyses are required to assess the contribution of the HM system to a reconfiguration approach to fault tolerance for a safety critical system. The first relates to which failures should be addressed using a reconfiguration approach, where each of these failure should be addressed in the health monitoring system and where the decision to decide that a particular reconfiguration action should take place in response to the failure should be determined. In other words how can the requirements be elicited for the HM aspects of a reconfiguration on failure system? The second analysis is required to determine how failures of the HM system can contribute to failures of the reconfiguration on failure functionality as a whole. In fact the same technique can be employed to undertake both of these analyses. The chosen technique is SHARD (McDermid et al 1995), which analyses flows, such as data flows, through a system. The aim is to analyse the effects of failures that occur for a number of classes of failure namely omission, commission, early, late and value failures.

Suppose that a system is to be analysed to determine whether reconfiguration should take place as a result of a data communication bus producing a stream of incorrect messages. If the correct messages on that bus do not arrive because of the "chattering" of the bus then this is characterised as an omission failure in the SHARD technique. The extra messages may also be defined as a commission failure because they represent messages that were not required. The effects of this failure in the system context can be addressed using the SHARD technique. It may be for instance that the bus can delete all the messages thus removing the commission failure. The failure has been transformed into an omission failure. The bus may not be able to do this and the messages will then be propagated to other elements of the system. It might be for instance that in the context of the system such extra messages can only be identified at the application level in which case this would be the appropriate level to trigger a reconfiguration.

The SHARD analysis allows the system designer to track the propagation and transformation of failures through the IMS to the end level effects. Decisions as to which failures need reconfiguration, where the failure should be identified and which element of the system should have responsibility for initiating the reconfiguration can then be determined. In this way the reconfiguration on failure approach becomes an integral part of system development. In our chattering bus example the appropriate response may be to reconfigure the system so that a redundant bus sends the messages. The sending and receiving processes would need to be able to switch from the existing bus to the new bus and timing / performance requirements would still need to be met.

Take a different example. Suppose that the system design had a smart sensor that could undertake fault diagnosis on a number of its failure modes. It is able to shut itself down or in some circumstances reconfigure itself to overcome the failure. It is able to send a message that it has done so to the IMS HM system. In this case the designer must decide whether the sensor should be given the authority to undertake shut down or reconfiguration locally. The designer will also need to consider the effect of an omission failure using the SHARD approach. The designer may also wish to consider a simple sensor and placing the failure identification and reconfiguration authority within the IMS. The analysis needs to be flexible enough to consider alternative design solutions.

There is another aspect that needs to be considered. So far our analysis has concentrated on failures in the hardware and functionality of the system, what about failures in the HM system? SHARD can help here to. Suppose that it is determined that a reconfiguration is required for the chattering bus example. Now suppose that there is a failure in the HM system and in some circumstances it erroneously identifies that the bus is in the chattering failure mode and initiates the reconfiguration. What is the effect of this at the system level? Can the system be put in a hazardous state as a result of this failure? Can another part of the HM system identify this failure? A SHARD analysis can be undertaken to determine the potential effects of such a failure mode. As another example, suppose that there is a failure mode inside the smart sensor that erroneously initiates a shut down of the sensor. Is this a safety issue or merely an availability issue?

An alternative approach, that in reality may be complementary to the SHARD analysis, is to undertake an initial system FMECA at the system design stage. (Kacprzynski and Hess 2002) argue that FMECA is a perfect link between the critical overall system failure modes and the health management system designed to help mitigate those failure modes. However, this approach does not address health management technologies for diagnosing faults and typically focuses on subsystems independently.

Current work is focusing on producing examples of SHARD analysis for a variety of hardware and software failures in a case study. It is hoped that results will be available by the conference to show how SHARD analysis can aid the designer in determining an appropriate reconfiguration on failure approach for a given system and to analyse the potential effects of failures in the proposed reconfiguration approach with respect to health monitoring.

4.2 Certification of HM for reconfigurable IMS

The system level at which a HM is employed and the type of failures addressed by reconfiguration partly determines the amount of effort required to certify the reconfiguration system. A full authority HM would require a significant effort to certify, as it is potentially a single point of failure. Commensurate validation and verification activities need to be determined.

The correlation between software criticality levels of the applications hosted on the IMS and HM depends on the level of authority that will be implemented for HM. There is thus a correlation between HM authority levels with software criticality level as per DO178B (RTCA/DO 1992) of the functionality being monitored. For example, if HM has full authority to initiate a reconfiguration of a system with software of criticality level A then the HM system must also be at criticality level A. Table 2 lists the likely correlation between HM authority levels and software criticality levels. It suggests the appropriate HM criticality levels.

Authority	Software criticality level of system				
	Catastrophic	Hazardous	Major	Minor	Non-essential
Full	A	A/B	C	D	E
Semi	A/B	B/C	C/D	D	E
Maintenance	C	C	D	D	E
No	D	D	D	D	E

Table 2: HM authority Versus Criticality

So in this section the requirement to consider the safety effects of a decision to employ a reconfiguration on failure approach to fault tolerance on a particular IMS has been investigated. First, it is proposed that a design time SHARD analysis should be undertaken to identify the failures that will trigger a reconfiguration and the appropriate level in the HM system hierarchy to place the reconfiguration decision. Secondly, a SHARD analysis should also be undertaken to assess the safety implications of a failure in the HM system. Finally, validation and verification activities commensurate with the authority of the HM and the safety criticality of the applications it can affect should be undertaken.

5. Conclusions

This paper has considered the first steps towards implementing a reconfiguration on failure-based approach to fault management in an IMS. It has concentrated on the scope, authority and safety / reliability analysis of a HM system required to initiate reconfiguration on failure. A four level HM is proposed with some elements being given full authority to initiate a reconfiguration and others only able to implement local actions. Safety analysis is via two SHARD analyses. The integrity level that would need to be associated with each level of HM depending on the authority of each level has also been addressed.

A significant number of unresolved issues have emerged as a result of this work that must be addressed before this approach can be used in real systems. For example, will the GHM have the final responsibility for initiating a reconfiguration based on the actions of other HM or can lower level HMs do this? How can the HM be improved to predict failures and what sort of reconfiguration would be appropriate in these conditions? How can the HM be removed as a potential single point of failure to a hazardous system state? How will the reconfiguration approach be certified?

Furthermore, what is the impact of a change to the system on the HM regime? Once a system is in operation it will be subject to change throughout its lifetime. Indeed one of the perceived advantages of IMS is the ability to implement incremental change. The aim here is for a change to have a minimal, and well defined, impact on elements of the IMS not directly affected. Work is needed to determine how the HM system can respect this approach as much as possible. This will imply that the impact on the HM system should be minimal if a change is made and that the amount of reworking of the safety analysis should be as proportionate to the size of the change as possible.

These issues present a significant challenge to the reconfiguration on failure approach put forward in this paper and may dilute the gains in reliability / safety that can be achieved as a result of the graceful degradation ability provided by reconfiguration on failure approach. Nevertheless, there is a strong incentive to resolve these problems.

References

ARINC (2003). ARINC SPECIFICATION 653-1 Avionics Application Software Standard Interface, 2003

ASAAC (2002). ASAAC Phase II Stage 2, Second draft of proposed guidelines for system issues - Volume 2: Fault Management, REF-WP: 32350, 2002

Bates SA, Bate IJ, Hawkins RD, Kelly TP, McDermid JA (2003). Safety Case Architectures to Complement a Contract-Based Approach to Designing Safe Systems. In Proceedings of 21st International System Safety Conference, Ottawa, Canada, 2003.

Eurocae (2004). Modular Avionics Guidance Document revision F. Ref: EUROCAE WG60 / RTCA SC 200, Aug 2004

Globalsecurity (2004). F-22 Raptor Flight Control Systems. www.globalsecurity.org/military/systems/aircraft/f-22/fcas.htm, 7th October 2004

Jolliffe G (2004). "Exploring the Possibilities of Safety Case Production for IMA Blueprints. MSc Project, Department of Computer Science, University of York, 2004

Kacprzynski GJ and Hess AJ (2002). Health Management System Design: Development, Simulation and Cost/Benefit Optimization. IEEE, Big Sky, MT, March 2002

Lisagor O, Pumfrey DJ & McDermid JA (2004). Safety Analysis of Software Architectures - "Lightweight PSSA", Proceedings of the 22nd International System Safety Conference, Providence, RI, System Safety Society, P.O.Box 70, Unionville, VA 22567-0070, USA, 2004

McDermid JA, Nicholson M, Pumfrey DJ & Fenelon P. (1995). Experience with the application of HAZOP to computer-based systems, COMPASS '95: Proceedings of the Tenth Annual Conference on Computer Assurance, Gaithersburg, MD, pp. 37-48, IEEE, ISBN 0-7803-2680-2, 1995

Nicholson M, Hollow P and McDermid JA (2000). Approaches to Certification of Reconfigurable IMA Systems. INCOSE 2000, Minneapolis, USA, July 2000

RTCA/DO (1992). RTCA/DO-178B - Software Considerations in Airborne Systems and Equipment Certification. RTCA/DO, 1992

Tanner and Crawford (2003). Aircraft Airborne Condition Monitoring. British Energy. IEE meeting, Gloucester, United Kingdom, 14 May 2003

Trapp M and Schurmann B (2002). On the Modelling of Adaptive Systems. Sigsoft 2002/FSE10, Charleston, SC, USA, 2002

You S and Jalics L (2004). Hierarchical Component Based Fault Diagnostics for By-Wire Systems. SAE white paper, SAE, 2004-01-0285, 2004

VICTORIA (2001). VICTORIA project on the Europa website. europa.eu.int/comm/research/growth/gcc/projects/in-action-victoria.html, 2001

Exploring the Possibilities Towards a Preliminary Safety Case for IMA Blueprints

Authors

Graham Jolliffe MSc CEng MRAeS;
QinetiQ, MoD Boscombe Down; Salisbury, Wiltshire, UK

Dr Mark Nicholson;
Department of Computer Science, University of York, Heslington, York, UK

Abstract

Keywords: Integrated Modular Avionics, Blueprints, Safety

The Aim of this paper is to show how a safety argument could be constructed for the use of blueprints in platforms using Integrated Modular Avionics (IMA). It is assumed that the IMA system will contain safety-critical elements. Given current safety analysis techniques, there is no certainty that this can be achieved satisfactorily.

Initially there is a need to define a blueprint: once this is done, the blueprints will be considered by looking at the impact of Blueprints on IMA Safety. The ultimate objective of IMA is to produce a reconfigurable system. Whilst this has potential safety benefits, there are substantial problems with the ability to argue that a reconfigurable IMA is safe. Consequently, this project will concentrate on a 3 Step Approach towards developing full IMA capability. The three steps are:

1. Fixed number of prioritised configurations (e.g. lookup table)
2. Ground (static) reconfiguration (between operations)
3. Dynamic reconfiguration

This approach is progressively more complex, but will enable confidence to be gained from success at each step. The safety argument that is produced in this paper is generic and has been produced as part of an MSc project. However, the overall IMA safety argument needs to consider many other issues and factors, which may affect the safety of blueprints. This is not covered in this paper, but is expanded in more detail in the MSc project (Jolliffe 2004).

1 Background

Before describing the background to this paper, it is worth spending some time explaining what IMA is and, importantly, providing a definition for an IMA blueprint. Most current avionic architectures are federated systems with each function located within its own processor or Line Replacement unit (LRU), connected to each other by an avionics data bus. A typical federated system is shown in the diagram below (Fig 1) (Kemp 2000).

IMA is a term to describe a distributed real-time computer network aboard an aircraft. This network might consist of a number of computing modules capable of supporting many applications, which in turn may have different safety criticality levels.

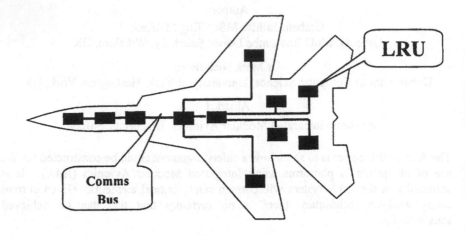

Figure 1 Typical Federated System Architecture

The diagram below (Figure 2) (Kemp 2000) shows what a typical IMA architecture might look like. Each module contains an application that 'services' either a sensor or output or both. A common shared network connects the sensors, modules and outputs.

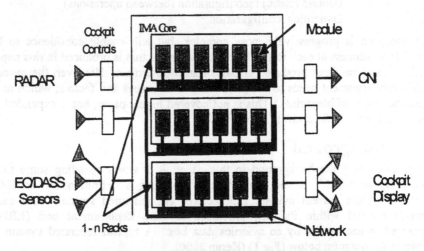

Figure 2 Possible IMA System Architecture

There are a number of benefits in progressing towards this type of architecture compared with that shown in Figure 1. The civil and military sectors have already clearly identified the benefits of IMA and (Kemp 2000, Conmy 2003, Tudor 2002, Aviation Today Magazine Website 2003, MoD ADAS(Air) Website 2002, and

Thales' A380 website 2003) are just a few of the many papers and articles that highlight the advantages of adopting this technology.

The IMA concept permits greater flexibility with each function capable of being run as software in any of a number of processors. However, this flexibility is intended to allow reconfiguration of all or part of the systems resources, which has two significant benefits. First, the system can be modified to fulfil different roles or missions. Secondly, the same ability can be used to maintain system safety or integrity, by transferring a safety critical application from a failed component to one that is serviceable. This will also enable more efficient and effective use of processing power and reduce the impact caused by obsolescence. Consequently, IMA promises to be both cheaper and more effective than the existing federated systems. It will also lend itself to a variety of platforms in various environments.

2   IMA Safety

Demonstrating safety is already a complicated task for federated systems, but for IMA the number of permutations of configurations could be a very large number. If traditional safety analysis approaches were to be utilised for this type of architecture, then the amount of time taken to conduct such analysis would be prohibitive. So an alternative approach needs to be found that will permit safety to be demonstrated adequately, but will not impede the development and exploitation of IMA systems.

The allocation of the applications to hardware in an effective and efficient way is a critical issue, when safety, reliability and real-time requirements have to be met. This has long been realised by most of the agencies and consortia that are considering how best to apply this technology including Eurocae WG60, RTCA SC200 and the Allied Standard Avionics Architecture Council (ASAAC). There are a number of viable methods for implementing IMA, and IMA is currently proposed for a number of new platforms including F22, and Airbus A380. There are also other platforms that claim to be developing IMA systems such as the Boeing 777, but they only partially meet the full objectives and aspirations of IMA as outlined above. Consequently, with so many variations, it might be difficult to prove IMA safety without knowing which 'sort' of IMA is in question.

However, all of the technology groups listed above have the same aspirations for IMA, therefore it can be argued that examining the safety aspects of one group should enable read across to the others. This paper will primarily concentrate on the work carried out by the ASAAC. The full aims of the ASAAC programme, and description of the standards and guidelines is not provided in this paper but are outlined in the supporting MSc project (Jolliffe 2004) and further information can be obtained from (Kemp 2000 and ASAAC 1999).

An approach to this problem that a number of these organisations, including ASAAC, are considering is the use of a concept called 'blueprints' to describe the system. It is worth noting that ASAAC does not specifically propose the use of blueprints, but it is generally accepted that blueprints will provide an expedient way of implementing IMA. The definition of 'blueprints' is provided below, however, the safety of a blueprint needs to consider normal operation of the system (including different modes), what are the blueprint hazards, and what hazards can blueprints contribute too and how. It also needs to consider the contribution of blueprints to safety during system failures.

3 Blueprint Definition

Some work has already been completed on blueprint generation by personnel at QinetiQ Farnborough (Stevens 2002 and Murray 2002), who were consulted on their view of what a blueprint is. Similar consultation was made with individuals from industries, who have also been pioneering work within the IMA area. A consensus was reached by a wide selection of individuals representing a good cross section from industry, government agencies, academia and other trusted experts. They broadly concurred with the findings of (Stevens 2002) at a meeting held at Farnborough in June 2003.

Blueprints can take many forms to cover Hardware, Software and Configurations. Each is a generic template for that part of the system, with its own constraints (e.g. hardware performance limitations) from which an optimal solution can be produced, which effectively becomes the System Blueprint. Each blueprint will contain many features that may not all be utilised within the System (or Run-Time) blueprint. In effect it is intended to pick the 'best' bits from each blueprint and deliver the System Blueprint that can then be loaded on to the relevant platform. This will depend upon a set of constraints or 'rules', which may be either hard (essential) or soft (desirable). The diagram in Figure 3 below shows how this is designed to work conceptually.

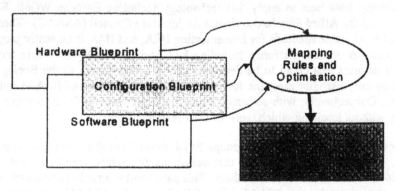

Figure 3 Blueprint Conceptual Relationship

From Figure 3 it can be seen that in addition to establishing the safety integrity of each blueprint, the mapping rules and possibly the algorithms used for optimisation must also be evaluated for integrity. As a result of the meetings and discussions mentioned above, the general consensus was that the blueprint model above is a hybrid, consisting of hardware, software and configuration blueprints, where:

a.   Software Blueprint – contains a description of each software application in terms of memory requirements (static and dynamic), scheduling requirements, communications requirements.

b.   Hardware Blueprint – contains a description of each type of hardware module in terms of available memory, processor type and speed, and available communications.

c.   Configuration Blueprint – contains a description of how the hardware and applications can be physically and logically connected together e.g. bandwidth, maximum number of connections, etc. This sounds similar to the mapping rules, and could be thought of as a high level 'filter'. This blueprint predefines how the hardware and software blueprints physically communicate with one another.

d.   System Blueprint – also known as a Run-time Blueprint, is the output from the mapping (optimisation) algorithm, and can implemented on a target system or platform.

e.   Mapping Rules – optimises the Software, Hardware and Configuration blueprints against a set of constraints.

It is this definition that will be used in this paper.

4   Approach and Current Research

In addition to considering the safety of blueprints when the system is performing normally, safety also needs to be assessed when failures occur, for which the failure modes of a blueprint need to be evaluated. Using the 3-step approach, safety considerations can be investigated, and the safety arguments can then be built up incrementally. Because IMA and the use of blueprints demand an alternative approach to safety analysis, it is easy to conclude that safety will be adversely impacted. However, there may well be positive safety benefits and these will be highlighted.

4.1   Modular Safety Cases

Modularity has been proposed as a more efficient means of constructing safety cases for complex systems and it would be sensible to examine work in this area to determine its applicability to IMA blueprint certification. A number of papers have been written on this subject. This includes (Rushby 2002) who first explains that certification is really concerned with abnormal behaviour of systems i.e. if a system can be shown to be fault free then it is safe. However, it is possible that a system could comprise of perfectly 'safe' components that were not designed to operate together. Such a system would still be unsafe. Even if components are designed to operate together, the ability to show that they are fault free has traditionally been difficult and is not a practical approach for IMA. Rushby acknowledges that cascade failures are more complex to evaluate, because they may well extend beyond the system module boundary and interfaces. Potentially, the failure can emerge in any other system module that has a dependency. Therefore, for this approach to be practical, module interdependencies must be kept to a minimum. That may be easier said than done, since some modules will have executive functions that extend to all other modules. Therefore, there is a need to conduct a Common Mode/Common Cause analysis. This is not specifically addressed in this project, but needs to be addressed in the overall IMA safety argument.

Kelly introduces GSN and its benefits as a tool for arguing system safety (Kelly 1998). It is also argued (Kelly and McDermid 1998) that the production of safety cases using Goal Structured Notation (GSN) often results in similar patterns emerging. It makes sense to reuse these patterns when appropriate, since this will save effort and there will already be confidence that the pattern works and has 'pedigree'. These patterns can be used to effectively capture solutions that have evolved over time, company expertise, successful certification approaches and 'tricks of the trade'. However, patterns only avoid duplication of effort. They need to be applied in a particular context in order to be useful in a larger safety case. Kelly (Kelly 2001) establishes the mechanisms for managing and representing safety cases as a composition of safety case modules. This requires the module interface to be defined as follows:

a. Objectives addressed by the module
b. Evidence presented within the module
c. Context defined within the module
d. Arguments requiring support from other modules
Inter-module dependencies:
e. Reliance on objectives addressed elsewhere
f. Reliance on evidence presented elsewhere
g. Reliance on context presented elsewhere.

Clearly, the relationship with other modules can be complex, with supporting evidence being derived from multiple sources. It, therefore, becomes important to understand the objectives, evidence and context defined for each module, since this could jeopardise a safety case argument if there are inconsistencies. Therefore, the support from other modules and the reliance needed to provide that support should not contradict the first three items in the above list. In (Kelly 1998) extensions to GSN are introduced to enable the concept of Safety Case 'Modules' to be represented. He also introduces the concept of 'Away Goals'. The Away Goal forms part of the argument for a particular safety case that requires the support of another module.

This requires the relationship between various modules to be well defined. It is recommended that an 'away goal' always be first satisfied by a single module. Only if this is impracticable, should combinations of sub-goals from multiple modules be used. However, in order for these modules to be integrated into a larger safety case or argument, some rules need to be established. For instance, it would not be acceptable to use an ALARP pattern as a solution to a Safety Margin Pattern. This is because the safety margin is likely to be a fixed target, whereas the target for ALARP will vary according to a number of system criteria. In other words, the two arguments have goals that do not match.

4.2　Safety Case Contracts

Kelly (Kelly 1998) recommends that once a successful match has been achieved, this should be recorded as a 'contract'. This should include the participants and the relevant goals, context and evidence that each participant brings to the contract. A suggested format for such a contract as shown below in Table 1.

Safety Case Module Contract			
Participant Modules (e.g. Modules A, B, C, etc.)			
Goals matched between Participant Modules			
Goal	Required By	Addressed By	Goal
(e.g. Goal 1)	(e.g. Module A)	(e.g. Module B)	(e.g. Goal 2)
Collective Context and Evidence to be held Consistent between Participating Modules			
Context		Evidence	
(e.g. Context C1, Assumption A2, etc.)		(e.g. Sn1, Sn 3, etc.)	
Resolved away Goal, Context and Solution References between Participating Modules			
Cross-Referenced Item	Source Module		Sink Module
(e.g. Away Goal AG3)	(e.g. Module B)		(e.g. Module A)

Table 1 - Proposed Format for Safety Case Contracts

An explanation of how a contract-based approach can be used to help design safe systems has been proposed (Bates et al 2003). They argue that sensibly chosen modularity can considerably benefit a system when under change. This should be beneficial for system changes as a result of upgrade, replacement through obsolescence and reconfiguration, all of which are objectives of IMA systems. The contract format proposed by Kelly and shown above in Table 1, is a good starting point in terms of broad safety integrity objectives. However, this information would only form part of the overall data needed to enable reconfiguration to occur. For instance, we have already determined that performance and resource requirements will be needed. There also needs to be some form of weighting or prioritisation allocated to safety information and performance information in order to determine how best to optimise the system.

5   IMA Methods of Reconfiguration

As previously described, this paper covers an incremental approach to arguing the safety of reconfiguration in an IMA system commencing with manual reconfiguration, followed by static automated reconfiguration, and finally, dynamic automated reconfiguration. This approach will enable safety experience to be gained through the increasing levels of reconfiguration complexity. Each of these methods is described below in more detail, but it is emphasised that these descriptions are not definitive, and each method may have variations in reality.

5.1   Manual Reconfiguration

This will consist of a limited number of predetermined configuration options. In its most basic form, a new configuration is chosen that best suits the intended use by the operator. However, variations of this method might include the possibility of limited automatic reconfiguration depending on certain faults. A decision making process that selects which configuration is best to use is required. This may be relatively straightforward for a small number of configurations, but may need the use of procedures for larger numbers of configurations. So, for instance if there is one configuration for each role of the platform, then it is simply a matter of choosing the configuration that matches that role. For more complex configurations, the operator might have to follow a flow chart that asks a number of questions that lead him to the best configuration depending on the answers supplied.

5.2   Static (Ground) Automated Reconfiguration

This is the next stage in the 'incremental' approach to IMA reconfiguration and represents an increase in the number of possible configurations that is too large to select manually as described above, hence, the need for automation. This brings a number of additional safety problems to resolve. First, it will be impossible to analyse all of the possible configuration permutations; therefore, it may not be possible to positively determine that the product (configuration) is error free. Consequently, there needs to be a combination of evidence showing that the process of reaching a particular configuration is error free, coupled with any testing of the configuration that can be achieved prior to use.

Secondly, a choice as to which optimisation algorithm to use has to be made. From the algorithm review (Jolliffe 2004) and the conclusions of (Stevens 2002), it would appear that Simulated Annealing has a consensus in its favour. However, the rationale for this conclusion is not particularly strong, and is dependent on its benefits for handling hard and soft rules. Another factor is the amount of time available to perform the optimisation process, which in turn has to be balanced with the need to conduct some testing of the chosen configuration.

5.3   Dynamic Reconfiguration

Dynamic reconfiguration is the final step in the proposed phased approach, and will be the most difficult version to argue that sufficient safety assurance can be achieved. This method of reconfiguration has all of the characteristics that the Static reconfiguration method offers, but the intent is that this can be achieved whilst the aircraft is operating. The technique will enable a change in the role of the aircraft in flight, thus enabling the aircraft to complete different missions without the need to return to base. Similarly, the aircraft will be able to automatically substitute for systems that have failed. This has the double benefit of maintaining some mission capability, though probably reduced, and adding another layer of safety. However, these two benefits could be applied at each other's expense, so a balance of priorities will be needed. Although these benefits are clearly advantageous, there are a number of problems that need to be addressed. These are discussed more fully (Jolliffe 2004), but include the current lack of processing power to run the optimisation algorithms quickly enough to enable reconfiguration to occur in real time. However, for the purposes of this paper it will be assumed that this technical obstacle has been overcome, so that the numerous safety issues can be discussed and subsequently addressed. Dynamic reconfiguration also has to take into account the need for a safe transition between configuration states. One other safety benefit of Dynamic reconfiguration is the possibility of fault reporting. If a system has detected a component failure that warrants a system reconfiguration, it should be able to record the information to enable maintainers to quickly locate and replace the failed component when the aircraft returns to base.

6   Other IMA Safety Issues

There are a number of IMA safety issues that do not directly affect IMA Blueprint safety. These are covered in some detail (Jolliffe 2004), but are simply listed below in order to emphasise that Blueprints are not the only IMA safety issue. They include:

Priority Deconfliction, Platform Roles (Peacetime or Wartime Scenarios), Operating System integrity, Communications integrity, Processor integrity, and there are also existing Safety Case constraints. The Safety Case will usually contain argument and evidence that demonstrate the safety of a system. This will include evidence from the Hazard Log and Hazard Tracking System, but is also concerned with other risks associated with the product including compliance failure with standards or contract terms. (Storey 1996) contains a suggested list of contents that might be expected to make up a typical safety case. Missing from this list is the overall safety argument, which should draw upon the individual pieces of evidence to produce a convincing rationale that the system is demonstrably safe.

The safety case also needs to be updated to reflect changes to the system, the problem for arguing reconfigurable IMA safety, is that the system is potentially always in a state of continual (or at least regular) change. Current safety analysis techniques can deal with this as long as the changes are predictable. Without this predictability, it will be impossible to present a reasoned safety argument for IMA. The reality is that the configurations that the IMA system can attain should be deterministic. However, the potential for IMA means that the number of configurations is potentially huge. Thus preventing timely or expedient analysis of the complete configuration set. Given this situation a number of potential solutions are discussed later for both the static and dynamic reconfiguration scenarios.

7 Progressing an IMA Blueprint Safety Argument

7.1 Technical Openness

The need for technical information to be made readily available in order to provide some agreed measure of integrity is well recognised, especially if modularity is to be an accepted means of developing Safety Cases for IMA systems. Such modules will require the use of safety contracts to enable goals to both be supported and requested depending on where the module resides in the overall safety argument. Therefore, if a subordinate module is offering support for a higher module, it needs to be able to express a means of providing that support. Ultimately this will take the form of evidence, which will include technical information where necessary.

However, even without the need for this information in support of the safety case, a lot of information will be required by the operating system to enable configuration optimisation and reconfiguration to occur. For example, a whole range of metrics will be needed to enable the optimisation algorithms to function correctly. In addition, this information will have to be provided in a common format, or at least a format that is readily understood by the algorithms. Currently, the need to provide this information is restricted to only those components that require access to each other. For IMA, however, this information needs to be available to the whole system in order that the system, through using the algorithms, can determine how it should reconfigure itself. This is potentially an area of very high risk for IMA, because existing federated systems are bound in an intricate web of contracts involving, design authorities, suppliers, customers, certification agencies, auditors and independent assessors. It is essential that these barriers to openness be broken down. Without a free exchange of information, it will be difficult to make an argument in favour of its safety, and there will certainly be insurmountable technical difficulties.

7.2 Fault Investigation

The need to correctly identify faults is paramount to the overall safety argument for blueprints, and hardware blueprints in particular. The implication is that in addition to the system being able to reconfigure itself to the next optimal configuration solution, the system should also have the ability to identify, and record the nature of the fault.

7.3 Search Algorithms

The ability to reconfigure these systems to enhance performance, mission capability and safety will be very restricted unless a means can be found to enable optimised configuration solutions to be quickly identified and implemented. Such processes need to be automated in order to cope with the complex factors that require consideration, and achieve an optimal solution within very limited time constraints. There are a number of algorithms that can be used for searching for optimal solutions of configurations. Each has different characteristics and, therefore, each has different advantages and disadvantages. The properties of some of these algorithms have been examined (Jolliffe 2004) to establish their relative merit in terms of demonstrating integrity.

7.4 Measurement of Optimisation

This is essential for determining if an optimal solution has been found, but it can also be a method of ensuring that minimum safety requirements have been met. So, for instance if a search reaches a point where a required set of conditions has been met, then the search terminates. To enable this, it is necessary to measure the value of each solution in some way, in order to compare it with the required value. Many attributes will need to be assigned values, which act as a means of prioritisation. These attributes or constraints need to be satisfied and this could be achieved by setting the optimisation algorithm some constraint targets to be met. So for instance if safety and performance are two such constraints, then the target for a peacetime mission scenario might have a high safety target, and lower performance target. This also assumes that both safety and performance can be measured to compare against the target set. In reality, providing such metrics is problematic, particularly for software.

8 IMA Blueprint Safety

This section takes those issues that are pertinent to IMA blueprint safety and attempt to construct a generic safety argument to support the use of IMA blueprints. As previously discussed the potential for complexity with IMA systems is likely to overwhelm the traditional approach taken for federated systems. However, it should be possible to show what a safety case should look like, or at least how safety for IMA can be argued. The approach taken below uses hazard analysis to determine the required integrity level of each IMA component using the ASAAC model as a basis. This information can then be used to determine what safety evidence is required.

8.1 Top-Level GSN Safety Argument

The GSN diagram below attempts to show the safety argument for IMA in each of the three methods of implementation. This is developed in much more detail (Jolliffe 2004). However, not all goals need to be achieved for each method, G4 is needed for additional goals required for static and dynamic reconfiguration, and G8 for additional goals required for dynamic reconfiguration.

Figure 4 is a top-down approach to arguing safety for IMA and there are a number of key elements that will determine ultimately whether a total safety argument can be constructed. Of the context boxes C1-3, C2 is likely to be the most awkward to fulfil, because the IMA system cannot properly be defined until its configuration is known. However, there will be a certain amount of system knowledge available, including the role requirements, which should be able to assist with identifying underlying system safety requirements. For instance, there will be certain safety issues on an aircraft, which will apply regardless of the actual system configuration used. An example might be that the undercarriage is not to be retracted when the aircraft has landed. However, care still has to be taken even with something as obvious as this if the aircraft in question is amphibious.

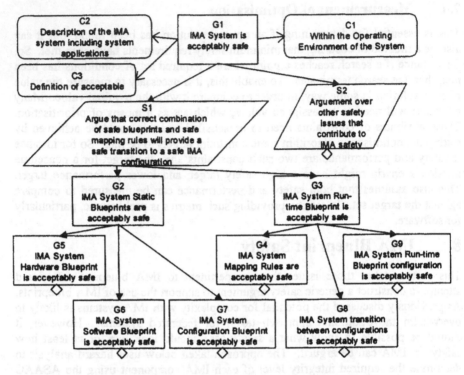

Figure 4 Top-Level GSN Safety Argument for IMA

Some of this ambiguity can be overcome when C2 is used in conjunction with C1. However, these gaps in system knowledge can be filled by information supplied and assumptions made for individual components of the static blueprints under goal G2. The strategies S1 and S2 are key to a successful overall safety argument. However, S2 is included to capture the issues that are not pertinent to IMA blueprint safety. S1 is based on what safety evidence is likely to be available. It is theoretically possible to produce product safety evidence that incontrovertibly demonstrates the safety of a particular configuration. This is the basis for current system certification. However, it is impractical to cover all potential configurations in this way, so S1 attempts to argue that there is sufficient evidence from the blueprints, the mapping rules and transition between configurations to demonstrate IMA configuration safety. These goals are shown at G2-4. Of these, G3 is likely to be the most difficult to satisfy, because of the unknown properties of optimisation. It may be possible to show that the final Run-Time configuration is safe without the need to demonstrate integrity of the optimisation process, but this becomes increasingly difficult with automated and dynamic reconfiguration. If it can be assumed that any reconfiguration on the ground is safe, then G4 is only applicable to dynamic reconfiguration.

The remainder of the goals deal with the safety of blueprints. The most important of these is G8, which covers the safety of the Run-Time blueprint. It will certainly not be sufficient to argue that the process integrity for determining the Run-Time blueprint is, by itself, sufficient evidence of safety. Apart from anything else, the process is far too complex to enable to support an argument based upon process evidence alone. Some form of product evidence is also required and the development of this goal (Jolliffe 2004) makes some recommendations as to how this can be achieved.

8.2   Safety Aspects of Blueprints

Looking more closely at the safety aspects of blueprints, particular attention to their safety is needed when the system is in one of the following modes: Power-up, operating normally, faulty, shut down and changes state (between configurations).

However, these aspects do not apply to all of the blueprints defined. In particular the Software, Hardware and Configuration blueprints are effectively fixed at any one point in time, since they represent availability of resources. However, the Run-Time blueprint will need to consider all of the above conditions. Of course if the software is modified, or the hardware updated, then they too may change, but that does not need to be taken into consideration when assessing integrity at one moment in time. Therefore, it is assumed that none of these blueprints will change state, though we do need to demonstrate that faults do not propagate and invalidate the required integrity of the Run-time blueprint. The Software, Hardware and Configuration blueprints will still need to be able to demonstrate their safety properties. This is not only to enable certification agencies to approve their use, but perhaps more importantly, to enable the safety properties to be used by the optimisation algorithms, through which the correct level of system integrity can be maintained. Before we can attempt to develop a safety argument for blueprints, there needs to be an analysis of the hazards associated with blueprints.

The HAZOP technique was used for each of the four types of blueprint and is detailed (Jolliffe 2004). The HAZOP technique has been chosen because it is a structured method of hazard analysis, which is less likely to overlook potential hazards. It is also the MoD's preferred technique (Defence Standard 00-56 1996). The choice of guidewords has been determined by those recommended by (Defence Standard 00-58). It is not feasible to guess what components might be included in any one blueprint, so this analysis is based upon generic hardware, software and configuration components. These can be treated as separate entities for these blueprints, but the Run-Time Blueprint will also have to consider how the components from each of the other blueprints might combine with one another. Again, this will be treated generically at this stage, since the number of permutations will make a full analysis impractical for this paper.

8.3   Blueprint Context

Although IMA probably has most potential in aircraft platforms, it can equally be applied in a number of other operating environments. A number of generic Safety Case Patterns (Kelly 1998) can be used in a variety of domains, however, all of them require some knowledge of the system hazards and/or system description. Unfortunately, such a description will not be known until it has been configured, so a Top-Down approach would not appear to be of much benefit at this stage. It also implies that ALARP is not a sound method for arguing IMA safety. From a system perspective, there are three main reasons for not using ALARP. First, there is the problem of identifying system hazards. Second, for automated reconfiguration, there is the problem of trying to achieve the optimal solution, when an acceptable solution is all that is required. Finally, it will be impractical to assign a proportion of safety to each component, when it may not be possible to determine how that component is likely to be used in any given configuration. For instance, it may be used in isolation, in parallel or in series with other components, or it may even be used to enable system redundancy.

This paints a somewhat pessimistic picture of the ability to define operating context, but there are ways of overcoming this. There is an argument that the choice of mapping rules can be used to define the operating context. Another approach to this problem is to consider a component of a blueprint that has been designed with a particular system-operating environment in mind. If such information or evidence is available then the gap between the top-level context C2 in Figure 4 and the blueprint safety argument can be bridged.

8.4   Blueprint Safety Claims

If this gap cannot be bridged then an alternative Bottom-Up approach may be required, because it can make use of safety claims. Now as Kelly, points out, this can only be used as supporting evidence, in other words, there needs to be some form of over arching argument that can be used to demonstrate blueprint integrity. Kelly has also identified General Construction Safety Case Patterns that include Diverse Argument and Safety Margin. Both have potential for arguing blueprint safety. However, of the two, the diverse argument will probably be the more difficult to prove in reality, partially due to the difficulty of defining diversity and also because it is notoriously difficult to demonstrate the complete absence of common mode failures. Hence, the need to include Common Mode/Cause Analysis as discussed earlier.

The Safety Margin pattern has much greater potential for IMA for two reasons; first each component of the blueprint in question, can be shown to have a 'safety margin', secondly, that safety margin can then be used by the optimisation algorithms to achieve overall system safety requirements. However, the weakness with this approach is that individual components may only be just safe enough in a given operating context. Outside of that context, there may be insufficient safety for that same component. Even if it remains just safe, there may still be a problem if the overall safety margin cannot be achieved. It is pointed out (Kelly 1998) that there is a danger of over-engineering if there is an excessive safety margin, which traditionally has been resolved by applying experienced judgement. That is more difficult to achieve with optimisation algorithms because as yet, there is little by way of experience to form such a judgement.

Although safety margins are relatively easy to apply with only one criterion, IMA uses a mixture of hardware and software components, whose means of measuring safety differ substantially. The means of connecting this mixture of components will also have a bearing on the overall safety integrity. Some are quantitative others are qualitative. Therefore, it would seem that some form of common denominator is required in order to measure safety and determine overall integrity of a blueprint. All four parts of the blueprint process will be looked at since each will impact on the overall integrity of the IMA system. However, ultimately it is the Run-Time blueprint that has to be demonstrably safe. Conceivably, there may be elements of the software and hardware blueprints that are not safe individually, but when combined in a particular configuration by the mapping rules, provide sufficient integrity. This will be explored later, but as already stated this project is looking at IMA in three steps, and it is simplest to consider the ground or manual reconfiguration case first.

8.4.1   Phase 1 Manual Reconfiguration

Each of the static blueprints was assessed from a safety argument perspective, using simple generic models. The models and the detail of these blueprint arguments were then found (G Jolliffe 2004). The hardware blueprint was examined at power-up, under normal operating conditions, at power down and under failure. The safety of the latter is considered most important and it was shown that the ability to identify faults is critical, thus requiring high integrity health monitoring. Maintaining an 'image' of the system configuration was also seen as a necessary requirement, in order to act as a reference point for any further reconfiguration. It may also assist with subsequent fault rectification.

A detailed generic HAZOP has been produced for each of the static blueprints (Jolliffe 2004), demonstrating how Hazards relating to these blueprints can be identified and assessed. The results can then be used to determine which goals are needed in the safety argument to address the hazards. The hardware HAZOP assumes that each (safety critical) component receives information and power and outputs data. Note that the processing of the information will be carried out by a suitable component in the Software blueprint, and the transfer of that information (or data) will be controlled by a suitable component in the Configuration Blueprint.

The examination of the software blueprint identified that specific safety targets could not be applied. However, in order to produce a rigorous safety argument, it is necessary to ensure that the development and testing processes are of the highest integrity. This includes the need for independent verification and validation. Although this is no different from the requirements for current high integrity software, it should be appreciated that IMA is likely to require greater dependence on high integrity software components to allow greater reconfiguration flexibility. It should be appreciated that software reconfiguration should only occur where the reconfigured software is of a similar or better integrity, unless it can be shown that not reconfiguring degrades integrity further.

The configuration blueprint safety argument identified the need for safety contracts, which should be completed as part of the initial system safety analysis and updated as the system is changed. However, there is a need to ensure that the optimisation algorithms can utilise this contract information via an information model. This should be considered for further research. Fundamentally, it is this blueprint more than any others that has to be proven to be safe. The preceding blueprints can all provide evidence of safety that can help with the overall safety argument, but the Run-time blueprint is what will determine the actual software configuration on the aircraft. However, for manual reconfiguration, it can be assumed that the system is safe prior to and post reconfiguration, since the system will be unpowered. A go/no go test will be required post reconfiguration, but the only other safety consideration for the manually reconfigured run-time blueprint is that any rigs or equipment used are also safe.

Similarly, for the Mapping Rules, the manually reconfigured system is not truly being optimised. Instead, a configuration is chosen from a limited number of predefined and pre-evaluated configurations. The main issue here is that the evaluation of each of the configurations will require considerable effort. This effort could be made more efficient with the use of modular safety cases and the use of safety contracts.

8.4.2   Phase 2 Static Reconfiguration

Since the Hardware, Software and Configuration Blueprints can be assumed to remain the same as for the Manual/ground reconfiguration case above, there will be no additional safety requirements for the Static Reconfiguration case. The principal additional safety consideration for the run-time blueprint is that the reconfigured system needs to be demonstrably safe. This is primarily because there are many more permutations of configuration compared with the manual reconfiguration scenario that cannot be pre-assessed for integrity. Post reconfiguration testing and a 'sanity' checking are recommended, however, neither can be considered foolproof.

Some additional confidence can be gained by comparing a reconfigured system with known configuration patterns that have been proven to be safe. If a particular configuration can be shown safe, then variations of that configuration could have implied safety characteristics if the variation provided a safety benefit. As long as the differences can be shown to be either similar or to improve safety, then an 'at least as safe as' argument can be made that the new configuration is also safe. Nevertheless the run-time blueprint safety argument is still relatively weak and needs evidence of integrity from the optimisation process to provide additional reassurance of overall integrity.

The choice of algorithm must be made based on a number of factors including; the type of problem; the size of the problem; computing power available and the importance of optimal against near optimal solutions. For example, it may be quite acceptable to produce a near optimal solution as long as mission requirements are met and safety requirements are not compromised. These are called System Design Factors (SDFs) (Nicholson 1998). Once these have been identified, it is then possible to address other issues such as the granularity of measures used for evaluation, and the speed at which the evaluation is to occur.

8.4.3   Phase 3 Dynamic Reconfiguration

As previously stated, dynamic reconfiguration is still largely aspirational. Though some limited automatic reconfiguration is technically achievable now, the computational power to permit full system reconfiguration is still some way off. Unlike the scenarios for the previous phases, dynamic reconfiguration has to take due account of the initial system state, the transition between states, the correctness of fault detecting and reporting and the selection of appropriate an optimisation algorithm. Fault reporting has already been mentioned under the hardware blueprint summary above and prior to the need for change, the initial system state can be assumed safe. A further factor is the need to complete the reconfiguration in real time; thus, optimisation time is now a constraint. However, this imposition makes it more likely that an optimal solution will take too long to identify, and there is a higher risk that a solution may not even be acceptable.

The transition between states may be achieved using a maintained 'image' of the initial configuration, such that system settings, data values, etc can be synchronised before transition occurs. However, an incorrect reconfiguration is more problematic and can occur for two reasons. The first of these reasons is the occurrence of a hardware fault, which should be detectable, and thus prompt a subsequent reconfiguration. The second reason is due to a failure to achieve the correct reconfiguration as a result of an algorithm error. This is much more difficult to detect, unless the error is obvious to the operator. Clearly, much depends upon the integrity of the optimisation algorithm. Although there is a very real potential improvement in safety through the use of reconfiguration, it needs to be argued and correctly prioritised.

In summary, of the four additional safety criteria that need to be considered for Dynamic reconfiguration listed above, only the safety of the initial state is without any major problems to resolve. The transition between states has to overcome the potential step change in real time data whilst the transition is occurring. Fault reporting relies upon fault detection, which is satisfactory for hardware faults, but an incorrect reconfiguration solution will be difficult to identify unless the error is obvious to the operator. The selection of the optimisation algorithm is made more difficult due to the time constraint imposed by the real time environment. This will lead to compromise solutions, and it could be deduced that the potential for erroneous solutions will increase as a result.

Apart from further research in this area, the best means of achieving integrity is probably through the phased approach proposed in this report. As confidence in the use of these algorithms grows through the previous phases, so an argument can be built based upon previous experience. Currently, however, this remains a weak argument. In the meantime, the technical difficulties of implementing dynamic reconfiguration can be advanced by the use of look-up tables, which is akin to a semi-automatic Ground Reconfiguration condition.

9 Conclusion of IMA Blueprint Safety Progress

The aim of this paper was to explore the possibilities of developing safety cases for IMA blueprints. The ultimate objective of dynamic reconfiguration is both technically difficult to achieve and difficult to determine safety integrity. Therefore, it was proposed to adopt a three phased approach. For each phase, each of the various blueprints defined were subjected to a hazard analysis, using the HAZOP process. From there, a safety argument can be produced for each.

9.1 Conclusion of Overall IMA Safety Issues

A number of alternative approaches to IMA safety were discussed which include Safety in Concept and Technical Openness. Safety in Concept is advancing the notion that if safety can be incorporated at the design stage, then it should follow that it can be incorporated within the conceptual stage as well. This requires further thought and consideration, but the fact that IMA can potentially be fault tolerant already demonstrates that safety is part of the system concept.

Technical Openness stresses the need for sharing information. This is an ongoing requirement for evaluating system safety currently, but for IMA, the need to share information will be essential to not only determine system integrity, but is likely to be necessary to achieve technical success as well. Although this is a very high-risk issue for IMA, no recommendations have been made at this time. This is because each stakeholder has a personal stake in overcoming the current problems regarding the withholding of information. Therefore, they will need to work together to solve this problem, but it would be inappropriate to provide advice on how this should be achieved, since much will depend upon the relationships developed between individual suppliers and their customers. However, efforts are already being made to address this, which should resolve this issue.

References

ASAAC Phase II Stage 1 - Stage 1 Executive Summary, 1999.

Aviation Today Magazine Website, http://www.aviationtoday.com/cgi/av/show_mag.cgi?pub=av, 2003.

Bates S et al (2003). Safety Case Architectures to Complement a Contract-Based Approach to Designing Safe Systems, Proceedings of 21st International System Safety Conference, Chicago, 2003.

Conmy P (2003). Philippa Conmy's Home page, http://www-users.cs.york.ac.uk/~philippa/IMA_LINKS.html , 2003.

Defence Standard 00-56 Safety Management Requirements for Defence Systems (Pt 1) Iss 2, 1996.

Defence Standard 00-58 HAZOP Studies on Systems Containing Programmable Electronics Iss 2, 2000.

Jolliffe G (2004). Exploring the Possibilities Towards a Preliminary Safety Case for IMA Blueprints, MSc Project, Department of Computer Science, University of York, 2004.

Kelly T P (1998). Arguing Safety – A Systematic Approach to Managing Safety Cases, Department of Computer Science, University of York, 1998.

Kelly T P, McDermid J A (1998). Safety Case Patterns - Reusing Successful Arguments, In Proceedings of IEE Colloquium on Understanding Patterns and Their Application to System Engineering, 1998.

Kelly T P (2001). Concepts and Principles of Compositional Safety Case Construction, Department of Computer Science, University of York, 2001.

Kemp J (2000). ASAAC – An Overview Issue: 01, 2000.

MoD ADAS(Air) Aviation Support Vision Website, www.ams.mod.uk/ams/content/docs/fse/fse-avs/inmodavs.htm, 2002.

Murray T (2002). Specification for a Run-Time Blueprint Generator, QinetiQ Report, 2002.

Nicholson M (1998). Selecting a Topology for Safety-Critical Real-Time Control Systems, Department of Computer Science, University of York, 1998.

Rushby J (2002). Modular Certification – CSL technical report, June 2002.

Stevens B (2002). IMA Configuration – Preliminary Blueprint Description, QinetiQ Report, 2002.

Storey N (1996). Safety Critical Computer Systems, Addison Wesley 1996.

Thales' A380 website http://www.thalesgroup.com/all/pdf/a380avionics.pdf, 2003.

Tudor N (2002). Realising Integrated Modular Avionics In Military Aircraft, 2002.

Modular Certification of Integrated Modular Systems

James Blow, Andrew Cox and Paul Liddell
BAE Systems, Warton Aerodrome
Preston, Lancashire, PR4 1AX

Abstract

This paper presents ongoing research into the modular certification of Integrated Modular Systems (IMS) within BAE Systems. An IMS is an open systems approach to the construction of systems from a set of standard hardware and software modules. Modular certification is the modular safety assessment of such systems. The aim is to reduce the certification costs of a system following a change to the system. To achieve this, a strategy has been proposed that is based on the concept of change isolation through the use of rely/guarantee contracts. The strategy advocates a more product-oriented approach to the development of safety cases for IMS.

1 Introduction

This paper discusses the modular certification of Integrated Modular Systems (IMS). IMS is an open systems approach to the construction of systems from a set of standard hardware and software modules, each of which has well defined interfaces.

It is often currently the case that the cost of re-certifying a system following a change is related to both the size and complexity of system and the size and complexity of the change. As systems increase in size and complexity the ability to identify and to justify that the minimum re-certification work necessary to ensure the required levels of safety have been maintained following change becomes increasingly difficult. This can prove to be very costly.

In order to address this, BAE Systems has developed a strategy for IMS that is based on the concept of change isolation. Such an approach should enable reduction in the impact of system size and complexity from the cost of re-certification such that, for a majority of change scenarios, the cost of re-certification is proportional to change size. This is achieved by minimising the level of architecture safety analysis required to re-validate and re-verify an IMS architecture within the overall system certification argument following a change.

The strategy proposes to use existing safety assessment techniques but to restructure the safety argument so that the IMS architectural aspects of the safety analysis are insulated from change. The impact of this strategy on lifecycle costs is expected to be that initial certification costs are not expected to reduce, but the cost of re-certification is expected to reduce.

To be able to restructure the safety argument, however, requires an alternative to the existing process-oriented approach, where safety is determined by appealing to the quality of a recommended or prescribed development process. These techniques, while sufficient, are at the equipment level and consequentially system focused. Following a sizeable change the impact on system safety can only practically be assessed by the re-application of significant elements of the process to ensure all potential safety impacts have been assessed. This is potentially very costly.

To address this issue, the certification strategy primarily, but not exclusively, involves looking at the use of certification evidence, rather than its production, as is currently the case. In other words, a product-oriented approach is more likely to be successful. This is particularly true for military systems given the likely changes in Defence Standard 00-56 Issue 3 (which has not been formally issued at the time of publication) [Def Stan 00-56 1996].

By considering the evidence it is possible to structure the safety argument using modules. The IMS architecture components can then be generic and the safety and certification evidence associated with the architecture inserted into the overall system safety argument without demanding system wide re-validation and re-verification. Product oriented safety assessment is the application of best practice within the safety community.

Due to its product basis, the product oriented safety case will reflect the modularity of the proposed architecture. The safety dependencies that the components place upon each other should therefore be made more explicit to assist identification of a reduced re-qualification activity to support any particular change. This is achieved by the strict definition of interfaces between modular components of the architecture. For safety assessment, these module interfaces are defined in terms of rely/guarantee contracts, which describe guaranteed services to other modules based on assumed receipt of services.

The structure of this paper is as follows. Firstly, an overview of IMS is presented. The paper then looks at rely/guarantee contracts in some detail, including their development, definition, representation, composition, validation and violation. Their use, both by directly by engineers and within the safety argument, is also addressed. Finally, conclusions are made and future work detailed.

2 Integrated Modular Systems

A correctly used IMS architecture should enable effective management of system complexity, obsolescence, system upgrades and improved system availability.

IMS hardware consists of a number of Line Replaceable Modules (LRM) connected to a common backplane that provides electrical power and optical communication paths. The LRMs and backplane are housed in an enclosure called a rack, which provides cooling to the LRMs and a degree of protection from the external environment. For example a set of standard core processing LRMs might include a Data Processing Module, a Signal Processing Module, a Graphics Processing Module, A Power Conversion Module, a Network Support Module and a Mass Memory Module.

The software architecture in IMS is three layered:

* Application Layer (AL), which consists of the software applications that provide the platform specific software functionality.
* Operating System Layer (OSL), which includes a system independent real-time operating system that provides a standard set of basic services such as process scheduling and communication. These services are made available to the applications via a standard interface (APOS) that is independent of the application software language. The OS provides the Application Layer with hardware independence.
* Module Support Layer (MSL), which is a set of hardware-specific services presenting a standard interface (MOS) to the OS that provides the OSL with hardware independence for the application software.

Blueprints are standard format descriptions of application requirements, resource capabilities and acceptable system configurations that map applications onto resources. As such, the blueprint captures the behavioural characteristics, performance and interfaces of the system and its components. There are two types of blueprints:

* Design Time Blueprints that are used in the process of developing an IMS
* Run Time Blueprints that are a component of the final system, providing the run time system with the information required to configure the system and control the scheduling of processing and communication.

Software applications consist of a set of processes, defined as being a unit of code that can be analysed and scheduled, which are connected and communicate via virtual channels. The channels enable process location transparency, meaning a process can read from and send to other processes without knowing the location of these other processes. Furthermore, they enable application abstraction and are predictable in terms of time and resource consumption. For inter-module communications transfer connections are used, providing a unidirectional means of communicating with the various device drivers contained in the MSL.

3 Rely/Guarantee Contracts

To motivate the use of rely/guarantee contracts, consider the flow of a message being sent from a Process A to a Process B. Whilst conceptually the flow is directly between them, in reality the flow of the message is through the architecture on which they have been placed. Safety analysis must therefore track any safety properties onto that specific implementation. This is a very detailed activity that is very brittle in the presence of change. Placing contracts, which constrain the use of the component such that a predictable response can be guaranteed, on the interface between the functional layer and the architecture on which the functions reside limits these problems.

Although all the analysis is still required, it is now in the context of the guarantee, not the detailed implementation of the architecture. This provides better insulation under changes since any changes do not affect the guarantee. Furthermore, the guarantee can then be used in the construction of a high-level safety argument for the system.

Since safety is a system-wide property, individual system components such as an IMS hardware module or operating system cannot be certified as safe in isolation. Any stand-alone certification of the underlying IMS operating system layer and hardware infrastructure can only be partial with respect to the whole system safety case, identifying the effect of IMS infrastructure failures on its ability to uphold its contractual obligations/guarantees as defined by the interfaces.

Full certification can only be performed once the consequences of these contract failures can be followed through for a specific application hosted on the IMS architecture within the system's environmental and operational context. Therefore, for service level guarantees to be a viable concept around which a safety case can be constructed the services provided by the IMS infrastructure must be correctly implemented and its guaranteed behaviour must be shown to be safe. Furthermore, applications, and their use of the IMS infrastructure, must be shown to be safe.

3.1 Contract Definition

A rely/guarantee contract is an abstract representation of a mutual agreement between a consumer component and a producer component, which specifies what will be done by both (consumer - rely, producer - guarantee). It should only specify on what a service is reliant and what is guaranteed by the architecture, but not specify how the guranteed behaviour is achieved. Two types of contract have been identified:

- *Primitive* contracts, which are against the basic elements of a system. For example, a contract on a specific APOS service call.
- *Composite* contracts, which are against a system property. They are formed from the composition of multiple primitive contracts.

The abstract behaviour represented by a contract can be service driven (i.e. direct calls through an interface), configuration driven (i.e. dependent on the system's configuration data) or a combination of both. Furthermore, contracts can potentially be produced at all system interfaces, throughout the engineering hierarchy. Consequently, the types of behaviour against which properties can be contracted include:

- Functional, temporal and failure behaviour
- Physical environment (for example thermal, vibrational, EMC)
- Resource usage

This raises issues to do with meaningful and sensible scoping of contracts. For instance, the focus of this paper is on the IMS architecture. At this level it is not sensible, nor indeed feasible, to be considering issues such as electromagnetic compatibility. At module or higher levels, however, it may be advantageous to do so.

3.2 Contract Representation

To represent primitive and composite contracts a tabular representation has been adopted, as shown by Table 1.

All contracts for system components are represented in this way. For some of these components certain behaviours will be uniform, i.e. the functionality will be the same. This essentially means a library populated with different ways to achieve the same functional behaviour. Different components, however, are differentiated by their non-functional properties.

For example, the service Send Message (blocking and non-blocking) could be implemented using ATM, Optic or Copper. For each of these, the non-functional (timing, resource and failure) behaviour is very different but their contracts are still represented in a uniform way. Similarly their functional implementation is very different but their contracts are represented in a uniform way and they have the same behaviour.

Example Contract				
RELY				
Condition	*Description*	*Detectable*	*Rely not Satisfied Behaviour*	*Analysis*
GUARANTEE				
Clause	*Post-condition*			*Result*

Table 1. Example Contract Table.

The rely of a contract has one or more measurable and testable conditions, each of which is a necessary condition for establishing the guarantee clause. Each rely also:

- Has an identifier (*Condition*) and associated description (*Description*)
- Identifies whether run-time or static analysis is required to detect the rely condition (*Detectable*)

- Records the behaviour in the case when the rely condition does not hold (*Rely not Satisfied Behaviour*)
- Records the analysis necessary to demonstrate the rely condition holds (*Analysis*)

Each guarantee clause has:

- A single *post-condition*, which defines the guaranteed behaviour within the scope of the conjunction of the rely conditions
- A *result*, which gives the value/result returned from the provisioning layer

3.3 Contract Development

To develop rely/guarantee contracts at least two artefacts have been required: a definition of the interface over which the contract applies and a definition of the behaviour of the service providing layer on which the interface resides. The following generic steps have been undertaken:

- Specification of primitive contracts (the derivation of the primitive contracts is project specific)
- Validation of primitive contracts (their completeness, consistency and correctness)
- Identification and specification of composite contracts.
- Validation of composite contracts
- Production of checklists. A checklist of Boolean conditions which, if shown true, demonstrate that the desirable system level behaviour has been achieved.

Each of these stages are discussed in the following subsections. The principal outputs of the method described above will be a set of valid primitive contracts, a set of valid composite contracts, derived by composing valid primitive contracts and a set of checklists.

3.4 Contract Composition

Composite contracts are system level contracts that are formed from the combination of multiple primitive contracts to produce a contract against a system property. They are required since a single primitive contract will be insufficient to mitigate a system level hazard.

They are deduced by reasoning 'backwards' from a desired post-condition through the consideration of the dependencies between the rely conditions of one contract and the guarantee clause of the contract with which it is being composed. The composition process takes into consideration issues such as scheduling and the trusted function call mechanism.

3.5 Contract Validation

Validation of contracts will consist of arguing their completeness, consistency and correctness.

Completeness is concerned with showing that *all* rely conditions have been identified. In practice it is not possible to achieve this, either arguing informally or through mathematical analysis. It is vital, however, that the rely conditions identified are as complete as they practically can be. This means having techniques and processes that can be used to effectively drive out the conditions.

It will also be necessary to demonstrate the *internal* and *external* consistency of a primitive contract. Internal consistency is concerned with demonstrating that a primitive contract's rely conditions are not contradictory. External consistency aims to demonstrate that contracts of different services do not contradict each other.

Finally, it will be necessary to argue the correctness of a contract by showing that the primitive contract as a whole is valid.

Since composing already validated primitive contracts creates composite contracts, the validation of composites will need to focus on 'emergent' properties introduced during the composition process. Furthermore, it will be necessary to validate the 'compatibility' of the primitive contracts that are being composed.

3.6 Contract Violations

Whilst contracts can capture all normal behaviour, the same cannot be said of abnormal behaviour. To address this potential problem, the use of contract *violations* and architectural classifications based on hazard classifications (for example, catastrophic, critical, etc), as a means of passing faults in a generic fashion, has been proposed. Abnormal behaviour can then be classified according to whether or not it can be captured in a contract.

A further problem, however, is that a system's context is not available when analysing the IMS target contract violations in isolation, and so their severity cannot be assessed in terms of the effects they have on the system's operational environment. Contract violation severities are therefore defined for the IMS architecture in terms of the "level of containment of the deviation" from the contract guarantees (i.e. by defining the degree to which a contract failure has the potential to propagate throughout the system).

A contract violation is therefore similar to a traditional hazard, however it only measures the *'potential'* risk to system safety of each contract violation; the actual safety risk can only be determined when the full system context is known.

3.7 Use of Contracts

Since contracts will have been derived from extensive requirements analysis, they will contain much detailed information. A project engineer will not, however, have the time to assess the contracts or contract compliance. Consequentially, the contracts are used to derive checklists. A checklist is effectively a set of Boolean criteria with which to demonstrate a system's compliance with the contracts. Checklist information will include a description of the test, the type of evidence required and whether or not the check can be automated (either initially or subsequently).

Use of contracts within a system means that testing will therefore become a checklist directed activity, which will ideally fully automated. Such a change will inevitably have some impact on process. The set of checks that need to be undertaken, however, is likely to remain largely unchanged to the current set. It is possible, however, that it will be necessary to identify additional information and, as such, it will be necessary to identify where this information exists.

4 Safety Case Development

To argue that a system has met its safety requirements, a safety case must be constructed. To use the rely/guarantee contract in a safety case:

- The guaranteed behaviour is 'assumed' in the safety argument. The system designer will have to argue that safety depends in part on a predictable computing architecture. In other words, the safety argument is constructed on the assumption that the behaviour at the IMS interfaces is in accordance with the guarantee.
- The guaranteed behaviour is demonstrated as a one-off exercise, with the limiting condition that the rely conditions are satisfied (although, of course, the safety case must undergo continued maintenance in respect of changes to functionality). The behaviour of the IMS components must be shown to be predictable at some point in the safety argument. Using the rely/guarantee approach a generic argument for predictability is generated within the limits of the rely conditions. This relies on the explicit identification of the rely conditions.
- The system verifies that its use complies with the rely constraints. Having shown that the safety case of the system is dependent on the assumed (i.e. guaranteed) behaviour of the IMS architecture, and that the IMS architecture has been shown to comply with the guarantee if the rely conditions are satisfied, the final part involves verifying that the system's use of the IMS architecture is compliant with the rely constraints.

The first two bullet points above should be reasonably stable over time since the safety assumptions on the IMS architecture should not change frequently, neither should the demonstration that the IMS components satisfy the rely/guarantee contract. With respect to life cycle costs, the recurring cost of the certification activity will be the final bullet point, which checks that the rely constraints have been satisfied.

Figure 1 shows the architecture of the modular safety case and the existence of safety arguments, presented using the Goal Structuring Notation (GSN) [Kelly 1998], for each of the modules within the software architecture. The OSL safety argument is based on the assumed receipt of guaranteed services from the MSL, whilst the Application Level argument is based on the assumed receipt of services guaranteed by the OSL.

A template safety case fragment has been produced for each primitive contract, which argues the contract's validity (with respect to the requirements documents from which they were derived) and its correct implementation. Since the fragment is generic, the key difference between each different contract's fragment is the required evidence.

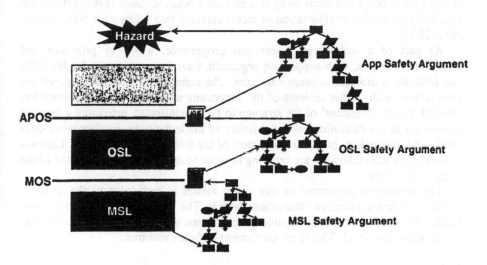

Figure 1. Modular Safety Case Architecture

5 Conclusions and Future Work

This paper has described an approach to the modular certification of IMS that is based on the inherent modularity of such systems and the use of rely/guarantee contracts between system components.

Earlier the paper identified the types of behaviour for which it is possible to contract (for example, timing, functional and failure). BAE Systems has so far focused on the production of functional contracts, although good progress on the development of temporal contacts through collaboration with the BAE Systems funded Dependable Computing Systems Centre at the University of York.

Although an approach has been proposed to address the issue of contract failures, the work does require further attention. The specification of physical/environmental contracts, meanwhile, is outside the scope of this paper. The issue of the mathematical formality of the contracts is another issue for future consideration.

Rely/guarantee contracts are an established technology (the classic example being [Meyer 1992]) and the approach advocated in this paper represents another useful application of such constructs. The Defence Aerospace Research

Partnership (DARP) is also looking at the use of contracts but specifically within a Model Driven Architectures (MDA) framework for high integrity real time systems (HIRTS) [Conmy 2003]. QinetiQ are also undertaking work related to contracts, particularly within the context of systems that contain COTS components [Pygott 2003].

The safety argument for the modular system has been produced using standard GSN [Kelly 1998]. A modular version of GSN [Kelly 2001] has been produced and further investigations need to be conducted to ascertain whether there are any advantages to be gained from using this extended notation. Such investigations are also likely to involve consideration of recent research into safety case architectures [Bate 2003].

As part of a technology maturation programme, a set of primitive and composite contracts, with supporting argument, have been produced for the OSL and MSL for a modular mission computer. The contracts have been validated via peer review, with further reviews of the supporting argument. The experience has enabled 'proof of concept' of the strategy to be demonstrated, providing a level of confidence in the suitability and practicality of the techniques. Further work does need to be undertaken, however, in respect of the integration of modules. Liaisons with certification authorities are ongoing in order to achieve their acceptance of the proposed strategy.

The modularity expressed in this paper relates in particular to the avionics architecture and application interactions with it. The same techniques can be used to identify interfaces between application processes, ensuring robustness to change at the application level. This is another aspect of future research.

References

Bate I., Bates S and Hawkins R. (2003). Safety Case Architectures to Complement a Contract Based Approach to Designing Safe Systems, Department of Computer Science, University of York, TN/2003/5, March 2003

Conmy P, Nicholson M, and Mc Dermid J. (2003). Safety Assurance Contracts for Integrated Modular Avionics, 8th Australian Workshop on Safety Critical Systems and Software, Canberra, CRPIT Vol. 33, pp69-78, October 2003

Defence Standard 00-56 (1996). Safety Management Requirements for Defence Systems, Issue 2, United Kingdom Ministry of Defence, December 1996

Kelly T P. (1998). Arguing Safety – A Systematic Approach to Safety Case Management. PhD Thesis. Department of Computer Science, University of York, 1998

Kelly T P. (2001). Concepts and Principles of Compositional Safety Case Construction. COMSA/2001/1/1. Department of Computer Science. University of York, 2001

Meyer B. (1992). Applying Design by Contract. IEEE Computer 1992; 25:40-52

Pygott C H. (2003). Compositional Safety Cases for COTS Assessment, QinetiQ, QinetiQ/KI/TIM/TR021996, March 2003

TECHNOLOGIES FOR DEPENDABILITY

The Effects of Timing and Collaboration on Dependability in the Neonatal Intensive Care Unit

Gordon D. Baxter
Department of Psychology, University of York
York, UK

Juliana Küster Filipe
School of Informatics, University of Edinburgh
Edinburgh, UK

Angela Miguel
Department of Computer Science, University of York
York, UK

Kenneth Tan
Department of Paediatrics, St James's University Hospital,
Leeds, UK

1 Introduction

Computer-based systems are now routinely deployed in many complex dynamic domains, such as aviation and industrial process control. The critical nature of these systems means that their operators rely on them to do the right thing at the right time when called upon. In other words, they are expected to have a high level of what Laprie (1995) defines as dependability. To date dependability research has largely focused on developing techniques for improving the dependability of hardware and software in safety critical applications (e.g., Leveson, 1995). Dependability, however, is a property of the whole socio-technical system: people, computers and context. It is therefore important not only to understand these components, but also how the interactions between them affect dependability.

A wealth of research into human-machine interaction (HMI) has emerged over the last two decades (e.g., see Baecker & Buxton, 1987; and Baecker, Grudin, Buxton, & Greenberg, 1995). One obvious aspect of HMI that affects dependability, is the temporal properties of the interaction. Delays in system response times, for example, can make tasks more complex, and may lead to errors (Johnson & Gray, 1996). Such issues are present in most complex dynamic domains, but particularly in real-time systems, including medicine (e.g., Combi & Shuhar, 1997).

This paper considers how timing issues in HMI affect dependability in one specialised branch of medicine: neonatal intensive care. A case study was carried out in the Neonatal Intensive Care Unit (NICU) at St James' University Hospital (SJUH), Leeds. An expert system, FLORENCE (Fuzzy LOgic for REspiratory Neonatal Care Expert), is being developed at SJUH (Tan et al., 2003) to help less

195

experienced staff make decisions about changes to the ventilators that are regularly used in treating premature babies.

One of the goals of the study was to identify any timing issues involved in the current socio-technical system that implements the practice of neonatal intensive care. More particularly, the aim was to identify and analyse those aspects of timing that affect how staff interact with the equipment in the NICU which places requirements on the design and use of FLORENCE. Once FLORENCE is in place, the dependability of the new system (including FLORENCE) should be at least equal to the dependability of the system without FLORENCE.

Section 2 of the paper provides an overview of the NICU environment at SJUH and an overview of the case study. Sections 3 and 4 highlight and analyse the timing and collaboration issues identified by the study and how they contribute to the dependability of the system of patient care. Section 5 examines how the introduction of FLORENCE could affect the timing and collaboration aspects of dependability. Section 6 briefly discusses the completeness of the case study methods in identifying timing and collaboration issues and considers the available alternatives. Finally, Section 7 summarises the work and suggests how it could be extended in the future to evaluate the impact of FLORENCE.

2 The Neonatal Intensive Care Unit

When a premature baby arrives in the NICU it is often placed on mechanical ventilation to help it deal with respiratory ailments, particularly Respiratory Distress Syndrome (RDS). This is a self-regulating disease, caused by the lungs not having developed sufficiently to produce the levels of surfactant required to facilitate gaseous exchange during respiration (e.g., Rennie & Roberton, 2002). The main aim during the period of ventilation is to stabilise the baby, such that its blood gas and pH levels remain within some predefined range. These parameters which are continuously monitored using a Neotrend multi-parameter intra-arterial sensor (Philips, 2001), cannot be directly controlled. They are affected by the baby's respiration, however, which is controlled using a Babylog 8000+ ventilator (Bartholomew, Newell, Dear, & Brownlee, 1994).

Much of the front line care of the babies is performed by nursing staff and junior doctors (Senior House Officers, SHOs). The SHOs normally only work in the NICU for six months as part of their job rotation. In general, the SHOs perform most of the interventions on the ventilator in acute situations where the baby has RDS, calling on more experienced members of staff as appropriate. One of the goals of FLORENCE is to empower the front line carers by helping them to more rapidly learn to make correct decisions about which interventions to make.

A Cognitive Task Analysis of the work in the NICU was performed in three stages (for full details of the methods see Baxter, Monk, Tan, Dear, & Newell, Submitted). First, domain and context familiarisation was carried out. Second, the Critical Decision Method (CDM; Klein, Calderwood, & MacGregor, 1989) was used to analyse decisions surrounding use of the ventilator. Third, naturalistic observation of the use of the ventilator in situ was carried out. These stages are briefly summarised below.

The first stage involved bootstrapping into the domain. In order to understand the language of the domain and the physical and social context in which FLORENCE was to be deployed, a lightweight version of the rich picture method was used (Monk, 1998). Eight members of staff at the unit were interviewed (including one administrator) to identify their roles and responsibilities.

In the second stage the CDM was used to analyse the decision making processes involved in making interventions using the ventilator. Semi-structured interviews were carried out with eight members of staff: four front line carers (nurses and SHOs) and four experts (registrars and consultants). The interviewees were asked to recall incidents where they had been involved in making decisions about changes to the ventilator settings.

The final stage involved a period of observation of work at the unit, focusing solely on a single baby. An earlier neonatal care study which used observation periods of between one and two hours, found that interactions with computerised equipment were fairly infrequent (Alberdi et al., 2001). Their observations were carried out at various times of the day over several months, and related to the unit as a whole, rather than just the NICU. Alberdi et al. were concerned mainly with the way that people used computerised monitoring equipment in neonatal care per se, whereas the goals of this study are more tightly constrained. Here, the main aim was to identify timing issues around use of the ventilator in dealing with RDS, with a view to informing the development of FLORENCE. Since RDS is a self-regulating disease which only lasts a matter of a few days, the baby normally recovers within about a week. Any interventions involving changes to ventilator settings will thus tend to be concentrated within that period. It was therefore decided to use observation sessions lasting two hours on each of the days when a baby was connected to the ventilator.

The findings of the case study are summarised in Table 1 as implications for the design and use of FLORENCE. In addition to these findings, several timing and collaboration issues were also identified which relate to the wider socio-technical system of the NICU. These issues are described in more detail below, where their implications for dependability are also considered.

3 Timing

In health care, the introduction of new technology often disrupts the socio-technical system in which the technology is embedded. The way that information is distributed, and the tasks that are performed are adversely affected, which has a knock-on effect on the relationships between health care professionals and other staff (Berg, 2001). It is therefore important to understand the timing and collaboration issues that exist before the new technology is introduced, so that the impact of the new technology can be properly evaluated. The main concern here is to understand how these issues influence the dependability of the socio-technical system.

Staff need to be aware of any contingencies (such as ignoring anomalous data) before implementing FLORENCE's suggestions.
FLORENCE should prompt staff to follow the DOPE mnemonic.
The FLORENCE audible alarm needs to be distinctive.
Staff need to be trained how to respond to a FLORENCE alarm.
The size of the text used to display FLORENCE's advice needs to legible when staff are stood at the ventilator.
The wording of FLORENCE's suggestions needs to be clear and unambiguous (e.g., PIP Up by 2 to 16)
Space needs to be made available for the PC running FLORENCE, and a mouse (unless a touch screen is used).
Consideration needs to be given to what data from FLORENCE needs to be included with existing paper records.
It must be possible to print data from FLORENCE for inclusion with the other patient records.
There needs to be a power socket available for the PC running FLORENCE.
The limitations of FLORENCE need to be made explicit to staff.
FLORENCE should check the current ventilator settings before deciding what changes are required.
Staff need to be made aware of the potential data redundancy problem, because FLORENCE will display trends of data that are available on the ventilator and Neotrend.
FLORENCE should be able to explain its decisions on request.
Staff should be able to override FLORENCE's suggestions, as long as they can supply a reason for doing so.
FLORENCE should attempt to avoid generating intermittent alarms.

Table 1. Implications for the design and deployment of FLORENCE identified by the case study.

The control of a baby's blood gases has some similarities to industrial process control. The basic control loop of perceiving, deciding and acting, for example, is common to both. The situation in the NICU is, in several respects, more complicated, however. Whereas continuous data sampling has been routine in process control for many years, it is only through the recent introduction of the Neotrend that reliable blood gas data can be collected continuously. Staff in the NICU have to effect control by monitoring the babies condition and, where appropriate, adjusting the ventilator settings and administering the necessary drugs.

The situation in the NICU is also somewhat more complex because the problems faced by an individual baby are partly determined by its gestation period at birth, and its birth weight. Generally, the closer a baby is to the normal term of a pregnancy (40 weeks) at birth the less likely it is to suffer from RDS, because its lungs will be more fully developed. These factors affect how long it takes to treat an individual baby and stabilise its condition.

After the ventilator has initially been configured, it will normally only be changed in response to acute situations. The decision to change the ventilator settings is normally made after discussions between a team of people. This is followed by the physical action of changing the settings. There are obvious timing and collaboration issues involved here.

3.1 Timing Issues

Examples of the timing issues that were explicitly described by clinical staff during interviews are listed in Table 2. It should be noted that the results of the CDM emphasised that the overriding concern of the NICU staff is the clinical outcome, rather than the amount of time available to stabilise the baby's condition.

3.2 Timing and Dependability

In dynamic complex domains such as medicine, time is an inherent determinant of system dependability: if the system cannot produce a safe outcome in a timely manner, then it cannot be regarded as dependable. There is a trade-off that needs to be made in the NICU between time and the quality of the decision making (and the associated action). So, for example, if a better decision can be made by waiting for a short time to get access to some more data, this may be preferable to starting on one course of action and then having to radically change it shortly afterwards.

The areas of dependability in the NICU that are most affected by timing issues are reliability and safety. If the system does not always produce appropriate responses in a timely manner, this could affect the well being of the baby.

The system has been developed on the basis of experience and best practice. In some cases timing issues have been introduced to impose a work structure that increases the system dependability. The use of deliberate delays before responding to alarms, for example, is a response to the inherently noisy data that is generated by the system (Miksch, Seyfang, Horn, & Popow, 1999). When a baby moves, for example, the heart rate increases, which causes the heart rate alarm to sound. In such situations the alarm may only sound a few times at most, so staff tend to wait to see if the alarm continues before responding. This allows any transient alarms to clear, but as a precautionary measure staff will also glance at the baby to check for any immediately apparent problems.

The pacing of work in the unit is the result of a trade-off between the temporal validity of data and the need to allow the babies to rest as much as possible. There are two main aspects of pacing. The first is the recording of hourly observations, which is implemented in a flexible manner. The observations for a particular baby can be brought forward or delayed as necessary to accommodate any changes in staff workload without adversely affecting the baby. The second is when the baby is not connected to a Neotrend. In this case a regime is put in place to take manual blood gases at regular intervals (3-4 hours), which involves pricking the baby's heel to collect the blood. This causes the baby some discomfort which partly explains the long interval between successive manual blood gas tests. Temporal validity is also an issue that affects the accuracy of the Neotrend readings which decay over time. When the data starts to decay, the Neotrend has to be recalibrated.

Category	Examples
Sequence	There is a sequence of systematic checks performed during diagnosis: DOPE (displacement of the ETT, obstruction of the ETT, pneumothorax, equipment failure). Manually bag the baby before carrying out suction. After changing the ventilator settings, take a manual blood gas to confirm the effect of the changes (after 15-30 min delay). Check the baby's status; decide if any action is necessary; take the appropriate action. Check the baby's Airway, Breathing and Circulation (ABC) in that order.
Delayed feedback	It takes 2-3 minutes before the rise in the PO2 brought about by the changes becomes apparent. The full rise takes about 20 minutes. The effects of the changes are not quantitatively assessed until a manual blood gas is taken. X-rays and manual blood gases have to be processed before the results are available.
Delays	A deliberate delay was introduced in the incident to allow the implemented changes to take effect and to let the consultant assess the changes that were made. Configuring the high frequency oscillator ventilator (HFOV) takes 20 minutes. This had to be considered when deciding whether to switch the baby onto HFOV. Staff deliberately wait before responding to alarms, to check whether the alarm is real.
Trends	Staff start looking for trends in the blood gases that show an improving situation after about 2-3 minutes. The Neotrend display shows the effects of the changes to the PIP and the TI as changes in PO2 and PCO2. Indications that the blood gases in particular are heading in the right direction.
Temporal validity	Manual blood gas data is only valid for about 20-30 minutes. Chest X-rays are only valid for a limited period of time. Manual blood gas data decays over time. The Neotrend is periodically recalibrated to maintain data accuracy.
Deadlines	If the oxygen level is critically low, then something has to be done in very few minutes, with an improvement in condition required in 10-15 minutes. Self imposed deadlines for detecting improvement in baby's condition.
Pacing	Observations of the babies condition are taken and recorded on an hourly basis. Where a Neotrend is not being used, blood gases are sampled regularly (normally every three or four hours).
Other	There are temporal aspects to the way that the ventilator operates, in that the inspiration and expiration time can be controlled.

Table 2. Summary of timing issues.

There are emergent timing loops in the work structure which reflect the defence in depth mechanism that allows cases to be referred to more expert staff in a timely manner. The front line carers tend to handle the smallest and simplest problems, which also take the shortest time. If a problem is more complex a registrar is typically called in to assist, and solving the problem will take longer. For the most complicated problems a consultant may also subsequently be called in, and these problems generally take the longest time to solve. Although these control loops are all based on competence, they are also characterised by their execution times.

The use of sequences is another example of an imposed feature. Although the DOPE mnemonic does not require a temporal ordering of the checks, the intention is to make the system safer by making sure that some of the common alternative causes of acute situations are not overlooked before changes are made to the ventilator settings. The ABC mnemonic sequence, however, does have a strict temporal ordering, based on getting the system into a safe state at the earliest opportunity.

Whenever staff were asked about deadlines and time pressures, they invariably replied with a range of values—a few minutes, seconds to minutes, and so on— rather than a hard deadline. It could be argued that this use of less tightly specified deadlines is an attempt to make the system safer and more reliable by not imposing unnecessarily strict time pressures on staff who are already working in a stressful environment. Furthermore, where deadlines were identified these tended to vary between babies, because they are largely determined by the individual baby's physiology.

The remainder of the timing issues can be considered as inherent properties of the components of the system, and hence need to be noted when assessing the system's dependability. There are natural delays between actions and the results of those actions being observable: the settle times of the equipment and the baby's physiology contribute to the delayed feedback and temporal validity of the data. When the ventilator settings are changed, for example, some effect can be observed shortly afterwards, but it takes 20-30 minutes for the full effects to become apparent. Similarly, X-rays take 20-30 minutes to be developed. Whilst these are aspects of the system that cannot be directly changed by staff they can be accounted for because they have known, relatively short limits. It is much more difficult, however, to gauge the full effect of some of the interventions when they are made. Where complications arise, due to oxygen starvation for example, the full extent of any problems may not become known until several months or even years afterwards.

The Neotrend displays trends of continuous blood gas data (partial oxygen and partial carbon dioxide pressures, and pH), which means that staff can be more responsive after changing the ventilator settings. This allows them to check that the changes are affecting the blood gases in the right direction at an appropriate rate and then respond accordingly.

4 Collaboration

In addition to the timing aspects of the interaction between the humans (NICU staff) and the technological equipment, the system also depends on the interactions between staff. Examples of the different collaboration issues that were identified are summarised in Table 3. These issues of human collaboration are considered in more detail below.

4.1 Collaboration Issues

The unit employs about 70 staff with varying levels of expertise. Collaboration between staff is essential to the successful functioning of the unit. The nature of this collaboration and how it is supported and facilitated by the infrastructure of the unit directly influences the system dependability.

Category	Examples
Organisational structure	Communication hierarchy. Decision making hierarchy in which nurses and SHOs make initial decisions, but can refer problems to registrars who can refer them to consultants.
Formal verbal communication	The ward round acts as the formal shift handover between the night shift and the day shift.
Informal verbal communication	Separate informal shift handovers for the nurses and the SHOs.
Formal non-verbal communication	Records are used extensively in the NICU by all staff.
Informal non-verbal communication	Overseeing Overhearing Changes to equipment settings

Table 3. Summary of collaboration issues.

4.2 Collaboration and Dependability

The organisation of work in the NICU makes it important that the staff work as a team to deliver an effective service of patient care. The corollary of this is that the need for sharing information and knowledge is critical to the system's dependability.

The main form of collaboration is communication between staff. Much of the information flow in health care takes place in the clinical communication space (Coiera, 2000). The unit operates a shift system, and communication takes place during and across shifts. Communication is also one of the major means through which other aspects of collaboration are achieved (Bardram, 1998). It is used to achieve coordination, cooperation, negotiation, planning, decision making and generally for sharing information. Decisions and actions concerning the ventilator settings are based on communication between staff, and the data values displayed by the monitoring equipment in the NICU.

Senior staff have several roles including clinical care, management and staff training. There is also some overlapping of roles. Some senior nursing staff, for example, have specialist training that allows them to perform more specialised medical tasks, like the SHOs, and the registrars may perform medical tasks like the SHOs, and make managerial decisions like the consultants.

In addition to the doctors and nurses several other staff play important supporting roles in the unit. These include technical support, ward clerks who collate various information sources generated by the unit, and a pharmacist.

The overlap between the roles and responsibilities of staff contributes to the reliability and availability of the system. If there is a shortage of SHOs due to illness, for example, their tasks can still be performed by the registrars, making the system resilient to single point failures.

The safety and reliability of the system are also helped by the hierarchical structure of decision making. This provides a defence in depth mechanism, in that if an SHO is having problems that they cannot solve with a particular case, they can refer it upwards to the registrars who can, if necessary, refer it to the consultants. The referral process is determined by the individual's level of expertise and the complexity of the case.

There are potential problems if knowledge is distributed too widely, at least in geographical terms. The staffing levels at the unit are coordinated in such a way that there is always an appropriate pool of knowledge available to deal with most situations. For the most difficult cases, the consultants are always available by telephone.

The sharing of information is used to generate the bigger picture for each case and to facilitate the coordination of staff. This is achieved through a combination of formal verbal communication—mainly the ward round—and informal verbal communication, such as the other shift handover meetings. These meetings allow work to be planned and co-ordinated for the next time period, and hence facilitate co-operation by giving staff an awareness of what others will be concerned with during the same period. The need for a shared up-to-date awareness of the situation is essential for dependability and provides a basis for the team to perform several tasks concurrently.

The main shift handover occurs during the ward round each morning, when the night shift hands over to the day shift. This formal handover is used to establish a care plan for the next 24 hours for each of the babies. The ward round is normally led by one of the consultants, and is attended by registrars, SHOs and nursing staff. Everyone is given the chance to contribute as individual cases are discussed and decisions explained at length. In this way the ward round also provides a means of in-service training.

Whilst the formal verbal communication provides staff with the key information needed to perform their work, it is the informal verbal communication that allows the system to continue to function effectively in the face of dynamically changing situations. Three examples of informal verbal communication are described below.

In addition to the ward round, the nurses, registrars and SHOs each have their own less formal staff handover meetings. These allow staff to share more detailed information using their own terms and decide how to achieve the care plans laid out during the ward round.

During the CDM several staff reported using explicit verbalisation by talking aloud when diagnosing a particular case. Verbalisation can save time because all of the staff who are present are simultaneously kept in the loop and hence can act immediately. Staff are also kept in the loop by overhearing the verbal communication of others.

Verbalisation also gives other staff some insight into the decision making processes for particular cases, and allows them to provide input to decisions. Furthermore, it provides a verbal audit trail which can be useful during subsequent discussions, enabling staff to reflectively learn from the handling of the case.

Whilst working, staff frequently talk to each other. Most explicit verbal communication is face-to-face because the people that could be required to perform a task are usually present on the unit. The main exception is when the on-call doctor has to be contacted by telephone or pager. Informal verbal communication is important for coping with changes in plans, either by sharing new information or negotiating new plans; for requesting help, and for discussing the specifics of how to achieve planned goals.

The consultants particularly rely on verbal communication with the front line carers to bring them up to date with the evolution of events. In acute situations this is the quickest way for them to get a current assessment of the situation. They utilise the communicated information together with the available data from the monitoring equipment, such as trends of the blood gases, and patient charts to help guide their decision making. There is lots of informal communication between the registrars and the consultants.

Both formal and informal verbal communication rely on the supporting infrastructure of the unit, particularly the patient records. Much of the communication in the NICU involves references to records. The records allow information to be shared between members of staff without them having to speak to one another. This can save time and reduce the amount of information that has to be remembered. Records are particularly useful for passing information between people who are present in one place at different times, as happens across shifts. This contributes to the reliability of the system because it supports the continuity of patient care. Over longer periods the records also provide a form of backup, which contributes to the integrity of the system.

Non-verbal communication is used to structure the work and record information for audit purposes, and provides a back-up of information. A written history of conditions and treatments is provided by the patient records, which can be used to resolve problems or ambiguities for individual cases; active problems are recorded using problem sheets (currently only for the doctors). The patient records also provide some level of data redundancy in that they are a written back up of staff knowledge about particular cases. The doctor's notes, for example, record relevant decisions made during the ward round, and details of subsequent events for the individual cases. Other documents contain information relating to the required treatment of the patient and any test results. Plans are not usually written down because they frequently have to be revised dynamically in response to changing situations.

There are several other informal ways in which non-verbal communication occurs. These alternatives to speech support verbal communication and provide faster ways of passing information when time is at a premium. Informal notes also allow information to be shared between people who cannot meet in person.

The main form of informal non-verbal communication used in the unit is passive communication. This occurs when one member of staff simply watches what another is doing, and when someone notes the changes that have been made to equipment settings and records and uses these to infer the actions of others. The latter can be triggered when somebody notices that the monitoring equipment is showing a change in the trend of the data values that are being recorded, for example.

The concept of dependability has recently been extended to take appropriate account of all aspects of socio-technical systems, such as patient care in the NICU (Dewsbury, Sommerville, Clarke, & Rouncefield, 2003). One of the aspects that has been added is learnability, and this is certainly applicable to the NICU. The SHOs only work in the NICU for six months on rotation as part of their general training to be a doctor. During that period they are expected to learn about patient care in the NICU.

The ward round provides a relatively formal way of learning about the system of patient care. The use of verbalisation by senior staff also contributes to learnability by helping the SHOs (and others) to understand about decision making task performance in the NICU. Even where verbalisation is not used, simply watching others provides another useful way of learning about the system.

The patient records also contribute to the learnability of the system by helping to structure verbal communication. The most obvious example occurs during the ward round where the daily update book is used as the source for discussions about each of the cases.

5   The Impact of FLORENCE on Dependability in the NICU

The way in which timing and collaboration features help to make the NICU dependable have been identified above. When FLORENCE is introduced, it should make the NICU even more dependable by helping front line carers to get babies into a more stable (safer) condition more rapidly. It should help to overcome the tendency of front line carers to be more conservative than experts when deciding on the magnitude of changes to the ventilator settings: the front line carer make smaller changes which means that they subsequently have to repeat the decision making and action processes.

What is not clear, however, is the impact of FLORENCE on the other aspects of work in the NICU, which could have a knock-on effect on dependability. Below, consideration is given to how FLORENCE could affect timing and collaboration in the NICU, together with how the impact can be assessed and appropriately managed.

The inherent timing issues identified in section 3 will not be affected by FLORENCE, because they depend on the properties of the equipment and the baby's physiology. FLORENCE could influence some of the other timing aspects, however. As noted above, the data in the NICU is inherently noisy; FLORENCE could exacerbate this problem if it generates more artefactual (false) alarms. The system of patient care has already developed a way to deal with this problem: staff generally do not respond immediately to alarms before checking the nature of the alarm.

Furthermore FLORENCE has been designed to remove some of the noise from the data used in calculating whether changes to the ventilator settings are required. These two defence mechanisms mean that FLORENCE should improve dependability by making the system safer and more reliable, because decisions will be based on better quality data.

There is a potential impact on learnability of the system. If it is fairly evident to staff what decisions FLORENCE is recommending and why, they may not verbalise the reasoning behind the decision to the same extent. This obviously reduces the scope for learning from other staff. This has been compensated for in FLORENCE by providing a facility to explain why it has made a particular decision. The system will become less safe, however, if staff always blindly accept FLORENCE's suggestions. The effects on learnability can be mitigated during the induction period for the SHOs when it needs to be clearly explained that FLORENCE is an *advisory* system, and that its decisions should not always be accepted without question.

By making learning faster, FLORENCE could reduce collaboration. This is because front line carers may become more self-reliant (if FLORENCE is trusted by staff) and able to respond to situations without needing to interact with others, particularly the more experienced staff. The corollary of this is that there will be fewer opportunities to learn from the more expert members of staff. This will affect the learnability of some parts of the system, and may also affect the safety and reliability if the front line carers do not learn about those subtler aspects of the system that are not encompassed by FLORENCE. These effects can also be addressed during the SHOs induction period. Staff should be encouraged to try and work out what changes they would make, and then explain the reasons why. Their suggestions could be compared to FLORENCE and any differences discussed with other staff.

Similarly, a reliance on FLORENCE could lead to fewer gatherings around the baby's cot to discuss interventions. Other nurses would therefore have fewer opportunities for picking up information through overhearing, hence reducing their overall awareness of what is happening in the NICU. The net effect could be a reduction in the system's safety and reliability if it means that it takes staff longer to get up to speed when they get called in to help with cases where they have not previously been directly involved. More senior staff in particular should be encouraged to make sure that they continue to discuss interventions and to encourage the SHOs to do so to, rather than just relying on FLORENCE.

There are two key aspects to ensuring that FLORENCE does not lead to a less safe system and, more generally, make it less dependable. The first lies in the education of the front line carers. During the SHOs induction training, the role and purpose of FLORENCE needs to be very clearly explained. The second is the monitoring of the use of FLORENCE. As part of the checking of the progress of the SHOs, senior staff will need to monitor the usage of FLORENCE to make sure that front line carers are not becoming too trusting or too reliant on FLORENCE. This will necessarily include checking how much SHOs are learning from communicating and collaborating with other staff. The process of monitoring the use of FLORENCE will obviously be an ongoing one.

6 General Discussion

The case study has highlighted several timing and collaboration issues that affect system dependability in the NICU. The way in which FLORENCE can affect the dependability has also been considered with respect to these issues. There may be some other timing and collaboration issues, however, which have not been identified by the methods used in the case study. It is therefore worth considering what other methods could be used to uncover those issues.

Timing issues in HMI are something that needs to be observed in situ. Routine timing issues, such as periodicity of work can be identified by observation. In acute situations, however, which is where most of the HMI takes place, it is more difficult to identify the precise nature of the timing issues. The CDM can be used to identify timing issues at a general level of abstraction, and in terms of the order of occurrence of events and actions. It is much more difficult to pin down the absolute times at which things happened in the recalled incidents, however. The main problem is that these events are unpredictable in terms of when they will occur, and how long they will last, since they are largely determined by the baby's physiology.

Detailed timing information can often be captured using video recording. In the NICU, however, where the occurrence of interesting events cannot be reliably predicted this would require video recordings over extended periods (possibly days). The NICU is a highly stressful situation for all concerned—babies, parents and staff—which is one of the reasons why the local ethics committee would not sanction the use of an intrusive method like video recording over long periods of time.

There is therefore a problem of how to get at the detailed timing and collaboration issues whilst avoiding potential problems of post hoc rationalisation about those issues. One obvious solution is to shadow the staff as they go about their daily work. This is a time and labour intensive approach and requires close co-operation with those people being shadowed. Perhaps the best described example of this approach is Hutchins (1995), who studied ship navigation by shadowing the operations on the bridge of a ship on various occasions over several months. This approach has also been successfully used to qualitatively explore communication patterns in the field of medicine by Coiera and Toombs (1998).

It is not clear whether all the collaboration issues were identified when using the CDM. This could be due to the method, but may also be attributed to the fact that during the incident being recalled there was so much happening that the interviewee could not physically track what everyone was doing, or whether collaboration was actually reduced. Interviewees also did not produce any detailed timing information associated with the coordination and co-operation of activities. The interviews to build rich pictures of roles, responsibilities and artefacts for non-verbal communication provide more information about collaborative work. They do not, however, provide information about the interaction between people and equipment that goes on at critical times.

7 Summary

Dependability is inherent in the NICU system. Contributions to the dependability of the socio-technical system are made by the humans (the NICU staff), the technology (ventilator, Neotrend and so on) and the context (social and physical). This study has focused more on those aspects associated with the humans, particularly the timing aspects of the human-machine interaction, and collaboration between the staff.

The study identified several examples of timing issues and collaboration issues that contribute to the dependability of the system before the introduction of FLORENCE. It is important that the system after the introduction of FLORENCE should be at least as dependable as it was before. Although there are often problems when new technology is introduced into clinical settings by outsiders (Coiera, 1999), this should not be the case in the NICU because it was the consultants in the unit who identified the need for FLORENCE, and they have been closely involved in its development. Furthermore they have the experiences of a previous expert system, ESNIC (Snowden, Brownlee, & Dear, 1997) to build on, where the issue of having to manually transfer the data readings from the equipment into ESNIC made it unacceptable to staff. The consultants took this into account in their requirement that FLORENCE had to be both clinically useful and acceptable to the staff for it to be successful.

Whether FLORENCE will improve the dependability of the system is an empirical question, albeit a difficult one due to the particular constraints of the NICU. SHOs are on rotation in the neonatal unit for only six months . This, coupled with the fact that the set of cases of RDS in the NICU changes considerably over time, makes it hard to directly compare the pre- and post-FLORENCE systems. The different rates of development of the babies also makes it hard to make direct comparisons across cases that are matched for gestation and birth weight at the start of their stay in the NICU for the pre- and post-FLORENCE systems.

Some of the ways in which FLORENCE could affect the dependability of the system have been identified here. In particular, the possible ways in which timing issues and collaboration could be affected have been highlighted. The next step is to return to the NICU after FLORENCE has been in place for some time to evaluate how the identified issues have really been affected.

Acknowledgements

The authors would like to thank the staff at SJUH Neonatal Unit for their helpful advice, assistance and co-operation during the study. This work was funded by the EPSRC (grant number GR/N13999) as part of the Dependability Interdisciplinary Research Collaboration (DIRC); the development of FLORENCE was funded by the SPARKS (Sport Aiding medical Research for KidS) charity.

8 References

Alberdi, E., Becher, J.-C., Gilhooly, K., Hunter, J., Logie, R., Lyon, A., McIntosh, N., & Reiss, J. (2001). Expertise and the interpretation of computerised physiological data: Implications for the design of medical decision support in neonatal intensive care. *International Journal of Human-Computer Systems, 55*(3), 191-216.

Baecker, R. M., & Buxton, W. A. S. (Eds.). (1987). *Readings in human-computer interaction: A multidisciplinary approach.* Palo Alto, CA: Morgan Kaufmann.

Baecker, R. M., Grudin, J., Buxton, W. A. S., & Greenberg, S. (Eds.). (1995). *Readings in human-computer interaction: Toward the year 2000.* Los Altos, CA: Morgan Kaufmann.

Bardram, J. E. (1998). Designing for the dynamics of cooperative work activities, *Proceedings of the 1998 ACM conference on computer supported cooperative work* (pp. 89-98). Seattle, WA: ACM Press.

Bartholomew, K., Newell, S., Dear, P., & Brownlee, K. (1994). *Babylog 8000 - Flow wave and volume monitoring .* Lübeck, Germany: Drägerwerk AG.

Baxter, G. D., Monk, A. F., Tan, K., Dear, P. R. F., & Newell, S. J. (Submitted). Using cognitive task analysis to identify requirements for the successful deployment of decision support systems in neonatal intensive care. *Manuscript submitted for publication.*

Berg, M. (2001). Implementing information systems in health care organizations: myths and challenges. *International Journal of Medical Informatics, 64*, 143-156.

Coiera, E. (1999). The impact of culture on technology: How do we create a clinical culture of innovation? *Medical Journal of Australia, 171*, 508-9.

Coiera, E., & Toombs, V. (1998). Communication behaviours in a hospital setting: an observational study. *BMJ, 316*, 673-676.

Combi, C., & Shuhar, Y. (1997). Temporal reasoning and temporal data maintenance in medicine: Issues and challenges. *Computers in Biology and Medicine, 27*(5), 353-368.

Dewsbury, G., Sommerville, I., Clarke, K., & Rouncefield, M. (2003). A dependability model for domestic systems, *Proceedings of 22nd International Conference on Computer Safety, Reliability and Security (SAFECOMP'03)* Heidelberg, Germany: Springer-Verlag.

Hutchins, E. (1995). *Cognition in the wild.* Cambridge, MA: MIT Press.

Johnson, C., & Gray, P. (1996). Temporal aspects of usability. *SigCHI Bulletin, 28*(2), 32-33.

Klein, G., Calderwood, R., & MacGregor, D. (1989). Critical decision method for eliciting knowledge. *IEEE Transactions on System, Man, and Cybernetics, 19*, 462-472.

Laprie, J.-C. (1995). *Dependable computing: Concepts, limits, challenges.* Paper presented at the 25th IEEE International symposium on fault-tolerant computing, Pasadena, CA.

Leveson, N. (1995). *Safeware: System safety and computers.* Reading, MA: Addison-Wesley.

Miksch, S., Seyfang, A., Horn, W., & Popow, C. (1999). Abstracting steady qualitative descriptions over time from noisy, high-frequency data. In W. Horn, Y. Shuhar, G. Lindberg, S. Andreassen, & J. Wyatt (Eds.), *Artificial Intelligence in Medicine. Joint European Conference on Artificial Intelligence in Medicine and Medical Decision Making, AIMDM'99, Aalborg, Denmark, June 1999, Proceedings. Lecture Notes in Computer Science 1620.* (pp. 281-290). Berlin: Springer.

Monk, A. F. (1998). Lightweight techniques to encourage innovative user interface design. In L. Wood (Ed.), *User interface design: bridging the gap between user requirements and design* (pp. 109-129). Boca Raton: CRC Press.

Philips. (2001). *Trendcare continuous blood gas monitoring system: Technical Overview* . Böblingen, Germany: Philips Medical Systems.

Rennie, J. M., & Roberton, N. R. C. (2002). *Neonatal Intensive Care.* (4th ed.). London: Arnold.

Snowden, S., Brownlee, K. G., & Dear, P. R. (1997). An expert system to assist neonatal intensive care. *Journal of medical engineering technology, 21*(2), 67-73.

Tan, K., Baxter, G., Brownlee, K. G., Newell, S. J., Dear, P. R. F., & Smye, S. (2003). Fuzzy logic expert system for ventilation of the newborn infant. *Archives of Disease in Childhood, 88*(Supplement 1), A47.

Applying Java™ Technologies to Mission-Critical and Safety-Critical Development

Kelvin Nilsen

Aonix Inc, Tucson, USA

Adrian Larkham

Aonix Europe, Henley on Thames, England

Abstract

As the complexity of embedded applications evolves, real-time Java is increasingly being used in large-scale applications that demand higher levels of abstraction, portability, and dynamic behaviour. Examples of such applications include management of network infrastructure, automation of manufacturing processes and control of power generating equipment. To meet these demands, real-time Java has moved increasingly into the mission-critical domain.

With the increased penetration into mission-critical and the expected eventual integration into safety-critical applications, the need to assure that Java can deliver reliable operation without exceeding resource constraints has increased. Ease of development and maintenance, support for dynamic behaviour, high performance, soft and hard real-time constraints, and reduction of physical footprint are just some of the requirements of mission-critical Java developers.

To meet these requirements, standards for both mission-critical and safety-critical software are being developed to assist developers in making the engineering tradeoffs necessary for components of such software.

1 Introduction

Originally designed as a language to support "advanced software for a wide variety of networked devices and embedded systems" [1], the Java programming language has much to offer the community of embedded system developers. In this context, we consider Java as a high-level general-purpose programming language rather than a special-purpose web development tool. Java offers many of the same benefits as Ada, while appealing to a much broader audience of developers. The breadth of interest in Java has led to a large third-party market for Java development tools, reusable component libraries, training resources, and consulting services.

Java borrows the familiar syntax of C and C++. Like C++, Java is object oriented, but it is much simpler than C++ because Java's designers chose not to support compilation of legacy C and C++ code. Because it is simpler, more programmers are able to master the language. With that mastery, they are more productive and less likely to introduce errors resulting from misunderstanding the programming language. Object-oriented encapsulation reduces interference between independently developed components and object-oriented abstractions reduce name collisions and other interference between components

The Java write-compile-debug cycle is faster than with traditional languages because Java supports both interpreted and just-in-time (JIT) compiled implementations. During development and rapid prototyping, developers save time by using the interpreter. This avoids the time typically required to recompile and relink object files.

Java application software is portable because the Java specification carefully defines a machine-independent intermediate byte-code representation and a robust collection of standard libraries. Byte-code class files can be transferred between heterogeneous network nodes and interpreted or compiled to native code on demand by the local Java run-time environment. The benefits of portability are several-fold:

1. Software engineers can develop and test their embedded software on fast PC workstations with large amounts of memory, and then deploy it on smaller less powerful embedded targets.
2. As embedded products evolve, it is easier to port their code from one processor and operating system to another.
3. Cross compiling is no longer necessary. The same executable byte code runs on Power PC, Pentium, MIPS, XScale, and others. This simplifies configuration management.
4. The ability to distribute portable binary software components provides the foundation for a reusable software component industry.

Certain features in Java's run-time environment help to improve software reliability. For example, automatic garbage collection, which describes the process of identifying all objects that are no longer being used by the application and reclaiming their memory, has been shown to reduce the total development effort for a complex system by approximately 40% [2]. Garbage collection eliminates dangling pointers and greatly reduces the effort required by developers to prevent memory leaks.

A high percentage of the CERT®/CC advisories issued every year are a direct result of buffer overflows in system software. Java automatically checks array subscripts to make sure code does not accidentally or maliciously reach beyond the ends of arrays, thereby eliminating this frequently exploited loophole.

The Java compiler and class loader enforce type checking much more strongly than C and C++. This means programmers cannot accidentally or maliciously misuse the bits of a particular variable to masquerade as an unintended value thus reducing programmer errors.

Developers of Java components can require as part of the interface definition for those components that exceptions thrown by their components be caught within the surrounding context. In lower level languages, uncaught exceptions often lead to unpredictable behaviour.

Another very useful Java feature is the ability to dynamically load software components into a running Java virtual machine (JVM). New software downloads serve to patch errors and add new capabilities to an existing embedded system. Special security checking is enforced when dynamic libraries are installed to ensure they do not compromise the integrity of the running system.

Though Java programs may be interpreted, it is much more common for Java byte codes to be translated to the target machine language before execution. For many I/O intensive applications, compiled Java runs as fast as C++. For compute-intensive applications, traditionally Java tends to run at one third to one half the speed of comparable C code.

2 Issues Regarding Java within Real-Time Systems

Although the initial design of Java was targeted to embedded devices, the first public distributions of Java did not support reliable real-time operation. There are several specific issues, identified here and discussed in greater detail in the reference material [3, 4].

2.1 Automatic garbage collection

Though automatic garbage collection greatly reduces the effort required by software developers to implement reliable and efficient dynamic memory management, typical implementations of automatic garbage collection are incompatible with real-time requirements. In most virtual machine environments, the garbage collector will occasionally put all application threads to sleep during certain uninterruptible operations while it analyses the relationships between objects within the heap to determine which objects are no longer in use. The durations of these garbage collection pauses are difficult to predict, and typically vary from half a second to tens of seconds, depending on characteristics of the virtual machine's configuration and the application. These problems can be addressed by using a virtual machine that provides real-time garbage collection, such as is described below.

2.2 Priority Inversion

To guarantee that real-time tasks meet all of their deadlines, real-time developers carefully analyse the resource requirements of each task and set the priorities of the tasks according to accepted practices of scheduling theory [5]. These real-time developers use thread priorities as a mechanism to implement compliance with deadlines. Unfortunately, many non-real-time operating systems and most JVM implementations view priorities as heuristic suggestions. This compromises real-time behaviour whenever the priorities of certain threads are temporarily boosted in the interest of providing "fair" access to the CPU or to improve overall system throughput. Another problem occurs when low-priority tasks lock resources that are required by high-priority tasks. In all of these cases, the real-time engineer describes the problem as priority inversion. It is important to deploy real-time Java components on virtual machines that honour strict priorities, preventing the operating system from automatically boosting or aging thread priorities, and that build priority inheritance or some other priority inversion avoidance mechanism into the implementation of synchronisation locks. Priority inheritance, for example, elevates the priority of a low-priority thread that owns a lock being requested by a high-priority thread so that the low-priority thread can get its work done and release the lock.

2.3 Timing Services

Standard Java timing services do not provide the exacting precision required by real-time programmers. Applications that use the Java **sleep()** service to control a periodic task will drift off schedule, because each invocation of **sleep()** is delayed within its period by the time required to do the periodic computation, and because the duration of each requested **sleep()** operation only approximates the desired delay time. Also, if a computer user changes the system's notion of time while a real-time Java program is running, any real-time threads that are using the system clock to drive their real-time activities will become confused because they assume the system clock is an accurate monotonically increasing time reference. JVMs designed for real-time operation typically provide high-precision and drift-free real-time timers that complement the standard timing utilities.

2.4 Low-Level Control

As a modern high-level programming language, Java's design intentionally precludes developers from directly accessing hardware and device drivers. The ideal is that hardware device drivers should be abstracted by the underlying operating system. However, given any hardware device, somebody has to write the device driver, and if Java were up to the task, many software engineers would rather do that development in Java than in assembly language or C. Most real-time Java implementations provide services to allow real-time Java components to store and fetch values from I/O ports and memory-mapped devices.

2.5 Hard Real-Time Tradeoffs

Developers of hard real-time systems tend to make different tradeoffs than soft real-time developers. In particular, hard real-time software tends to be relatively small, simple, and static. Often, economic considerations demand very high performance and very small footprint of the hard real-time layers of a complex system. To meet the demanding performance requirements, hard real-time developers generally recognize they must work harder to deliver functionality that could be realized with much less effort if there were no timing constraints, or if all of the timing constraints were soft real-time. Work is under way to define special hard real-time variants of the Java language [6-8]. One noteworthy difference between hard real-time and soft real-time Java is that the hard real-time variants generally do not rely on any form of automatic garbage collection.

3 Real-Time Garbage Collection

One of the most difficult challenges of real-time development with Java is managing the interaction between application code and automatic garbage collection. For reliable operation of real-time Java software, there are a number of characteristics that must be satisfied by the garbage collection subsystem. These are described in the sub-sections below.

3.1 Pre-emptive

Typical real-time Java applications are divided into multiple threads, some of which need to allocate memory and others of which only manipulate data in previously allocated objects. Both classes of threads may have real-time constraints. The threads that do not allocate memory may have tighter deadlines, and run at higher priorities, than the threads that do allocate memory. Garbage collection generally runs at a priority level between these two classes of priorities. Whenever a higher priority thread needs to run, it must be possible to pre-empt garbage collection. In some non-real-time virtual machines, once garbage collection begins, it cannot be pre-empted until garbage collection has completed its execution.

3.2 Incremental

To assure that garbage collection makes appropriate forward progress, it is necessary that the complete garbage collection effort be divided into many small increments of work. Whenever garbage collection is pre-empted, it must resume with the next increment of work after the pre-empting task relinquishes control. Some garbage collection systems allow pre-emption but restart either the complete garbage collection effort or the current garbage collection phase when they are resumed. Real-time garbage collectors avoid the need to restart operations when garbage collection is pre-empted.

3.3 Accurate

We use the term accurate to describe a garbage collector that always knows whether a particular memory cell holds a reference (pointer) or holds, for example, numerical representations of integers and floating-point values. In contrast, conservative garbage collectors do not always keep track of this type information. Whenever there is any uncertainty as to the meaning of the information held in a particular memory location, the conservative garbage collector makes the assumption that the data represents a pointer. If, interpreted as a pointer, there is an object that would be directly referenced by this pointer, that object is conservatively treated as live. Because conservative garbage collectors cannot promise to reclaim all dead memory, they are less reliable for long-running mission-critical applications.

3.4 Defragmenting

Over the history of a long-running application, it is possible for the pool of free memory to become fragmented. A fragmented allocation pool may have an abundance of available memory, but the free memory is divided into a large number of very small segments. This prevents the system from reliably allocating large objects. It also complicates the allocation of smaller segments, because it becomes increasingly important to efficiently pack newly allocated objects into the available free memory segments (so as to reduce further fragmentation). In general, a real-time virtual machine intended to support reliable long-running mission-critical applications must provide some mechanism for defragmentation of the free pool.

3.5 Paced

It is not enough to just be able to pre-empt garbage collection. In large and complex systems, certain activities depend on an ability to allocate new memory in order to fulfil their real-time-constrained responsibilities. If the memory pool becomes depleted, the real-time tasks that need to allocate memory will necessarily become blocked while garbage collection is carried out. To prevent this sort of priority inversion from occurring, a real-time virtual machine must pace garbage collection against the rate of memory allocation. The ideal is for the system to automatically dedicate to garbage collection activities enough CPU time to recycle dead memory as quickly as the application is allocating memory, without dedicating to garbage collection any CPU time that has already been set aside for execution of the real-time application threads, and without dedicating so much CPU time to garbage collection that it completes way ahead of schedule. In a soft or firm real-time system, heuristics are applied to approximate this ideal. The driving considerations are (1) to prevent out-of-memory conditions from stalling execution of real-time threads, and (2) to maximize the efficiency of garbage collection by delaying as long as possible in order that each fixed-cost collection reclaim the largest possible amount of dead memory.

4 Real-Time Java Technologies

Within this paper, the term soft real-time is used to describe systems where there is imprecision or uncertainty regarding timing deadlines, resource requirements, budgeting, and enforcement.

The term firm real-time is used to differentiate from soft real-time. With firm real-time a disciplined development in which software engineers carefully analyse deadlines, resource requirements, and schedulability is used. Firm real-time differs from hard real-time in that, for the most part, resource requirements are determined empirically, by measuring the behaviour of individual components rather than theoretical analysis. Generally, empirical evaluation provides statistical confidence but does not offer absolute guarantees.

The term hard real-time is used to describe systems that are proven through mathematical analysis to always meet all deadlines. Such proofs, which necessarily depend on intimate knowledge of the RTOS implementation, the CPU's pipeline and cache architecture, the organisation of the memory subsystem, and the compiler's code generation model, are extremely difficult and are generally only practical for very small and simple real-time systems.

Since it was first publicly released in 1996, Java has evolved into several different versions to serve the needs of different audiences. J2SE™ is the "standard edition" that is used by nearly all Java developers [9]. This is the version that typically runs on personal desktop computers, and this is the version that almost all of the software components available for licensing from 3rd parties or downloadable as open-source components. J2EE™ is the enterprise edition [10].

It includes all of the J2SE libraries, and has additional server-specific libraries to support, for example, secure transaction processing. J2ME™ is the micro edition, which is available in two configurations, the Connected Device Configuration (CDC) and the Connected Limited Device Configuration (CLDC) [11]. J2ME is designed for memory-limited systems like cell phones and set-top boxes.

To enable Java to address both firm real-time and hard real-time systems the following technologies, specifications and initiatives have been produced or are in progress:

- J2SE based technologies
- The Real-Time Specification for Java
- The Open Group Standardisation of Safety and Mission Critical Java

4.1 J2SE Based Technologies

Several vendors have developed J2SE based technologies suitable for the development of systems that have firm real-time requirements ranging from one to tens of milliseconds. Using the conventional J2SE libraries and JVM but with tightened semantics for garbage collection, synchronisation, and scheduling provides a portable, and scalable development environment for large, complex, and dynamic firm real-time applications. PERC® is an example of such a technology [12]. It provides

- Paced real-time garbage collection with high reliability achieved through accurate scanning and automatic defragmentation of the memory heap
- Optional extended priority range (1-32). Strict scheduling of Java threads (based on priority) to ensure consistent fixed-priority dispatching (without priority aging). Synchronisation implemented using priority inheritance.
- Enhanced timing services. A special Timer class implements the same services as **java.util.Timer** with but is not affected if the system's real-time clock drifts or is modified by human operators. SleepUntil() and waitUntil() methods are provided which can be used to implement non-drifting periodic execution and absolute timeouts. The enhanced timing services provide nanoseconds granularity and the capability to set the tick period and the duration of each time slice.

4.2 The Real-Time Specification for Java

The Real-Time Specification for Java (RTSJ) [6] is a collection of APIs in combination with a tightening of the semantic requirements for standard Java APIs. It can be combined with any of the existing Java platforms (J2ME, J2SE, or J2EE) to allow development of both soft and hard real-time software in "Java". The RTSJ requires, for example, that traditional Java threads honour strict priority scheduling as determined by the Java thread priorities and not by system heuristics that occasionally age the priorities of certain threads, boosting their priorities if they have not recently run and lowering their priorities if they are seen to be consuming more than their fair share of CPU resources. The RTSJ also requires the implementation of Java's synchronisation constructs to provide a means of avoiding priority inversion.

The RTSJ introduces certain new APIs that are not in standard Java. Among the extensions, RTSJ introduces two new thread types: **RealtimeThread** and **NoHeapRealtimeThread**. Unlike traditional Java threads, these threads respond to asynchronous interruption and cancellation requests. These threads are also able to run at priorities higher than the traditional virtual machine's 10 thread priorities. And the **NoHeapRealTimeThread** is guaranteed to never be pre-empted by garbage collection.

Within the RTSJ specification, the scheduling behaviour of **RealtimeThread** is not well defined. If a particular RTSJ implementation offers some form of real-time garbage collection, then the developer can expect predictable scheduling behaviour. But if it doesn't, **RealtimeThread** threads will experience unpredictable interference from garbage collection activities.

NoHeapRealtimeThread threads achieve highly predictable real-time scheduling behaviour by avoiding all access to heap-allocated objects. Whenever they need access to a dynamically allocated object, they must allocate this object either from an **ImmortalMemory** or **ScopedMemory** region. **ImmortalMemory** objects live permanently and can never be reclaimed. For applications that are expected to run reliably for years at a time, the only objects that can be allocated in **ImmortalMemory** are the ones allocated during initial start-up. Objects allocated within a **ScopedMemory** region are all reclaimed simultaneously, at the moment the reference count for the **ScopedMemory** region itself is decremented to zero. **ScopedMemory** regions may nest, and objects within one **ScopedMemory** region may refer to objects in outer nested **ScopedMemory** regions, but not the other way around. Run-time checks accompany every assignment to reference fields of objects to make sure that these constraints are not violated.

Synchronisation between **NoHeapRealtimeThread** and traditional Java threads is problematic given that a traditional Java thread may be pre-empted by garbage collection while it holds a lock on a shared object. If a **NoHeapRealtimeThread** subsequently requests access to the same synchronisation lock, it may be forced to wait for garbage collection to complete before the traditional Java thread can relinquish its lock to grant access to the **NoHeapRealtimeThread**. For this reason, the RTSJ programmer is told not to synchronize between **NoHeapRealtimeThread** and traditional Java threads. Instead, any information sharing between these two domains must be realised by copying the data into **ImmortalMemory** objects and passing the copies to the other domain by way of built-in wait-free queues.

The RTSJ designers have commented in discussing the rationale for various design trade offs that "real-time is not real fast." The primary criterion in designing the RTSJ was to enable predictable and deterministic execution. Some of the performance compromises that were implemented in order to achieve this include the requirement to impose run-time checks on reference assignments and to require copying of data between real-time and non-real-time domains whenever information sharing is necessary.

4.3 The Open Group Standardisation of Safety- and Mission-critical Java

The standards development that is being carried out by the Open Group's Real-Time and Embedded Systems Forum will establish a foundation that encourages competitive pricing and innovation among Java technology vendors while assuring portability and interoperability of real-time components written in the Java language. These standards, which are to be endorsed both by the Java Community Process and by ISO, will address a slightly different set of requirements than the existing Real-Time Specification for Java. In particular, the standard for safety-critical Java will address concerns regarding certification under the FAA's DO-178B guidelines [13]. And beyond requirements for real-time, the standard for mission-critical Java will address issues of portability, scalability, performance, memory footprint, abstraction, and encapsulation. Work within the Open Group is ongoing. The current plan is to deliver the safety-critical specification, reference implementation, and Technology Compatibility Kit (TCK) by Q1 2005. Open Group standardisation of mission-critical Java standards would follow successful completion of the safety-critical Java standard. Working documents describing the Open Group's Real-Time and Embedded Systems Forum's ongoing work standardisation activities related to real-time Java are available at http://www.opengroup.org/rtforum/.

The table below summarizes key differences between different proposed mission-critical Java approaches.

	Traditional Java	Mission-Critical Java		
		Firm Real-Time	Hard Real-Time	Safety-Critical
Library Support	J2SE	J2SE	Subset of CDC	Very restrictive subset of CDC
Garbage Collection	Pauses in excess of 10 seconds	Real Time	No garbage collection	
Manual Memory Deallocation	Manual memory deallocation is disallowed		Allows manual deallocation	No manual deallocation
Stack Memory Allocation	No		Safe stack allocation	
Dynamic Class Loading	Yes			No
Thread Priorities	Unpredictable priority clustering and aging	Fixed priority, time-sliced pre-emptive, with distinct priorities		Fixed priority, distinct priorities, no time slicing

	Traditional Java	Mission-Critical Java		
		Firm Real-Time	Hard Real-Time	Safety-Critical
Priority Inversion Avoidance	None	Priority inheritance	Priority inheritance and priority ceiling	Priority ceiling
Asynchronous Transfer of Control	No	Yes		No
Approximate Performance	One-third to two-thirds speed of C	Within 10% of traditional Java speed	Within 10% of C speed	

Table 1. Proposed Differentiation Between Java Technologies

The key points emphasized in this table are described below:

- The standard J2SE Java libraries are key to enabling high developer productivity, software portability, and ease of maintenance. Thus, it is important to provide all of these libraries to the firm real-time developer. Unfortunately, the standard J2SE libraries have a significant footprint requirement (at least 4 Mbytes) and depend heavily on automatic garbage collection, which is not available in the hard real-time environment. Thus, hard real-time and safety-critical Java cannot use the standard libraries. Java for hard real-time development will support the subset of the CDC libraries that is appropriate for a non-garbage-collected environment running on a limited-service hard real-time executive. Safety-critical Java will support an even smaller library subset, pared down so as to facilitate safety certification efforts.
- The approach to firm real-time development supports real-time garbage collection as described above. To improve throughput, determinism, and memory footprint requirements, hard real-time and safety-critical Java will not offer automatic garbage collection.
- In traditional Java and firm real-time Java, memory is reclaimed by garbage collection. There is no application programmer interface (API) to allow developers to explicitly release objects, as this would decrease software reliability by introducing the possibility of dangling pointers. With hard real-time Java, memory associated with certain objects can be explicitly reclaimed. This is a dangerous service that must be used with great care. It is necessary, however, to support a breadth of real-world application requirements. With safety-critical Java, manual deallocation of memory will be disallowed, as use of this service would make it very difficult to certify safe operation of the software system.
- Traditional Java and firm real-time Java allocates all objects in the heap. In the absence of automatic garbage collection, hard real-time and safety-critical Java will provide special protocols to allocate certain objects on the run-time stack. The protocol will include compile-time enforcement of

rules that assure that no pointers to these stack-allocated objects survive beyond the lifetime of the objects themselves.

- Dynamic class loading allows new libraries and new application components to be loaded into a virtual machine environment on the fly. This is a very powerful capability, and we desire to provide this expressive power as broadly as possible. However, current safety certification practices are too restrictive to allow use of this capability in a safety-critical system.

- In the specification for traditional Java, thread priorities are mere suggestions. The virtual machine implementation may honour these suggestions, or it may ignore them. It may, for example, choose to treat all priorities with equal scheduling preference, or it may even choose to give greater scheduling preference to threads running at lower priorities. In all of the real-time Java specifications, priorities are distinct and priority ordering is strictly honoured. Safety-critical Java will implement strict FIFO scheduling within priority levels, with no time slicing. This is the more common expectation for developers of safety-critical systems.

- Traditional Java does not offer any mechanism to avoid priority inversion, which might occur when a low-priority task locks a resource that is subsequently required by a high-priority task in order for it to make progress. Both hard and firm real-time Java will support priority inheritance, in which any thread that holds a lock to a resource requested by a higher priority thread will have its priority automatically increased to the highest priority level of any requesting thread until such time as the lower priority thread releases its lock on the shared resource. Additionally, hard real-time Java and safety-critical Java will support the priority ceiling protocol, in which particular locks are assigned ceiling priorities that represent the maximum priority of any thread that is allowed to acquire this particular lock. Whenever a thread obtains a lock, its priority is automatically elevated to the ceiling priority level. If a thread with higher priority than the lock's ceiling priority attempts to acquire that lock, a run-time exception is generated. The priority ceiling mechanism is most efficient and is simpler to implement and to analyse for static systems in which all of the threads and their priorities are known before run time. The priority inheritance mechanism deals better with environments that experience dynamic adjustments to the thread population or to their respective priorities.

- Asynchronous transfer of control allows one thread to interrupt another in order to have that other thread execute a special asynchronous event handler and then either resume the work that had been pre-empted or abandon its current efforts. This capability, missing from traditional Java, is very useful in many real-time scenarios. Safety-critical Java will not support this capability because the asynchronous behaviour is incompatible with accepted practices for safety certification.

- Because of the high-level services supported by Java, including automatic garbage collection, array subscript checking, dynamic class loading, and JIT compilation, traditional Java generally runs quite a bit slower than comparable algorithms implemented in, for example, the C language. Experience with implementations of firm real-time Java reveals that it runs slightly slower than traditional Java, because real-time garbage collection imposes a greater penalty on typical thread performance than non-real-time garbage collectors. The various compromises represented in the hard real-time and safety-critical domains are designed to enable execution efficiency that is within 10% of typical C performance.

- Because of the size of the standard J2SE libraries and a JIT compiler, which is present in a typical J2SE deployment, the typical J2SE deployment requires at least 16 Mbytes of memory. Of this total, about half is available for application code and data structures. Depending on the needs of a particular application, the memory requirements may range much higher, up to hundreds of Mbytes for certain applications. Hard real-time Java is designed specifically to support very efficient deployment of low-level hard real-time and performance constrained software components. Though different applications exhibit different memory requirements, targeted applications typically run from about 64 Kbytes up to a full Mbyte in memory requirements. Safety-critical deployments tend to be even smaller. This is because the costs of certification are so high per line of code that there is strong incentive to keep safety-critical systems as small as possible.

5 Conclusions

Java has matured greatly during the nine years since it was first released to the public. During this time, custom-tailored versions of the JVM have been developed to serve the special needs of mission-critical embedded development. Early adopters of firm real-time Java technologies have proven the software developer productivity benefits of using Java in place of legacy languages like C and C++. Successfully deployed products have proven that firm real-time JVMs serve as a strong foundation upon which to deploy mission-critical software systems that have demanding reliability requirements.

As market acceptance of Java technologies in the mission-critical space grows, there is increasing demand to broaden the reach and applicability of Java to components that are more tightly constrained by resource and time budgets. New standards are being developed to make mission-critical Java relevant to the hard real-time, safety-critical, and high-performance domains as well.

By combining hard real-time, firm real-time, and traditional non-real-time Java technologies, the Java programming environment serves as an excellent platform for all mission-critical development efforts. Since the trends in many computer engineering and computer science education programs are to emphasize Java over older languages like C and C++, we expect to see a gradual migration to Java for development of all new mission-critical functionality.

References

1. Sun Microsystems Inc., The Java Language Environment: A White Paper. 1995, Sun Microsystems, Inc.: Mountain View, CA. (http://java.sun.com/docs/white/langenv/)
2. P. Rovner. "On Adding Garbage Collection and Runtime Types to a Strongly-Typed Statically Checked, Concurrent Language", CSL-84-7, Xerox Palo Alto

Research Center. 1984. (See http://www.parc.xerox.com/about/history/pub-historical.html)

3. K. Nilsen. "Issues in the Design and Implementation of Real-Time Java", Real-Time Magazine. March 1998.(http://www.realtime-info.be/magazine/98q1/1998q1 p009.pdf

4. K. Nilsen. "Adding Real-Time Capabilities to the Java Programming Language." Communications of the ACM. Vol. 41, no. 6, pp. 49-56, June 1998. (http://doi.acm.org/10.1145/276609.276619)

5. M. Klein, T. Ralya, B. Pollak, R. Obenza. A Practitioner's Handbook for Real-Time Analysis: Guide to Rate Monotonic Analysis for Real-Time Systems. 712 pages. Kluwer Academic Publishers. November 1993. (http://www.sei.cmu.edu/publications/books/other-books/rma.hndbk.html)

6. G. Bollella, J. Gosling, B. Brosgol, P. Dibble, S. Furr, M. Turnbull. The Real-Time Specification for Java. 195 pages. Addison-Wesley Publishing Company. January 2000. (http://www.rtj.org/)

7. K. Nilsen, A. Klein. "Issues in the Design and Implementation of Efficient Interfaces Between Hard and Soft Real-Time Java Components." Proceedings of the Workshop on Java Technologies for Real-Time and Embedded Systems. Springer-Verlag. November 2003.

8. K. Nilsen. "Doing Firm-Real-Time With J2SE APIs." Proceedings of the Workshop on Java Technologies for Real-Time and Embedded Systems. Springer-Verlag. November 2003.

9. Zukowski, J. "Mastering Java 2, J2SE 1.4", Sybex. 928 pages. April 2002.

10. Keogh, J. "J2EE: The Complete Reference", McGraw-Hill Osborne Media. 904 pages. Sept. 6, 2002.

11. Keogh, J. "J2ME: The Complete Reference", McGraw-Hill Osborne Media. 768 pages. Feb. 27, 2003.

12. Differentiating Features of the PERC Virtual Machine, June 2, 2004 (http://www.aonix.co.uk/pdf/PERCWhitePaper.pdf)

13. RTCA/DO-178B, "Software Considerations in Airborne Systems and Equipment Certification," December 1, 1992.

AUTHOR INDEX

Baret, H.	51	Larkham, A.	211	
Baxter, G.D.	195	Lautieri, S.	65	
Blow, J.	183	Liddell, P.	183	
Cooper, D.	65	Miguel, A.	195	
Cox, A.	183	Nicholson, M.	149,	163
Fenn, J.	21	Nilsen, K.	211	
Filipe, J.K.	195	Payne, K.	79	
Froome, P.	37	Pierce, R.	51	
George, M.	111	Prince, M.	129	
Jackson, D.	65	Rygh, K.	93	
Jepson, B.	21	Smith, D.H.	3	
Jolliffe, G.	163	Tan, K.	195	

Printed in the United States
80870LV00001B/11

Printed in the United States
80870LV00001B/11